Wisdom of the Cloister

Wisdom

of the

Cloister

a monastic reader

John Skinner

IMAGE BOOKS

Doubleday

New York   London   Toronto   Sydney   Auckland

An Image Book
Published by Doubleday

a division of Random House, Inc.
1540 Broadway, New York, New York 10036

IMAGE, DOUBLEDAY, and the portrayal of a deer drinking from a stream are
trademarks of Doubleday, a division of Random House, Inc.

Book design by Donna Sinisgalli.

Library of Congress Cataloging-in-Publication Data

Skinner, John.
Wisdom of the cloister: a monastic reader / by John Skinner.—1st Image Books ed.
p.   cm.
1. Devotional calendars. 2. Monasticism and religious orders. I. Title.
BX2170.C55 S57 1999

242'.2—ddc21   99-28826

CIP

ISBN 0-385-49262-6
Copyright © 1999 by John Skinner
All Rights Reserved
Printed in the United States of America
October 1999
First Edition
1   3   5   7   9   10   8   6   4   2

For Charles

our firstborn

a man of silence and much wisdom

Foreword

I heard a startling statement from a senior Anglican priest recently. "The loss of the monasteries [in England] was tragic. We have still to recover from that wholesale destruction of a spiritual tradition. . . ."

Perhaps the wise and mighty politicians of Europe were making the same statement, albeit negatively, at the time of the Enlightenment, the French Revolution, and again at the end of the nineteenth century, when they were adamant that there was no sense in monasticism; it was nonsense. When man had at last understood the world as a whole, there was no longer room for those intent upon squaring the circle.

Even for us moderns, given our good will, it still remains hard to comprehend this escape into the desert. Giving up marriage, money, one's own ways—it all seems so negative, a retreat from reality. Yet this is not the place to argue against such reaction; rather, I would agree. On the face of it, joining a monastery *is* death. Otherwise it would make no sense. The whole point is to die: to oneself, to the world. Only then may one hope to discover the hidden, new life of Christ.

Yet why all this secrecy behind closed doors? If they have a special vision, why not share it, we complain. That is because the grasp every monk has upon his daily vision, attempted day by day, is always fragile. That is the stuff of it. So that he will never be able to burst out of the cloister crying "Eureka!"

Luke tells us it was just the same with Mary. She knew her Son better than any other human being ever would, yet she "kept all these things in her heart." So, too, the monk may not broadcast a secret which he scarcely glimpses for himself. He is, by and large, enfolded in a mystery, a rhythm of life that absorbs him to the exclusion of all else.

But monks have always written or been written about. From the time of the Emperor Constantine, who felt compelled to write to Antony, the first abbot, hoping against hope for reply, monks have fascinated the outsider. And in our day Thomas Merton is the classic example of the monk drawn ever deeper into a mystery of solitary life only to find himself more and more concerned with the world, its trouble and pain. For these two—world and cloister— are inextricably linked, precisely because of the mystery of God's birth among men. The monk who goes into the desert loses himself to find God in faith, but he also rediscovers the world. And at the heart of that rediscovery lies our fascination for the monastic way of life. What does he know about ourselves which we do not yet know? We may learn this mystery slowly and piecemeal, like all simple truths. Yet it can never be written up, packaged, and sold by *Reader's Digest*. We must work to find ourselves.

In order for any book to come about, its shape must first be found. At first, seeking the shape of this work soon became very frustrating. One shied from the obvious, a chronology beginning with Adam and Eve—as do all novice sermons. But then, slowly, it became apparent. Why not use the natural cycle of the year? Begin in

September with the wisdom of the Desert Fathers, then the Fathers of the Church, and allow the year to unfold into the present day. Many readers will wish to use this book as a daily reader that feeds them throughout the year. Others may prefer to pick and choose, finding favorite passages to which they will return again and again.

The butterfly's wing is made up of countless tiny patches of assorted bright colors. It is only when we see the whole that we begin to identify our butterfly. Newton, at the height of his fame, declared that he only knew himself to be standing on giants' shoulders. Great was his scientific stride, gravity had been determined in his mathematical formulae, but it was as nothing, he confessed, to those who had walked ahead of him.

In order to understand the simplicity of monasticism, its innate wisdom, we need to construct a patchwork of colors, beginning with the Desert Fathers, in order to arrive at our present day. We do not need very much. Just simple spot colors, vivid yet not entirely meaningful in themselves. It is only when we stand back and admire the pattern as a whole that we begin to glimpse its meaning.

This book is shaped as a daily reader. Some will prefer to use it that way. But certain passages will hold more for some readers than for others; each individual will seek his or her own path and find themselves returning again and again to certain readings. But slowly the story will unfold and the mysterious pattern reveal itself. From the extravagant antics of Antony, tussling with his devils in the desert, to the steely determination of Theresa of Àvila; listening to Meister Eckhart preaching in Cologne or reading Julian's limpid English as she writes from her anchorhold in fourteenth-century Norwich; staying patiently with Thérèse of Lisieux (who has been labeled a "spoiled brat") until she teaches us her own Little Way; or hearing the wisdom of Henri Nouwen, a European newly arrived in an alien New World: this is the butterfly wing. Bright, beautiful, immensely fragile, yet able to lift us to great heights or allow us to alight in some silent spot where we may find rest and warmth in the spring sun.

Wisdom of the Cloister

Sunday

THE JOURNEY BEGINS

Luke tells of Mary's response
to her messenger from God

In the sixth month the angel Gabriel was sent by God to a town in Galilee called Nazareth, to a virgin engaged to a man whose name was Joseph, of the house of David. The virgin's name was Mary.

And he came to her and said, "Greetings, favored one! The Lord is with you." But she was much perplexed by his words and pondered what sort of greeting this might be. Then the angel said to her, "Do not be afraid, Mary, for you have found favor with God. And now, you will conceive in your womb and bear a son, and you will give him the name Jesus. He will be great, and will be called Son of the Most High. The Lord God will give him the throne of his ancestor David, and he will reign over the house of Jacob forever; and of his kingdom there will be no end." Mary said to the angel, "How can this be, since I am a virgin?" The angel said to her, "The Holy Spirit will come upon you, and the power of the Most High will overshadow you; therefore the child to be born will be holy; he will be called Son of God. And now, your relative Elizabeth in her old age has also conceived a son; and this is the sixth month for her who was said to be barren. For nothing will be impossible with God." Then Mary said, "Here I am, the servant of the Lord: Let it be with me according to your word." And the angel departed from her.

September

Monday

IGNATIUS OF ANTIOCH (35–107)

Jesus Christ, our inseparable life:
thought of God

I do not presume to give you orders, as if I were a person of consequence. I am Christ's prisoner in chains, but I am not yet perfected in him. Indeed, I am but a beginner at this moment, and I write to you as fellow-disciples. It is I who need you to anoint me before the battle, with faith and encouragement, with patience and endurance. But love will not let me keep silence, and so I am taking the initiative in urging you to walk in accordance with the thought of God. For Jesus Christ, our inseparable life, is the thought of God, just as the bishops that are appointed to the ends of the earth are in the thought of Jesus Christ.

IGNATIUS OF ANTIOCH

Tuesday

You have only one physician,
for body and spirit alike,
born and unborn,
he is made flesh and he is God himself;
at the very heart of death, he is true life,
born of Mary, born of God,
at first subject to suffering,
but now beyond every pain:
he is none other than our Lord Jesus Christ.

CONTINUES . . .

Wednesday

Do not allow anyone to lead you astray; moreover you must never give way to betraying yourself, for you belong solely to God. If you refuse any place for quarrelling among you, which might so easily tear you apart, then you will truly live according to God.

All those who live according to the flesh cannot perform the works of the spirit, and those who live according to the spirit cannot do deeds of the flesh (Rom. 8:4). In the same way, faith cannot work infidelity, nor can unbelief treat with faith. But even the deeds you do that are of the body are deemed to be of the spirit: that is because everything you do is done in the name of Jesus Christ.

CONTINUES . . .

Thursday

Raised by the crane of Christ

You are the stones of the Father's temple, made ready for God's building, raised aloft by the crane of Jesus Christ which is the cross, with the Holy Spirit for the rope; your faith pulls you upwards and love is the way that raises you to God. You are also all to be companions on this road, bearers of God, temples of the Spirit, carriers of Christ, bringing with you holy gifts, you are adorned by the commandments of Jesus Christ.

I share with you your gladness, for I have been judged worthy to write to you and to rejoice with you that in your new life you love God alone. Pray for other men without ceasing. We may hope to see them being converted and meeting God; but until that happens allow them at least to follow your example and become your disciples.

CONTINUES . . .

Friday

Our God present in us

Nothing is hidden from the Lord, even our secrets are close to him. So as we go about our work, let us always remember that he dwells in us: so we will be his temples, and he will be our God present in us. For he *is* present in us, that is the plain truth of the matter, and it is precisely as we love him that he will show himself to our own eyes.

CONTINUES . . .

Saturday

Mysteries of God's silence

I am a victim of that cross which is a stumbling-block for unbelievers, but for us salvation and eternal life. Where is the sage? Where is the sophist? Where is the emptiness of the self-styled gnostic? Jesus Christ our God was carried in Mary's womb according to the divine plan, he was born of the lineage of David by the Holy Spirit. He was born, and later he was baptized to purify the water by his suffering. The prince of this world knew nothing of Mary's virginity, of her childbearing and of the death of the Lord—three resounding mysteries accomplished in God's silence. . . .

CONTINUES . . .

Week Two

Sunday

Breaking the one same bread

If Jesus Christ makes me worthy to do so thanks to your prayers, and if it is the will of God, I will explain to you in a second letter the divine plan about which I have begun to tell you, the plan that concerns Jesus Christ, the new man. It consists of faith in him and love for him, in his suffering and his resurrection. My explanation will be all the better if the Lord makes it known to me that each one of you individually and all of you at once, by the grace that comes from his name, come together in one same faith in Jesus Christ, who is of the lineage of David according to the flesh, son of man and son of God; if you obey the bishop and the priests in harmony; and if you break the one same bread, which is the medicine of immortality and the antidote to preserve us from death and make us live forever in Jesus Christ.

CONTINUES . . .

Monday

I have to run my course
Christians of Rome, blessed of God, at last I have gained from God by my eager and persistent prayers the boon of seeing you face to face.

In the chains I bear for Jesus Christ, I hope to greet you, if by God's will I am found worthy to go on to the end. But I fear that your charity may wrong me, if you speak to the authorities on my behalf. It is easy for you to do anything you wish, but for me it will be difficult to reach God, if you do not let me go.

My wish is that you should please not men but God; as indeed you do. Never shall I have another chance of finding God: and you, by keeping silent, are doing the best deed of your lives. If you say nothing about me, I am God's; if you love my flesh, I shall have to run my course again. Obtain nothing for me but to be offered as a sacrifice to God while the altar is still prepared.

In charity gather yourselves into a choir and sing a hymn to the Father in Jesus Christ, because God has deigned to make the bishop of Syria worthy to be found in him, he has brought him from the east to the west. It is good for me to set far away from the world, that I may rise in Christ.

CONTINUES . . .

Tuesday

I am God's wheat

You have never been jealous of others, you have been their teacher. I want you to put your lessons and your counsels into practice. Ask for me nothing but strength of spirit and of body, that I may not only speak but enact, that I may be Christian not merely in name but in deed. If I am a true Christian, that time for me to call myself one, the time when I am truly a believer, will be when I am no longer to be seen by the eyes of men.

Nothing that can be seen is good. And Jesus Christ our God, having returned to his Father, shows himself in still greater splendor. When the Christian religion is hated by the world, then it is no longer a matter of human eloquence, it is a work of the power of God.

I write to all the churches, and this is what I tell them: with a good heart I go to die for God, if you do not prevent me. I beg you, do not show me any untimely kindness. Let me be food for the beast: by their means I shall be able to meet God. I am God's wheat; I am to be ground by the teeth of beasts and become the pure bread of Christ.

IGNATIUS OF ANTIOCH

Wednesday

SAINT IRENÆUS (C.130–200)

I am who I-Am

He who is God and Lord of all things, he alone deserves the name God. He alone is called Lord.

It was he who said to Moses: "I am who I-Am. This is what you must say to the sons of Israel, I-Am has sent me." The same name belongs to his Son, Jesus Christ our Lord; and those, who believe in his name, Christ makes them sons of God.

Of old he said to Moses: "I have come down to deliver this people; for it was he and no other who came down and who went up again (Eph.4:10) to save mankind." So, through the Son who is in the Father and who has the Father in him, the God who is has revealed himself: "the Father who sent me bears witness to me himself" (John 5:37). It is the Son who announces the Father.

SAINT IRENÆUS

Thursday

I call upon you

I too call upon you, Lord God of Abraham, God of Isaac, God of Jacob and of Israel (Ex.3:15). You are the Father of our Lord Jesus Christ. In your infinite mercy you have loved us and made yourself known to us. You are maker of heaven and earth, Lord of all, the one true God—for there is none other above you. Through Jesus Christ, the Lord, you bestow upon us the rule of your Spirit; give to all those who read what I have written recognition that you are their only God, be their strength always and save them from all error and distrust.

CONTINUES . . .

Friday

Through the Word all things were made

No creature lower than God is to be compared with the Word of God through whom all things were made: Jesus Christ our Lord.

To take the angels, archangels, thrones, dominations, God, who is above them all, made and established them; indeed, through his Word he made them, as John tells us: speaking of the Word that was with God, he goes on: "through him all things came to be, not one thing had its being but through him" (John 1:3).

David too sings in praise of the Word: "Let heaven praise Yahweh; praise him, heavenly heights, praise him, all his angels, praise him, all his armies"; and he continues: "he has fixed them in their place forever; at his command they were created" (Ps.148). And through whom did he command this? Through his Word. And elsewhere he says as much: "by the Word of Yahweh the heavens were made, their whole array by the breath of his mouth" (Ps. 33:6).

Now that which is stood in being is not he who sets it there; what is created is not he who creates. The Creator is made by no one, he has no beginning, no end. He lacks nothing, he is sufficient in himself; he it is who gives being to all that exists. By contrast, the things that were made by him knew their beginning; and everything that begins bears with it the germ of decay; it is dependent, for it needs its Creator to continue.

CONTINUES . . .

Saturday

Christ as God's seed

The Word, only Son of the Father, is ever present to mankind; he is at one with the work that he has fashioned in his Father's knowledge: for he has impregnated it with his own divine seed (I John 3:9).

This has come about because being of our Flesh, he is our Lord, Jesus Christ; he has suffered for us, he has risen again for us; and it is he who will come once more in the glory of the Father to raise all Flesh. It is then that he will reveal his work of salvation to dazzle the universe; subject once more to his law, his justice will be praised by all.

There is then but one God and one only Father; there is but one Christ, who is Jesus our Lord: his coming impregnates the God plan of our salvation: He utters the universe in himself. Now within this universe there is man: Being made by God—thus Christ utters man in himself. And it is for this: He who is unseen may now be seen; the unknowable appears within our grasp; he who should not suffer, suffered. Thus did the Man who is Word gather all things to himself.

This then is the Word of God who rules the entire world of spirit unseen in high heaven: this Word is master, too, of our world that is seen.

As head of the Church he gathers all things to himself at the time that God has fixed.

CONTINUES . . .

Sunday

Always present to mankind

The Word, with God in the beginning, through whom all things were made, has always been present to mankind. This Word has made himself one with the work of his hands to become true man, able to suffer: this he has done in the last days, the true time already fixed by the Father. He has taken Flesh; assuming in himself the entire race and lineage of man, he offers us in his own person the sum of salvation. What we lost in Adam, we regain in Christ Jesus.

Once man, overcome by his disobedience, had become broken, he could never regain the prize of victory that had been promised him. Ever since he had fallen into sin, man could never on his own account attain once more that state of salvation. So it was the Son who achieved something we could never do for ourselves. He who was the Word of God came down from the Father's side and was made Flesh; he humbled himself even to accepting death and brought to its conclusion the plan of our salvation.

CONTINUES . . .

Monday

Generous physician

God's generosity is very great: he leads humanity through all the stages of salvation. First, man must be taught to know about death; then he must learn about resurrection from the dead. Knowing full well the prison from which he has been rescued, he cherishes an overwhelming gratitude towards his Saviour. And finding his immortality in Christ, he knows even greater love; "he will love more who is pardoned most" (Luke 7:42).

And so man has come to learn how weak he is under death's shadow; yet he is also taught that the God of wisdom and power will confer his life-giving vigor on man: "what was sown perishable will become imperishable" (I Cor. 15:53). He has also learned of the many other God-given energies that lie to hand for his help; and through them he can begin to discern something of God's grandeur. For now God has come to be recognized as man's glory: but man himself is merely the vessel in which God continually pours the wisdom and power of his workings.

God is like a physician exercizing his skills on his patient; he shows us plainly who he is as he attends to mankind's every need. As Paul puts it: "God has imprisoned all men in their own disobedience only to show mercy to all mankind" (Rom. 11:32).

CONTINUES . . .

Tuesday

The second Adam to be like the first

The work of the Word was set down long before it was brought together under Christ. Through the disobedience of one man sin made its entrance, bringing in train the rule of death; so by one man's obedience many will be justified and life will be brought to men long since dead (*vide* Rom. 5). The stuff of Adam, the first man to be formed, was from earth that was intact—"for Yahweh God had not sent rain upon the earth, nor was there any man to till the soil" (Gen. 2:5). And Adam was formed by the hand of God, that is by his Word: for it is written; "through him all things were made."

In the same way the Word, summing up in himself the person of Adam, came to be born of one who stayed a virgin, of Mary. Thus it was right that the second Adam be engendered in the same way.

For if the first Adam had had a human father and been born of human seed, then there would be good reason for claiming that the second Adam must also have been begotten, as son of Joseph. But since the first Adam had been taken from the earth and formed by the Word of God, it follows that the Word, in whom Adam was summed up, should have the same origin.

But why did God not take dust of the soil once more? Why did he work in Mary to bring to birth work that he himself could fashion? Quite simply, in order that the work he made should be no different from the first so that the first and no other might be saved: it would be exactly the same, recapitulating the first man and identical in kind.

CONTINUES . . .

Wednesday

Mary's words of obedience

According to Luke, the genealogy going backwards from our Lord's birth to Adam is made up of seventy-two generations. By means of it, he joins the end with the beginning and demonstrates how our Lord summed up in himself all those nations that had dispersed across the earth since man first appeared, all their languages, all their many tribes and including Adam himself.

That is why Paul names Adam "figure of the One who was to come" (Rom. 5:14): for the Word, the Craftsman who made all things, had planned beforehand what he would accomplish in himself, the design that would relate the human race to the Son of God.

God first formed the old Adam with the precise plan of saving him by means of the new, spiritual Adam. The Saviour already existed in God; so it follows that man must be made in order to be saved; or else the Saviour would be pointless.

Following out God's same plan, we come to understand Mary's words of obedience: "I am the handmaid of the Lord; let what you have said be done to me" (Luke 1:38). But Eve fell into disobedience and caused death to herself and all mankind; while Mary, virgin wife of a man chosen by God, by her obedience caused salvation not just for herself but for all mankind.

CONTINUES . . .

Thursday

The twofold truth

No one can know the Father without the Word of God, that is unless the Son reveals the Father; and no one may know the Son except it pleases the Father.

Now the Son has accomplished this good pleasure: the Father sends, the Son is sent and so he comes. To us the Father is unseen, but his own Word knows him fully; for he expresses this inexpressible mystery. And in return, the Word is known only to the Father. Such is the twofold truth our Lord teaches us. So that by showing us himself, the Son opens our path to knowing his Father: to see the Son is to uncover the source of our knowledge of the Father: in the Word the whole mystery is revealed. And to show us that it is the Son, by his coming, who brings this knowledge of his Father to birth in all who believe in him, Jesus told his disciples: "no one knows the Son except the Father, just as no one knows the Father except the Son—and those to whom the Son chooses to reveal him"

(Matt. 11:27). In these words he means us to understand who he himself is and who the Father is, so that we may know none other Father than him who is revealed by the Son.

CONTINUES . . .

Friday

The unseen mystery of the Son was the Father

It is through creation that the Word reveals God, the creator of the world. In the order there is within the world, he shows us the Lord who ordered the world. In man, fashioned and made from "the dust of the soil," he shows the Artist who conceived man. And as Son, he reveals the Father who begot the Son. All say the same as this; yet not all believe alike.

Or again, by the Law and the prophets the Word announced himself, as he announced the Father: all the people heard his word, but not all of them believed alike.

At length, the Word gave himself to be seen and touched; through him too the Father also showed himself. Yet although not all believed in him, none could avoid seeing the Father in the Son: for the unseen mystery of the Son was the Father, and the Father showed himself in the Son. That is why when they came into his presence, all alike recognized him as Christ and named him God. And even the demons, when they saw him, cried out: "we know who you are, the Holy One of God" (Mark 1:24). And tempter declared in his presence: "If you are the Son of God . . ." (Matt. 4:3). They alike saw the Son and with him the Father; all named him Son, although not all believed.

CONTINUES . . .

Saturday

Christ is sown throughout the Scriptures

In Saint John we see Jesus saying: "You study the Scriptures, believing that in them you have eternal life; now these same Scriptures testify to me, and yet you refuse to come to me for life!" (John 5:39). How could the Scriptures bear witness to him, if they did not stem from his own true Father, telling the world in advance of his Son who should come?"

Again, Christ said: "You place your hopes in Moses, and Moses will be your accuser. If you really believed in him, you would believe in me too, since it was I that he was writing about" (John 5:46). In fact, the Son is sown throughout the Scriptures in the writings of Moses. Here he talks to Abraham; there he gives Noah the dimensions of the ark; now he seeks Adam; later on he comes to judge the men of Sodom; or here again he shows himself to Jacob and guides him on his journey; now he is speaking to Moses from the burning bush. In each of these many texts it is Moses who shows the Son of God. Even the day of his passion was not unknown to Moses who spoke of it symbolically under the name of the Pasch. It was on this same feast, proclaimed so long in advance by the man of God, that the Lord endured his passion and so accomplished the true Pasch.

Moses did not merely prefigure the feast, he foretold where it would take place, and equally the fullness of time, too, signified by the setting of the sun: "You may not sacrifice the passover in any of the towns that Yahweh your God gives you," he writes, "but only in the place where Yahweh your God chooses to give his name

a home, there you must sacrifice the passover, in the evening sunset . . ." (Deut. 16:5).

SAINT IRENÆUS

Week Four

⌒

Sunday

THE LETTER TO DIOGNETUS

Born to some new life

Christians certainly are in the body, yet they do not live according
to that body. As their life on earth unfolds, they grow to be citizens
of heaven. They obey all the proper laws, yet their way of life is
more perfect than any law.

All men they love, but they are persecuted by all. They are misunderstood, they stand condemned: they are put to death, and
through death they gain life. They are poor, yet this makes them
rich. They lack everything, yet they have all things in abundance.
They are despised, but such contempt is their highest glory. They
are slandered: they repay it with honour; they do nothing but good
and are treated as criminals; receiving their punishment, they are
overjoyed as if they were born to some new life.

The Jews pursue them as a national nuisance; the Greeks per-
secute them; and those who hate them most cannot find words to
explain their feelings.

THE LETTER TO DIOGNETUS

Monday

God sets them a vital task

To say all this in so many words: what the soul is to the body, Christians are in the world.

The soul is present to every part of the body, and so too Christians are to be found in every city.

The soul dwells in the body without itself being that body; and Christians dwell in the world without being of the world.

The soul, unseen of itself, is a prisoner in the body that is seen; and so too, Christians, though they are to be found in the world, offer worship to God who is invisible.

The body hates the soul and wars with it all the time; not that the soul ever did it harm, but simply because it stands in the way of the pleasures of the flesh. And so too, the world hates Christians, who do it no harm, because Christians stand out against its pleasures.

The soul loves the body that hates it, loves each of its members; and so do Christians love those who hate them.

The soul is enfolded within the body; yet it serves to preserve the body: Christians, likewise, are held as prisoners of this world while they safeguard the world they are in.

The soul although immortal inhabits a mortal home: so too Christians must live in this passing and corrupt world as they await the everlasting life of heaven.

The soul grows in strength by being tested by hunger and thirst; Christians who are persecuted grow in number from day to day.

The task that God has set them is so vital, that on no account may they forsake it.

CONTINUES . . .

Tuesday

No earthly origin

The Christian tradition has no earthly origin; what we are so proud of, what we seek at all costs to preserve is not of man's making, our faith is not a mixture of human mysteries. But the Omnipotent in person, the Unseen Maker of the Universe, namely God himself has sent his Truth from the height of the heavens and convinced men of his holy Word that passes all understanding; he has established the truth of his Word in their hearts.

CONTINUES . . .

Wednesday

Unspeakable wisdom

This Master and Maker of the Universe, God who made and disposed all things in his order, showed himself to us not only full of love for all men but full of patience. He has always been what he is and will be: swift to help, kind, patient and the fullness of truth: he is rightful. But when he drew up his plan of unspeakable wisdom, he uttered it to us by means of a baby.

CONTINUES . . .

Thursday

He disposed all things

He who was sent as Craftsman and Master of the universe; through him God made the heavens and through him he confined the sea to its limits. The elements of the world faithfully obey his mysterious ways; the sun took from him the law that sets its daily course; the moon shines at night in obedience to him, and as the moon goes, so go the stars, all under his guidance. He fixed the bounds and hierarchy of all beings; he too it was who disposed all things: the heavens and all they contain, the earth and all it bears, the sea and all it enfolds, fire and air and abyss, the upper and the nether regions and the middle one contained between the two.

Such is He whom God sent among men.

CONTINUES . . .

Friday

He has prepared his reign of justice

All the time God kept his own wise mind and held this mystery in his own contemplation, he appeared to forget us, even to hold no interest in men. But when through this beloved Child he showed us plainly what he had determined from the beginning, he gave us everything all at once: a share in his bounty, the sight and understanding of his plan. Could any man have dared expect it to be so?

God therefore had already determined everything between himself and his Child; but until just lately he allowed us to remain slaves to our pleasures and to passion, swept along here and there by every disordered urge. That is not to say he took some spiteful pleasure when he saw us in such sin; yet he was content that wickedness should rule while he prepared his present reign of justice. And so, while the first interval of time showed us how unworthy of this life we were, now we are able to grow worthy of life through the goodness of God's gift; we have known how impossible it is to enter the kingdom by our own efforts, but now we may do so by the power of God.

CONTINUES . . .

Saturday

Imitate the Father's goodness

If you also desire to embrace this faith, if you would long to understand it, then you must begin to know the Father. For God created men, for them he created this world; he placed under their rule everything that exists upon this earth. He gave them reason, he offered them wisdom; and he gave them the right to lift their eyes to heaven. He made them in his own image. And finally, he even sent his only Son to them who promised the Kingdom of heaven as his gift to those who love him.

And once you know him, think what joy will fill your heart. How you will learn to love him who first loved you. And as you love him, you will come to imitate his goodness.

Do not think it strange that man may imitate his God: It is meant to be, and it is possible, for God wills it so. Lording it over other men, wielding power over the weak, putting down the poor and meek—there is no happiness in such deeds, men do not imitate God in such a way; for those deeds are far removed from God's greatness. But the man who takes upon his own shoulder the burden of another, who tries to offer those who have less some share of his own advantages, who gives to the needy without thinking all that God has given him: such a man is playing the same role as God to those to whom he gives: He is a true imitator of God.

THE LETTER TO DIOGNETUS

--------- *W e e k F i v e* ---------

Sunday

SAINT CLEMENT OF ALEXANDRIA
(C. 150 – 215)

His chosen lyre, tuned by the Holy Spirit
God has given to the universe a musical arrangement; he has placed the dissonant elements under the discipline of harmony, that the whole world may become a symphony to his ears. He has left the sea unbridled but has not failed to forbid it to encroach on the land; the land that itself was once a flux he has hardened and set up as a frontier to the ocean.

He has tamed the icy cold of the air by passing fire through the midst of it, and all these conflicting voices of the world he has finely blended together. From centre to the periphery, from the periphery back to the centre, he has orchestrated this pure concert of the universe that keeps all beings in mutual harmony. Its melodious flow he has regulated not by the rules of Greek music derived from the invention of Jubal (Gen. 4:21), but by the fatherly will of God, which was David's concern.

And so, that descendant of David, the Word of God who was existing before David, despised the unspiritual harp and lyre; his chosen instrument was our world, and particularly man, body and soul, who is the world in microcosm. This is his lyre, tuned by the Holy Spirit, and on it he plays the accompaniment to his own voice as he sings his song for God.

SAINT CLEMENT OF ALEXANDRIA

Monday

Playing the drama of our salvation

With matchless speed and a goodness that could not hold aloof, the divine power illuminated the earth, filling everything with the seed of salvation.

Never without a divine providence would the Lord have accomplished this vast work in so short a time. His appearance invited scorn (Isa. 53:3), but his acts demanded worship; he was the Word of God, to cleanse, to reconcile and to save. He made it wholly clear that he was truly God, the equal of the Master of the universe; for he was his Son, and the Word was in God.

There were some who came to believe the ancient preaching by which he had been proclaimed beforehand, and when he took the form of a man and was fashioned in flesh to play out the drama of our salvation, he did not remain unknown; he entered the lists as a loyal fighter coming to the help of the creature he had formed.

From the bosom of the Father's will he rose, and swifter than the sun's rays he spread over the whole human race. Effortlessly he bathed us in light; his teaching and his signs led us to God from whom he came and who by his very nature he was; for he was the Word, the messenger of peace, the mediator of the Covenant, our Saviour. He is the source, the giver of life and peace, spread over the surface of all the earth, transforming all things into an ocean of goodness.

CONTINUES . . .

Tuesday

Gift of knowledge from the Father

The man who has true knowledge of God is a man both religious and holy: he gives fitting worship to the majesty of God, and is loved by him. He has learnt in all things to honour that which is first: in the visible world, our fathers and the governors of the state; in the invisible world, he goes back to the firstborn, the eternal unborn Beginning, the Origin of all things, the Son.

Through the Son we may learn to know the ultimate Source, the universal Father, who is older than all and who distributes his benefits to all. No creature can find words to describe him: in silence and holy dread we revere him, to whom we owe fealty above all. The Lord speaks to us of him in language that we can understand; the chosen disciples receive the gift of knowledge from the Father. There are they whose judgement, as the apostle says, is trained to discern good and evil (Heb. 5:14).

This, then, is authentic worship: to be constantly vigilant over our soul, and to place God in the forefront of our lives in an unfailing love.

CONTINUES . . .

Wednesday

The Son: the living activity of the Father
In the nature of the Son dwell the height of perfection, absolute holiness, supreme and most royal majesty, universal well-doing; no other being is closer than he to the Father, the Sovereign Lord.

As he is above all, the Son orders all things according to the will of his Father; he guides the universe wonderfully, working everywhere with an untiring power, his eyes fixed on the mystery of God's plan. The Son watches without failing; he does not move from place to place, he does not split himself up nor share himself out, but is everywhere at once and knows no limit. He is all spirit, all light streaming out from the Father, all vision; he sees all, he hears all, he knows all. His power pervades the powers that govern the world, and he is universally obeyed.

Word of the Father, he makes manifest God's plan, to the glory of him who put all things under his feet. All men belong to him, some as friends, some as faithful servants. Our Lord's function is referred to in its entirety as the Sovereign Father; the Son is as it were the living activity of the Father.

CONTINUES . . .

Thursday

We honour his Son by offering ourselves in sacrifice
The soul that possesses spiritual knowledge works within itself a transformation and as it were a re-creation; it grows in likeness to

God and can be the sower of the inner harmony in those that seek its company.

It has learnt by asceticism to control its passions and has reached the highest possible degree of resemblance to him who is Unchanging by nature. More than this, it is in habitual converse with the Lord and is always with him.

Now the soul grows towards likeness with God to the extent that it is good and loving towards others and profoundly religious. These virtues, I insist, are the sacrifice which is pleasing to God: they lead to simplicity of heart, and when they are joined to a sound knowledge, they make up the true holocaust of which Scripture speaks. For God reserves men to himself to make them holy, and they receive the light of knowledge that they may be one with him and never parted.

It is at the heart of the gospel, it is the whole teaching of the Apostle, that we should give ourselves up as captives to God, that we should inflict death upon the old man who is on the way to corruption through his passions, and that from him we should bring the new man to birth.

This explains why we offer no victims to God; he has no need of anything, indeed it is he that gives to all beings all that they have. But we honour his Son who sacrificed himself for us, and we do so by offering ourselves in sacrifice after his example. This offering comes from him who possesses all things, and to him it returns; its source is the Unmoved, which Unmoved is also its good.

CONTINUES . . .

Friday

Image of the image

The only offering that pleases God is our salvation. Why do the heathen imagine that he is a beggar, to be seduced or to be bribed?

He is plenitude; he provides for every need of every being that comes into the world. The heart of God is not taken prisoner by victims sacrificed or honours paid; he shows himself only to upright men who cannot bring themselves to betray justice, to be swayed by threats, or to yield to corruption.

The soul of the just is a divine image, as close to God as can be; it is obedient to the Commandments, and in it the sanctuary is being built of the Sovereign Master of all beings, mortal and immortal. In it the king himself comes to dwell, who is the source of goodness, the true law, the holy precept, the Word of eternity, the only Saviour of each human person and of the community of the universe.

He is the true and only Son, the imprint of the Father's glory and his Sovereign Majesty; on the enlightened soul he imprints the seal of perfect contemplation in the image of his own nature; and so the soul becomes image of the image, as like as can be to the Beginning, born of the Beginning, and to the true life by whose gift we truly live.

CONTINUES . . .

Saturday

God is everywhere, an enveloping presence
The man who truly knows God honours him not in a place set apart
or a chosen temple, nor on the feastdays set by a calendar, but
everywhere and all day long, whether he is alone or in the company
of brethren in the faith.

The presence of a holy man always inspires in those who seek
his society such respect and veneration as may make them better
men: the believer then, who is continually seeking God through an
enlightened faith, a life guided towards him and incessant thanksgiving, how much more will he be raised above himself in all his acts
and words and feelings?

His inmost conviction is that God is everywhere: no particular
place marks his limits, and nowhere, by day or by night, can we
imagine that he is absent and allow ourselves to grow lax. In this
belief that God is everywhere, an enveloping presence whichever
way we look, our life becomes an unending solemnity; we praise
him as we till the fields, we sing of him as we sail the seas; whatever
we do, this is the wisdom that is our guide. The spiritual man
lives close to God; never therefore under any circumstances does
he lose his gravity nor his gladness; gravity because he is turned
towards God, gladness at the thought of all the good things that God
in his kindness has given us. Such is the royal man, the holy priest
of God.

CONTINUES . . .

≈

Sunday

Prayer without ceasing, struggling to be with God
Prayer is, if I may use the phrase, a conversation with God. Even if
we whisper, even if we do not open our mouth, a cry rises within
us. And God never fails to hear this inner conversation.

Knowing this, we raise our eyes and lift up our hands to the
heavens, at the end of the prayer we stand for the acclamation and
fervently stretch out our soul towards God who is Spirit. We wish
that the body itself could follow our thought and tear itself away
from the earth; for the soul, raised up by the longing for better
things, looks heavenward; with all our energy we desire to go
through into the holy of holies, despising the bonds of flesh that tie
us to the world.

Some are accustomed, to be sure, to consecrate fixed hours to
prayer, as for example the third, the sixth and the ninth, but the
spiritual man prays without ceasing; prayer is the way by which he
struggles to be with God, and with this in view he leaves aside all
that is useless.

CONTINUES . . .

≈

Monday

Fulfilling the promise of the Psalmist
The Word of God,
born of the house of David, yet of far more ancient
lineage,

refusing harp, lyre and suchlike mindless instruments,
attuned the whole Universe to himself in the Holy Spirit,
in particular, the tiny world of man, his mind, his soul,
   his body.
And on this instrument, small yet with many voices, he
   sings to God,
and plays to his instrument, man.
"You are my harp, my flute, my sanctuary";
my harp for all your fine harmonies,
a flute by your breath,
my sanctuary for your memory and your mind.
May this harp sing at his every touch,
this flute breathe with his life-giving Breath,
may this sanctuary be the Lord's abiding home.

SAINT CLEMENT OF ALEXANDRIA,

PROTREPTIKON

Tuesday

ORIGEN (C. 185–C. 254)

He became the light of men

God is absolutely one: God is simple. It is his creatures who are diverse: thus our Saviour becomes many, for God predestined him to be the victim that earns pardon by offering himself as first-fruits of the whole of creation. Indeed, it seems only natural that on behalf of these creatures he came to deliver, he himself should be everything they could need.

He became the light of men: for men that are blinded by their wickedness need this light to shine in the darkness, which that darkness could not overpower. He would not have become the light of men if men had not been in darkness. The same consideration applies to his title first-born from the dead. Suppose the woman had not yielded to seduction and Adam had not fallen: suppose that man had taken possession of that incorruption for which he was made; then Christ would not have "lain in the dust of death" (Ps. 21:16). Had it not been for that sin which his love for men made him die, he would not have lost his life, nor would he have been the first-born from among the dead.

ORIGEN ON JOHN

Wednesday

On this way we need no sandals

We may understand how Christ is the way if we consider how we make progress in wisdom. We go forward seeking truth in the Divine speech, or the Word; and then by our actions we conform ourselves to true righteousness.

We may take nothing with us on this way, neither bag nor cloak; and we need no staff to walk with or sandals to wear. The way alone is enough: he will provide all we need for our journey. For the man who walks this way will lack nothing; he wears the guest-robe of one who is going to a wedding, and he will meet with no misfortune on his way. In the Book of Proverbs we are told the way of an eagle through the skies, the way of a snake over the rock is beyond comprehension (Prov. 30:19). And therefore a staff is useless when we are going by a way where such adversaries leave not so much as a trace; indeed, our way is so solid that it is called the rock and will repel all the attacks of the wicked.

CONTINUES . . .

Thursday

He is the peace between us

Our Lord is called Christ which means the Anointed. Now among creatures anointing is the sign of a king, or sometimes of a priest. Would this kingship of the Son of God have been given him as an afterthought? Would it not rather have been his at birth? Is it thinkable that the firstborn of all creation was not king from the beginning, or that he became king only after some period of trial and because he loved righteousness? As if he himself were not by nature righteous! Perhaps this is the explanation, that it was his manhood which received the anointing, the same manhood which felt troubled and afflicted in spirit because of his human nature; yet in his divinity he is king. This suggestion is supported by the words of Psalm 71: "O God, give the King your judgement, your righteousness to the King's son."

I think the title king is given to him who is pre-eminent by nature: he was born before all creatures and therefore judgement falls to him because of his transcendence. My reason for this is that the two are united in a single pronoun when the text goes on to speak not of two but of only one. "For he is the peace between us and has made the two into one" (Eph. 2:14); he did so perhaps because he had already brought into being the first and most fruitful union of two realities. And this mystery of union spreads to include all men, for the soul of each one is as it were so mingled with the Holy Spirit that all who are saved become men of the Spirit.

CONTINUES . . .

Friday

You are my servant

Jesus behaves with his disciples not as the one who is sitting at table but as the one who serves; he has taken on himself the condition of servant so as to deliver men from their servitude to sin. Consider these things and you will not fail to understand why the Father said to him: "You are my servant" and again "it is not enough for you to be my servant" (Isa. 49). For we must be bold and say that the goodness of Christ appeared greater and more godlike, more true to the image of the Father, when he abased himself and became obedient to death, his death on the cross. For this is what he chose to do; when instead he might have regarded his being equal to God as a treasure to be guarded jealously and as a result refused to accept the condition of servant who has come to redeem the world. He wanted us to know that this mission of service that the Father entrusted to him is a wonderful gift, as he declared: "I was honoured in the eyes of Yahweh, my God was my strength. And now Yahweh has spoken, he who formed me in the womb to be his servant, to bring Jacob back to him, to gather Israel to him: 'It is not enough for you to be my servant, to restore the tribes of Jacob and bring back the survivors of Israel; I will make you the light of the nations so that my salvation may reach to the ends of the earth' " (Isa. 49).

CONTINUES . . .

Saturday

I have begotten you this day

The only Son is Truth. For he grasps in its entirety and with perfect understanding the thought and intention of the Father for the universe. He is the Truth, and he gives each one of us a share of the Truth according to our merits. We might perhaps wonder whether our Saviour indeed knows all that is within the Father's comprehension, the full depth and measure of the riches of his wisdom and knowledge; on the pretext of giving glory to the Father, we might be tempted to assert that he knows certain things of which the Son remains ignorant. But in reality, the comprehension of the Son is equal to that of the Unbegotten God. We must remember that the Saviour is the Truth, and if the Truth is complete, there is nothing that it does not know; otherwise, this so-called Truth would fall short, shut off from those mysteries reserved to the Father.

As for the Son's high birth, hear these words which clearly spell it out: "You are my Son, I have begotten you this day." It is God who is saying this, and for him today means always. For in God, it seems to me, there can be neither evening nor morning; the same time which, dare I say it, measures his life as eternal and unbegun is that same today, when the Son was begotten. Therefore we can discover neither the beginning nor the day of his begetting.

CONTINUES . . .

❦

Sunday

The image of the invisible God

It may also be perhaps that the Son is Word in that he proclaims the secrets of his Father, who is Thought in the same way as the Son is called Word. For just as amongst ourselves, words proclaim the thoughts of our minds, in the same way the Word of God, knowing the Father whom no creature can come near without a guide, reveals the Father that he knows. For no one has known the Father save the Son, and him to whom the Son has revealed him.

As eternal Word, he is the angel of mighty counsel, and the government rests upon his shoulder; he has obtained the kingship by his suffering on the cross. In the Apocalypse it is said that the Word, faithful and true, is seated on a white horse; and this, I think, points to the clear voice in which the Word calls our attention to his coming. And just as in speaking we breathe out invisible breath into the open air, so also, it may be, the Father does not keep enclosed within himself the Truth on which he gazes, but breathes it out and passes on its shape to his Word, who for this reason is called the image of the invisible God.

CONTINUES . . .

❦

Monday

His victory over death

"Destroy this temple, and in three days I will raise it up" (John 2:19). There is an interpretation that I could give that sees both the temple and the body of Christ as images of his church. The church is built of living stones, and so it has become the spiritual home of a holy priesthood. Moreover, with apostles and prophets for its foundations, it is called a temple and Christ is its cornerstone.

You too are the Body of Christ and therefore his members, each of you has his part to play. Even if stones and fabric of the temple appear cracked and broken apart; even if, as is written in Psalm 21, those who rage against the unity of the temple plot and conspire together so that all the bones of Christ seem to be scattered as a result of this persecution and oppression; yet still the temple will be rebuilt, the Body raised up on the third day. After the day of unhappiness that breaks upon the Body (Sirach 7:14), and after the next day, when all seems lost, there will be a third day. Then there will be a new heaven and a new earth, when those bones, which are the whole house of Israel, stand upright again for the great day of the Lord (Ezek. 37), after his victory over death. You can see how the resurrection of Christ, which follows his sufferings on the cross, embraces within itself the mystery of the resurrection of his whole Body in its entirety.

ORIGEN ON JOHN

Tuesday

SAINT CYPRIAN (D. 258)

They are become children of God
"Our Father who art in heaven."

Man is made anew, born again; he is reconciled to his God by grace. And so his prayer begins with the word Father, for now he is

God's son. "He came to his own domain and his own people did not accept him. But to all who did accept him he gave power to become children of God" (John 1:11). Therefore anyone believing in his name, who has become a child of God, should first give him thanks; he should acknowledge he is God's child and that his Father is God, the God of heaven.

My dearest brothers, we should not stop short at merely knowing that we give the name Father to him who is in heaven, nor at knowing the reason why. For we say also that he is Our Father, that is the Father of all who believe, all who are made holy by him, all who are made new by being born into grace so that now they are become children of God.

ON THE LORD'S PRAYER

Wednesday

Impatient to be present

"Thy Kingdom come."

By the Kingdom of God, we should understand Christ himself; for we long for his coming every new day, we are impatient to be present before him. Just as he is our resurrection, since in him we will rise again, so too we can say that he is in person the Kingdom of God, for we will reign in him. It is only right that we should pray for the coming of God's Kingdom, that is to say the Kingdom of Heaven; true there is also a kingdom of this earth, but the Christian who has turned aside from the world has greater honours and riches than any it can provide. So whoever gives themselves to God and to Christ looks forward to the heavenly kingdom, not for any kingdom of this world.

And we continue to pray, "Thy will be done on earth as it is in heaven": not meaning that God should do his own will, but that we should be given strength to do God's will. For who could possibly stop God from doing his will? Yet the devil puts every obstacle in our way when we try to obey God in our every thought and deed. That is why we pray that God's will may be done in us. And this can only happen if God wills it, that is if he gives us his continual help and protection.

CONTINUES . . .

Thursday

This bread belongs to us

"Give us this day our daily bread."

We can understand this literally and also in a spiritual way. Either sense means our prayer is answered by help coming from God that is so vital for our salvation.

The bread of life is Christ: This bread is not for every man, it belongs only to us. In the same way, we say: Our Father; because he is Father to those who understand the faith, so we say: Our Bread; for Christ is the bread of those who have access to his Body. And we ask for this bread day by day; we who are in Christ, we receive the Eucharist every day to be the food of our salvation. But we fear that a grave sin may surprise us and prevent us approaching the bread of heaven. Then we would be separated from the Body of Christ, who said: "I am the living bread which has come down from heaven. Anyone who eats this bread will live forever; and the bread I shall give is my flesh, for the life of the world" (John 6:51).

And so we ask for our bread, which is Christ, to be given us each day. As we dwell in Christ and have our life in him, so we want nothing ever to separate us from his sanctifying work or to cut us off from his Body.

CONTINUES . . .

Friday

Confess and he will forgive

"Forgive us our trespasses, as we forgive those who trespass against us."

First we ask for food, then we ask pardon for our faults. Fed by God, we long to live in him. We are aware not only of our present life in time, we look forward to our future eternal life. And we cannot come to this unless we win pardon for our sins, or debts, as our Lord tells us in the Gospel: "I cancelled all that debt of yours when you appealed to me" (Matt. 18:32). It is a lesson we need to learn for our own good; which is why our Lord wants us to remember our sinful state so that we ask all the while to be forgiven. When we seek God's mercy, we should first look at our conscience and confront our sins. It was to safeguard against our becoming self-satisfied and think we have nothing wrong with us that our Lord advised us to pray about our sins every day. For each day that dawns, we sin. This is what John too writes in his first letter: "If we say we have no sin in us, we are deceiving ourselves and refusing to admit the truth. But if we acknowledge our sins, then God who is faithful and just will forgive our sins and purify us from everything that is wrong."

CONTINUES . . .

Saturday

Living in the same Spirit

In this home of his, which is prayer, God wants us to find peace, joined one with another, living in the same Spirit. He wants us to live this new life that we have been given in baptism.

We are now become children of God; let us live in his peace. We have been given the one Spirit: let us have one heart, and a single thought. God will not accept the offering of someone who has cut themselves off from the rest. He bids such a person leave the altar and first become reconciled with his brother, so that God will be pleased by the prayers of a heart that has found peace. For the sacrifice most pleasing to God is that peace should flow between the brethren; then the divine union of the Trinity, Father, Son and Holy Spirit, joins us together.

God's just and peaceful servant Abel offered his sacrifice with a pure heart. He showed us how to bring our offering to the altar in the fear of God, simply at peace with an upright heart. Indeed such was his goodness of heart that he deserved to become a victim himself, giving us the first example of martyrdom. For just as he had first borne the image of God's rightfulness and peace, so he shed his blood nobly, and thus he prefigured the passion of our Lord.

CONTINUES . . .

Sunday

Eternal life is this . . .

"Deliver us from evil."

Once we have made this petition, there is nothing more to be said. For once he grants us this request, we will be safe, hidden away from every attack of the devil and the temptations of the world. For how can the world harm us when our protector is God himself? This is the prayer, my dearest brothers, our Lord has taught us to pray.

It is only short because it carries our Lord's meaning precisely: in one short, life-giving text, he gives us all we need to pray.

God's Living Word, who is our Lord Jesus Christ, came for all men; he wanted to draw all men to himself, wise and ignorant alike. He spoke to them his law of salvation, whatever sex they were or age. And he fashioned a wonderful summary of his law for them, to teach them the wisdom of heaven. Without over-loading their memories, he made it possible for them to learn in a very short time the simple elements of faith. Similarly, to teach us the basic nature of eternal life, Christ summed up life's mystery in a few simple, God-given words: "Eternal life is this: to know you, the only true God, and Jesus Christ whom you have sent" (John 17:3).

CONTINUES . . .

Monday

Our Lord prayed

It was not only with his words that our Lord taught us to pray, but also by his works; he too often prayed to his Father. He showed us how to pray by his own example; in the Gospel, we may read how he went into the desert to pray. And in another place we find, he went apart onto the mountain to pray and there he spent the entire night in prayer with God. If it was his practice to pray, he who knew not sin, then what of us who are sinners? How much more do we stand in need of prayer. If he would spend whole nights in prayer, are we not duty bound to make our vigils into the night?

Our Lord prayed: he pleaded with his Father, not on his own account, for he needed no forgiveness, but on behalf of us sinners. In those words he spoke to Simon Peter: "Simon, Simon! Satan, you must know, has got his wish to sift you all like wheat; but I have prayed for you, Simon, that your faith may not fail" (Luke 22:31). And elsewhere he prays to his Father for the salvation of all men: "I pray not only for these, but for those also who through their words will believe in me. May they all be one. Father, may they be one in us" (John 17:20).

CONTINUES . . .

Tuesday

We lift our hearts to the Lord

Brethren, when we set out to pray, let us do so with all our care and concentration. We should put aside every earthly and fleshly thought to let our mind be filled by God alone.

In the same way, the priest also, before he begins the Eucharistic prayer, captures our attention with the words: "Let us lift up our hearts." To which the people reply: "We lift them up to the Lord." Thus they are reminded that they should forget every concern they may have and care only for the Lord. We should close the door of our heart to the devil and open it to God alone. We must not allow our enemy to come near at our time of prayer. For he can so easily worm his way deep inside us and cunningly turn our prayer away from God, so that our heart is no longer in tune with our lips.

On the contrary, we must seek the Lord in purity, calling on him not only with words but with our hearts and minds. How cowardly to let our minds wander in time of prayer so that they lack any devotion, any progress. Is anything more important to us than God; is this little thing about to deprive you of him? How ever can you expect God to listen to you when you are incapable of listening to yourself? Why should he remember you, when you forget him? It is good advice to listen to Saint Paul's warning: "Be careful when you pray and when you give thanks."

CONTINUES . . .

Wednesday

Continual prayer

Scripture speaks of Christ as the true Sun and very Day, so that there can be no time when a Christian should not be offering his continual and fervent prayers to God.

If we are one in Christ, who is true Sun and very Day, we should strive to pray all day long; and so when night follows the day, according to the law that governs the universe, those who have prayed will have nothing to fear from the darkness. For the children of light, night and day are alike.

How can you be without light, if there is light in your heart? How can the sun be absent, when Christ is your Sun? If then we remain continually in Christ, who is light, let us not cease to pray when it is night. For if we remember the new life that grace has brought us, then night itself will be our daylight. Let us know that we are always walking in the Light, and so we must never again let ourselves be caught up by the darkness that we have left behind.

We should never undervalue our night prayers, nor be lazy or careless as we pray them. God's love has made us new creatures: let us be at this present moment what we will become. In the Kingdom there is but perpetual day which gives no place to night. So learn today how to spend the night as vigil of that day. If our future is to give thanks without end, let us give God here and now our continual prayers and thanks.

SAINT CYPRIAN ON THE LORD'S PRAYER

Thursday

ANTONY ABBOT (250–353)

I no longer fear God, I love him,
and love chases fear out of doors.

ANTONY ABBOT

Whenever a large crowd such as this came to his cell, Antony was never put out. He listened patiently to all they had to tell him and treated each person gently and with immense courtesy. And they recognized that the Living Word informed all his actions and his every utterance. Among those who came to him were many who had all manner of afflictions both of mind and body; and Our Lord healed them by the hand of this blessed man. Moreover God graced his words to them so that everyone found consolation and fresh strength to suffer their particular lot. The sick endured their illness in patience, the proud became humble, the arrogant changed their ways at the very sight of such a holy man. He used to tell them: "We should own nothing superfluous but love Christ alone: neither possessions, nor family, not even our own soul. For if God himself did not spare his own Son, but gave him up for our sins, how much more just is it that we, having tasted and known his Divine grace, should surrender our souls to him. And this we should do, not for his sake for that is not what is wanted: but to save our very lives!"

When he spoke in this way, many were persuaded to give up the world and all its busy ways and hide themselves away where monks lived.

ATHANASIUS OF ALEXANDRIA,

LIFE OF ANTONY ABBOT

Friday

He would teach his brethren in these words:

It is only right that we should continually seek the food of our souls. The soul collaborates with our spirit in striving to overcome the enemy. So it is necessary for the body to be subjected and put to the test, for it so easily gets above itself due to the urgings and flattery of the evil one. Rather than look after our body, we must care for our soul. We should always put our soul before the body otherwise it will dominate us with its constant physical demands. Our Lord taught as much when he told the Apostles: "Do not fret, asking, what are we to eat? what are we to drink? It is for the heathen to busy themselves over such things. You have a Father in heaven who knows that you need them all. Make it your first care to find the kingdom of God and his approval, and all these things will be yours without asking" (Matt. 6:31f.).

CONTINUES . . .

Saturday

He would tell all the monks that their most important duty was to confess gladly their faith in Christ; and they should love to perform this task with all their strength. They should also purge their hearts of evil thoughts, and turn aside from the lusts of the body. They should avoid at all costs vain boasting but pray without ceasing. They should always be ready to sing the psalms and perform their office before they slept. As soon as they awoke, they should call to mind the words of Scripture which was their life staff. They should meditate especially on the acts and lives of the Apostles. They should also consider who they were before they had met Christ; also what sort of man they had become now that they had drawn near to him. How in the former state they were despised: how as monks they were now revered and held in high honor both in this world and in the world to come. But that it was none of their own efforts which had achieved all this, but the grace of God alone. Antony used admonitions like these to advise and enlighten their minds and make their hearts zealous.

CONTINUES . . .

Sunday

This is how he spoke:

Since we are monks, we must be on our guard against being overtaken by anger. Satan will steal all our good works away from us if we neglect this. And our Lord tells us, "If you are bringing your gift to the altar and you remember you have a quarrel with your brother, go straightaway and be reconciled with him. Then bring your offering" (Matt. 5:23).

And we must remember Saint Paul's words: "Never let the sun go down on your anger" (Eph. 4:26). Yet this was not said merely to put us on our guard against anger alone, but against every kind of sin. It is very proper to warn us that the sun should not go down on our sin; or that the moon should not rise over our sin. Otherwise we might find ourselves in the service of the evil one, our thoughts taken up in his affairs. We should take to heart the Apostle's words:

"Examine yourselves to find whether you are living in the faith. Test yourselves" (II Cor. 13:5). Let each one of us examine our deeds and our conscience daily both in the morning and in the evening. Let everyone be honest in scrutinizing his soul aware that one day he must appear before the Son of Man to be judged (Matt. 16:27). Those who have resisted sin, he will encourage. The man who stands in all truth, he will encourage to new efforts. But he will also admonish him for fear all his virtue be lost in boastfulness or leached away by overconfidence. Or in case he despise this man and make another his favorite. And as the Apostle Paul tells us, "Let us do these things until such time as the Lord comes" (I Tim. 6:14) who will reveal all that is hidden.

CONTINUES . . .

Monday

For it may come about that we ourselves lose sight of our way of life and our daily practice; but although this may happen, God is well aware, for he sees all things. So let him be our Judge. Let us, at all times, carry each other's burdens; let us suffer for one another just as our Lord suffered for us; but let us continue to examine our consciences without cease, so that we can be quick to make good any ground we may have lost. And as a protection against sin, let everyone write down, or at least commit to heart, each one of his sins as if he were about to manifest them to his brethren. Remember how utterly ashamed we would be to have them made known in public. Then we will hold back from such sins and allow no evil thoughts to entertain our hearts. For who would want to be seen in the act of sinning? For who would not lie about some evil they have done, rather than have it discovered? Take a carnal sin: we would never commit that in the sight of others. And so if we record our thoughts as if we were about to tell them to another, we will more easily avoid such evil thoughts for fear they might be discovered. So when we write down such things about our sinful thoughts and actions, that can stand in place of our brethren's watchful eyes. Then blushing to write such matters as if we had been caught in the act, we will avoid even thinking of them. Putting this into practice, we will more easily control our bodies; then shall we please the Lord and defeat the enemy's tricks.

ATHANASIUS OF ALEXANDRIA,

LIFE OF ANTONY ABBOT

Tuesday

THE JESUS PRAYER

And Jacob asked him and said: "Tell me, I pray thee, thy name." And he said: "Wherefore is it that thou dost ask after my name?" And he blessed him there (Gen. 32:29).

The Name of Jesus may either be used alone or be inserted in a more or less developed phrase. In the East the commonest form is: "Lord Jesus Christ, Son of God, have mercy upon me, a sinner." One might simply say: "Jesus Christ," or "Lord Jesus." The invocation may be reduced to a single word, "Jesus."

The last form—the name of Jesus only—is the most ancient mould of the invocation of the Name. It is the shortest, the simplest, and, as we think, the easiest. Therefore, without depreciating the other formulas, we suggest that the word "Jesus" alone should be used.

A common mistake of beginners is to wish to associate the invocation of the Holy Name with an inner intensity or emotion. They try to say it with great force. But the name of Jesus is not to be shouted, or fashioned with violence, even inwardly. When Elijah was commanded to stand before the Lord, there was a great and strong wind, but the Lord was not in the wind; and after the wind an earthquake, but the Lord was not in the earthquake, and after the earthquake a fire, but the Lord was not in the fire. After the fire came a still small voice, "And it was so, when Elijah heard it, that he wrapped his face in his mantle, and went out, and stood . . . " (I Kings 19:13).

As you repeat the Holy Name gather quietly, little by little, your thoughts and feelings and will around it; gather around it your whole being. Let the Name penetrate your soul as a drop of oil spreads out and impregnates a cloth. Let nothing of yourself escape. Surrender your whole self and enclose it within the Name.

THE JESUS PRAYER,

BY A MONK OF THE EASTERN CHURCH

Wednesday

THE PHILOKALIA

Wisdom from the Fathers
If you wish to pray as you ought, imitate the dulcimer player; bending his head a little and inclining his ear to the strings, he strikes the

strings skilfully, and enjoys the melody he draws from their harmonious notes.

Is this example clear to you? The dulcimer is the heart; the strings—the feelings; the hammer—remembrance of God and of Divine things; the mind draws holy feelings from the God-fearing heart, then ineffable sweetness fills the soul, and the mind, which is pure, is lit up by Divine illuminations.

PHILOKALIA, BLESSED CALLISTUS

ON PRAYER

Thursday

SAINT BASIL, "THE GREAT"
(330–79)

Moses goes on ahead of you

In the beginning, God made heaven and earth. The description of this task of creation in Genesis is full of meaning for us. The author starts by naming a beginning so that no one might imagine that the world had no such beginning. Then he uses these words: God made. And this seems to suggest to us that only a small part of God's power is given over to the task of making. It is rather like the potter who uses the same skill to make any number of pots without in any way exhausting his art or even his strength; in a similar way, the Maker of our universe, whose creative power is not to be measured against the world since its potential is always infinite, brought into being, by the sole movement of his will, all the multitude of splendours that crowd the living world we witness.

Now if the world had a beginning, and if it was created, look more closely to learn who it is who gave it this beginning, in other words seek out its Creator. Or rather, lest your own faltering human faculties fail you and you mistake the truth, Moses goes on ahead of you with his own teaching. It is as if he had marked our souls with a seal, a memory of the holy name of God; he said: In the beginning, God made.

He who in the beginning made heaven and earth is bliss by his very essence, he is goodness that overflows, the source of all being, light immaterial, wisdom unfathomable.

SAINT BASIL ON GENESIS,

"THE WORK OF SIX DAYS"

Friday

Carrying forward a purpose

You may reach some idea of the point in time at which the world began to receive its special shape and order if you move back from the way things are now to all those stages that went before. And now try hard to imagine for yourself that very first day when the world was born. In this way you may discover a glimpse of that initial impulse that was imparted at the very first moment in time. The heavens and the earth itself were laid down in their foundations; and next, Thought that was Art as well was present as the entire visible world was being set in order.

This was to be a universe conceived not by chance but with its own proper reason; it was to carry forward a purpose, it must respond to the basic needs of all its creatures. For this world is to become the school where thinking beings are to be taught, the place where they will come to learn about their God. The world is offered to our spirit so as to lead us by means of things visible and tangible towards the contemplation of the invisible. As the Apostle puts it: "ever since God created the world, his everlasting power and deity—however invisible—have been there for the mind to see in the things he has made" (Rom. 1:20).

CONTINUES . . .

Saturday

The light from the Father

"God said: let there be light."

The very first word of God was to make the nature of light. So it was that he scattered the darkness, putting an end to sadness and giving the world its zest; all that existed was suddenly clad in grace and charm. For now the starry heavens appeared which until then had been wrapped in darkness; its beauty was the same then that we still witness today. The air was clear; or rather, joined so intimately with the light that it transmitted its swift beams in every direction to the very limits of its extent. The ether also became more pleasing and the waters below became more clear; and this came about not merely because they held the brightness of the day but also because they reflected it into the far distance, breaking it into a thousand glitters sparkling off the surface of the waves. There is nothing that the divine creative word has not enriched with grace and his nobility.

Thus the Father of true light made the day beautiful with his heavenly splendour; he gives us the brilliant stars at night for he has prepared us a resting place to come in that light which is eternal and wholly spiritual. May this Father send light to your hearts and teach you his truth; may he grant you a safe passage in life's journey, so that you may walk openly in his sight while the day lasts. And then may you shine like the sun amidst the splendour of his saints, in Christ's own bright day, to whom be glory and power for ever and ever.

CONTINUES . . .

---------- *W e e k   T e n* ----------

Sunday

Finding God's beauty

"And God saw that his work was beautiful."

This is not to tell us that God himself is beguiled by his own works: beauty does not make the same impression upon him as it does on us. But just as we call something beautiful if it meets all that is required by art, and if it is perfectly suited to attain its end: so God, who has assigned a clear end for all beings, considered all the various parts of his work as they related to the demands of the whole as well as their common purpose, and he praised them.

A single hand lying by itself,[1] an eye apart from the face, the limb off a statue removed from the trunk, these would never give the semblance of beauty. But put them back in their proper place and at once their beauty returns. It is a question of their relationship or proportion to the whole; and this was missing all the while they

---

[1]The fragmented statue of Constantine lying scattered like a fallen giant can be seen in Rome today in the Palazzo dei Conservatori.

were separated. But now that beauty is self-evident even to the untrained eye.

The artist himself, however, is aware of the beauty of the parts even before their wholeness is realised; he praises each in turn as he contemplates the end he has in mind for them. It is in this way that Genesis reveals to us the Creator as skilful artist, full of praise for every detail of his works, one after another. Later on, his eulogy will find completion as he gives the praise it deserves to the wholeness achieved in the perfected universe.

SAINT BASIL ON GENESIS

Monday

What thoughts might we have, what words could there be so that we might glorify you, the God of all: you who made man from what is visible as well as that which is unseen; you who gave him the power to achieve every excellence and even the Divine likeness itself, so that there should be nothing of all the things which you have made which should not share in your gift of grace. So that even the very dust itself might become happy in contemplating your glory and might share in the blessings which the angels have received. So that now in all your works, we might marvel and honor you in utter silence.

Joining with the cherubim of countless eyes, with the six-winged seraphim, full of your knowledge and trembling before your invisible and unknowable Godhead, turning one to the other and absorbed in this invisible sight that may never be known, praising you and saying over and over: "Holy, Holy, Holy."

SEVERUS OF ANTIOCH, *ANAPHORA*

Tuesday

GREGORY OF NYSSA (330–395)

Put on Christ Jesus

Would you learn this mystery of the Song of Songs?

Then first, you should take Paul's advice and put off the old man—all his old ways and lusts: slip off that worn-out cloak that forever makes you hot and sticky. Next, by pure living, you would wear a very different garment, that dazzling coat our Lord showed us when he was transfigured on the mountain. Better still, put on our Lord Jesus Christ, wear his own holy coat of love; transfigured into his own image, now at last you will be free of your animal nature: you will become divine.

Once this has been done, begin to listen to this mystery of the Song of Songs, enter the bedroom of that holy marriage, clad only in a white robe of pure and honest thoughts. And let no one come here with feelings that belong to the flesh and the senses: for anyone who fails in spirit to dress properly for this divine marriage will stay trapped in thoughts of their own making. Such a person will poison all the pure words that pass between Bridegroom and his Bride, and reduce them to the level of mindless, animal passion. I make this solemn warning to myself as I strive to draw near the door of mystical contemplation. And we read in this book how the soul is to be clad, as it were, as a future bride; she looks forward to a spiritual union with God in which things of the body and the material world no longer have any part to play.

GREGORY OF NYSSA,

ON THE SONG OF SONGS

Wednesday

Here reality abides

Keep watch over yourself, say the friends of the Bridegroom to the Bride: for then you will keep safe all your possessions. Consider how your Creator honours every single created thing, yet how far your own share outmatches theirs. Not the sun nor moon, not even a single star in the heavens for all their beauty, no one single thing that may be discovered or marvelled at in the entire universe is made as you yourself are made, that is to say, in the image of God.

From the very beginning, you alone were made in the image of that Nature which lies beyond our understanding; you were made like this unchanging Beauty so that you bear the exact reality of the Divine imprint. You became a vessel of the life of bliss, a mirror that shines back the true light. You need only gaze at God, and you will become what he is: the radiance that shines back from your purity is a copy of the Splendour that shines in you.

Nothing else that exists may be compared with this greatness that belongs to you. God is able to measure the entire universe with the width of his hand, his grasp enfolds both land and sea: and yet, immense as he really is, he has placed himself completely in your own grasp, because he dwells within you; but at the same time he is not limited or confined as he journeys through life in your nature. "I will make my home among them and live with them," he says, "I will be their God and they shall be my people" (II Cor. 6:16).

Here reality dwells: and once you truly dwell upon it, your eyes will have no time for the things of this world. Not even heaven itself will claim your attention: how can it, for when you look inwards upon yourself you find a Presence that may never be moved.

CONTINUES . . .

Thursday

The mystery of the wine

The soul should run swiftly upon her divine course. She must leap and long for all that lies ahead, and never turn back to wonder how far on she might be. Yet her thirst is constant and may never be slaked at the cup of wisdom. For even were she to drink all it contains, she would still thirst just as much. But instead, she asks to be brought into the wine cellar itself, where she can see the grapes being pressed, and where the vine-dresser himself attends the true vine which has grown a vintage which is rich and satisfying.

No, she longs only to witness the Bridegroom's garment growing redder as he treads the winepress. As Isaiah asks: "Why are your garments red, your clothes as if you had trodden the winepress?" That is why she would enter the wine cellar, to know the mystery of the wine. And as she comes there, she leaps again to something higher still; she asks only to give way to his love. For as St John says, God is love. Or in David's words, "In God alone there is rest for my soul, from him comes my safety" (Ps. 62). Now that I have come to the wine cellar, the soul declares, subject me to your love: or rather, let your love rule over me.

CONTINUES . . .

Friday

The warmth of the Spirit

Our human nature had become hardened by the granite of paganism. Held fast in the ice of idolatry, it was unable to move towards anything higher. But now the blessed Sun has risen after so cruel a winter; it shines from the east and brings the south wind to melt all that had been frozen solid with the warmth of the Spirit and with the softening light of the Word: man becomes once more like water leaping up to eternal life. God will send out his Spirit and the waters will flow once more. What before was stone is turned into pools of water, the hardest granite is now a splashing fountain.

This is how the Church learns from the Word, even while the wall of the Law still stands: for it receives rays of the Truth through windows—which are the Prophets—set in the lattice-work of the Law. The Law itself could only teach in types and symbols and offer shadows of those good things to come with no clear image. But following behind the Law comes the Truth, with clear symbols of its own. First of all through the Prophets, it shows the Word to the Church; next it disperses all shadows with the Gospel's clear revelation. So now the wall between is pulled down, and the air within the house may mingle directly with this light from heaven. No more need for rays to filter through windows, for the Light of truth itself is shining rays of the Gospel upon all who are within.

CONTINUES . . .

Saturday

Imaging God's beauty

"Come then, my love, my lovely one, come. My dove, hiding in the clefts of the rock" (Song of Songs 2:10).

Let us note first how the words are linked and one idea follows the next. The Bride hears her summons; the Word fills her with new strength; she awakens, she goes out and draws near; for now she is fair, she is called a dove.

A mirror cannot reflect a beautiful image unless it has first received such a reflection from the object of beauty itself. So it is with us. Our human nature is like a mirror. It was not fair at the start, but as soon as God's goodness came near, it became an image of the beauty of God's own splendour. Before, when the Bride wore the likeness of the serpent, she lay upon the ground and averted her gaze; but now she stands upright and rejects evil, she can turn her face towards the Good. She may even put on the very Goodness at which she gazes. Face to face with timeless Beauty, she draws near to the Light; more, she herself becomes light. In this new light, a beautiful image begins to take shape, that of a dove—we recognize at once the presence of the Holy Spirit.

Now at last the Word is whispering to his Bride; he calls her fair, since she has come to him, he names her lovely in token of her new-won beauty.

CONTINUES . . .

Sunday

Ever beyond reach

God's Nature is simple, pure and untainted; unchanging and incapable of change: it remains forever itself. No trace of evil may enter; apart from all else, the fullness of his goodness is without
measure. Even as it draws the human soul so as to give of itself, the
Godhead transcends mankind by such measure that will always be
infinite. But the soul continually grows as it shares this Nature that
so exceeds it; and this growth too is never ending. The good it
shares remains as it is, while the soul, as it discovers more and
more, perceives that it is always beyond reach.

In this way, little by little, the Word guides his Bride towards
the summit by means of an ascending path of virtue. First, he sends
his ray of brightness through the windows of the prophets and the
lattice-work of the Law; he invites her nearer the light so that she
may grow beautiful and become changed into a dove in the very
heart of the light. And when she has received as much as she can,
the Word draws near once more and, as if she had received nothing
as yet, calls her again to share his overwhelming Beauty.

The more the soul travels step by step on her journey, the
longer her path appears, and yet the more her desire continues to
grow. At each step, she is overwhelmed by the good things she finds,
so that it seems to the soul as if she were only at the start of her journey. That is why the Word says repeatedly: "Come then, my love,
my lovely one, come." "Arise," when she has already risen; "Come,"
when she has already come far. For rising in this sense means to go

on rising without end; and to run towards the Lord is to run a
course that stretches onwards without end.

GREGORY OF NYSSA, *ON THE SONG OF SONGS*

A d v e n t

Monday

The Monastic Year
Long is our winter,
Dark is our night;
Come, set us free,
O Saving Light!

FIFTEENTH-CENTURY GERMAN HYMN

As we enter into the season of Advent, our winter days grow
shorter, the air grows colder, and a quiet stillnesss settles on the
physical world at large. All living things that must survive the winter out-of-doors draw deep into themselves. The trees retract their
sap, the forest animals hibernate, and the living creatures that continue to move around in the cold, snow-covered world take care to
conceal their food stores.

Just as nature retreats deep into itself during the winter
months, so the Christian is invited to turn inward during the blessed
time of Advent in preparation for the Lord's coming. The inner
preparation, helped by prayer, silence, Bible readings, and good
works, is essential if we are to celebrate in a worthy manner the
solemn commemoration of the Lord's birth on Christmas Day and
during the whole of the Christmas season.

Advent is a quiet contemplative time of waiting for the Light that will come and shine on us on Christmas Day, rescuing us from the great darkness and hopelessness we experience in our daily lives. Advent then is a very special season of hope that links the coming of the promised Messiah in Jesus with the coming of Christ into our own hearts after a period of preparation, and with the coming of Christ again at the end of time.

BROTHER VICTOR-ANTOINE D'AVILA-LATOURRETTE,

A MONASTIC YEAR

Tuesday

The Eastern Christian tradition sees the Advent season as a time of waiting for the light that will first shine forth at Christmas and reach its peak on Epiphany, the Feast of Lights. The beautiful Isaiah text is then proclaimed during the liturgy: "Rise up in splendor! Your light has come, the glory of the Lord shines upon you. . . . Upon you the Lord shines, and over you appears his glory" (Is. 60:1–2).

It is a lovely thing to see that in the northern hemisphere, Christ's birth coincides with the victory of light over darkness in the physical world. After the winter solstice, about December 22, daylight slowly begins to lengthen, filling us with a sense of expectancy and promise. Likewise, during our Advent journey, our longing intensifies for the true Light who will be revealed on Christmas Day, thenceforth dispelling the darkness from the innermost parts of our hearts. During the long Advent nights, the church of the East prays in one of its liturgical texts, "To those who are caught in the night straying into the works of darkness, grant, O Christ, your light and your blessings."

CONTINUES . . .

Wednesday

The Advent journey
Eternal God who made the stars,
Your people's everlasting light!
O Lord, Redeemer, save us all,
And hear your servants when they call.

You came with healing power to save
A world that languished, self-condemned:
The wounds of sin were wide and deep,
The cure for guilt was your free gift.

The evening time of life was near
For all the world, when you came forth,
A bridegroom from your nuptial bed
Within the Virgin's spotless womb.

"CONDITOR ALME SIDERUM,"

ADVENT HYMN FOR VESPERS

As one travels into the rural landscape of New York's Dutchess County during the early days of winter, one may glimpse from a distance the contemplative monastery of Our Lady of the Resurrection. Perched on a hilltop and surrounded by silent wintry woods, our small, secluded monastery lies only a few miles away from Millbrook, the nearest village. The brilliant incomparable foliage of autumn has disappeared, and the trees stand stark and bare. One of the delights of early winter is to gaze upon the sunset through the elaborate patterns of branches that partition the pink sky like the elegant tracery of a stained glass window. The trees, with their bare branches reaching quietly towards the light, seem to share in the pleading of our Advent prayer: "Come, Lord Jesus, come."

CONTINUES . . .

Thursday

In the monastery there is something special about Advent, and something of it is felt immediately the moment the Vespers hymn, "Conditor alme siderum," is intoned in the choir. Through the lilting Gregorian melody, one senses the deep inner joy that comes with the season. From the years of singing time and again the same melodies of the monastic chant for each particular feast or season, they have grown into us, giving the awareness of how beautifully they express the rich meaning of the season. The Gregorian chant, sanctified by centuries of monastic use, has its own unique way of conveying something of the mystery commemorated in our liturgical prayer. We must never forget the fact that the chant is not music or melody alone, but it is words *and* music, and the music was written to fit the words, not the other way around, thus making the chant truly a vehicle of prayer. The Gregorian Advent melodies, with their simplicity and serene beauty, have a way of transforming our vocal sounds into acts of praise and adoration to our eternal God, for all his wonderful deeds among us.

Among the antiphons there is one in particular that nurtures in me the Advent message of hope and reflects the loveliness of the season: *"In illa die stillabunt montes dulcedinem. . . ."* "On that day [of the Lord's coming] sweet wine will flow from the mountains, milk and honey from the hills, alleluia."

Advent is primarily about the coming of God, and only in a secondary way about asking, seeking, waiting, and longing. There is hope, because we are unconditionally loved, whatever may be our failures, our tepidity, or our secret despair. The word "Come" is a bearer of mystery.

MARIA BOULDING, *THE COMING OF GOD*

Friday

The Advent wreath
Holly and Ivy, Box and Bay
Put in the church on Christmas Day.

FIFTEENTH-CENTURY ENGLISH CAROL

Our small monastery chapel is quite austere (as it should be!), especially during Advent and Lent, when there are no flowers or decorations in it. The only exception is the Advent wreath.

The custom of the wreath—with its four candles, three purple and one pink—originated in antiquity in the Germanic countries and was passed on from paganism to Christianity. Burning lights and fires during the darkest month (December, or Yule, as it was called then) was part of the folk celebrations and enthusiastically anticipated by northern Europeans each year. In the early sixteenth century during the days of the Reformation, some Christians conceived the idea of introducing this ancient custom, with its symbolism of lights, into their Advent practices, changing it from a pagan custom into a Christian one, Christ being, of course, both the symbol of

Light and the Light of the world. In Germany the custom took hold among both Protestants and Catholics, was introduced to monasteries of the surrounding region, and spread from there to the rest of the world.

The lighting of the candle provides a moment of intense joy and anticipation, for the candle's peaceful light announces the approaching celebration of the Lord's birth. The cry of the early Church resounds again and again in the heart of the monk: Come, come, Lord Jesus. Come O Thou, the fulfillment of a promise!

CONTINUES . . .

~

Saturday

The O Antiphons

O Wisdom from the Father's mouth,
The Word of his eternal love,
Beneath whose firm yet gentle sway
This world is governed from above.
O come! O come!
And teach us all
The ways that lead to life.

MAGNIFICAT ANTIPHON

FOR DECEMBER 17

Beginning December 17, our sense of Advent expectation intensifying, our longing for the Redeemer finds perfect expression in the so-called O Antiphons, which are solemnly sung each evening at Vespers in all monasteries until December 23. These seven antiphons are known as the O Antiphons because each starts with the vocative O: "O Wisdom," "O Adonai," "O Root of Jesse," "O Key of David," "O Daystar," "O King of All People," "O Emmanuel."

Each begins with an invocation to the Lord that expresses his attributes or messianic titles, then culminates with a longing call and prayer or concrete petition: "O come! and set us free, delay no longer in your love."

The arrival of the beautiful O Antiphons is enthusiastically awaited each Advent in every monastery and sung with the utmost reverence and solemnity. Usually the antiphon is first intoned by the abbot or superior of the monastery, who is attended by two monks bearing candles as on the most solemn occasions. Then all the monks join in, while the altar is incensed and the monastery bells ring in sounds of joy and praise during the antiphon and the Magnificat. It is the highlight of the evening liturgical prayer of Vespers, and those who experience it even once never forget it.

O Daystar of unending light,
The Sun of God's pure holiness,
The splendor of the Father's face,
And image of his Graciousness.
O come! O come!
And lead us forth from darkness
And the gloom of death.

O ANTIPHON

FOR DECEMBER 21

Sunday

JOHN CASSIAN (C. 360–435)

The aim of our journey

Every art, each discipline has its own aim and objective. So too the soul has its aim to which the spirit attends without interruption. For unless it worked in this way, it could never attain its desired goal. Now the monastic way that we have chosen will lead us to this destination, which is none other than the kingdom of God. But what precisely is our purpose? It is a critical question: and if we cannot find the answer, we are working ourselves out for nothing. A traveller without a route suffers all the exhaustion of his journey and gets nowhere.

So, the aim of our journey is the kingdom of God, or the kingdom of heaven. And our purpose must be purity of heart, for without this, no one will gain the kingdom. Let us fix our mind on purity of heart; this will plot our path and enable us to run straight ahead, confident of where we are heading. And if our thoughts sometimes stray, let us return to this purity at once. This one aim will set us on a straight path, so that all our effort will contribute to our single goal. Then, if our spirit strays from the true path in any way, we will know without delay.

CONFERENCES OF CASSIAN

Monday

Rule of thumb

Fasting and vigils, meditating on the Scriptures, going without clothing, doing without, none of these add up to perfection, for they are merely steps towards perfection. The wisdom of monastic life never sees such activities as an end in themselves; for they are merely the means. It would be wasted effort to use practices and regard them as of the utmost priority, as if they were good in themselves; but we must bend all our energy in seeking the good towards which they are simply the instruments. One must be like a man who possesses the instruments of his art without knowing their purpose, which is itself the outcome of such an art!

Let us avoid therefore anything that threatens our purity and peace of soul, even when something appears useful or even necessary. Such a rule of thumb will prevent our thoughts from wandering and dissipating at the slightest event; it also ensures that travelling a path that is well-blazed we will arrive before long at that destination we so much desire.

CONTINUES . . .

Tuesday

Purity of heart

If we are to limit our asceticism merely to the body, that is no use: it would mean an exodus from Egypt in body alone. No: we have to win purity of the heart as well: that is an asceticism and renunciation more far reaching and beneficial than any other option.

Listen to Saint Paul on asceticism of the body: "If I give away all that I possess, piece by piece, and even if I let them take my body to burn it: but am without love, it will do me no good whatever" (I Cor. 13:3). The apostle would never have used such extreme language unless he had foreseen how many people, having given away all their goods to the poor, still remain unable to set out and climb the real heights; for the gospel invites us to the way of perfect love. These unfortunates are still wrapped in their pride, they so easily give way to impatience; small wonder they find themselves incapable of reaching out to the love that never fails.

CONTINUES . . .

Wednesday

Martha and Mary

Our first aim in all we do—and we should stand by it continually with all our heart's strength—is to hold fast to God and his ways. Anything that leads elsewhere, however important it seems at the time, should be thought of as irrelevant and futile or even positively harmful.

The gospel gives us a wonderful example of this frame of mind in the story of Martha and Mary. Martha busied herself performing a genuinely holy task, attending to our Lord and the disciples. In contrast, Mary fixed her attention on the spiritual teaching of Jesus; she clung to his feet which she covered with her kisses and anointed with the perfume of perfect faith. It was she whom our Lord preferred, because, as he told her, she had chosen the better part, a part that could not be taken from her.

CONTINUES . . .

Thursday

Why we are tested

All those feelings of spiritual aridity, dryness and despondency; they stem either from our own carelessness, or from the devil or from a will on God's part that we might be tested.

There are two reasons why he might wish this to happen. First, left to ourselves for a while, we are forced to realise the true poverty of our position; at the same time, we will find it harder to puff ourselves up with pride even if it follows soon after we have been visited by God and enriched by his grace and given purity of heart. And this apart, when left to ourselves, we discover by bitter experience that no pleas or effort on our side can return us to that former joy and state of well-being. And so slowly we come to realise what we appear to have lost is nothing to do with our own energies but quite simply the grace of God. And once more we need to ask for his help and his light.

The second reason is that this is his way of testing us, trying our inner resolve and our heart's true desire. He wants us to know how steadfast and unremitting our prayers should be asking for the return of the Holy Spirit when it seems he has left us to ourself. He wishes us to know what a precious thing it is to regain joy and peace of spirit having lost them. And so for the future, we will decide to safeguard these gifts of his grace and defend them within ourselves by watching ever more closely.

CONFERENCES OF CASSIAN

Friday

To follow God

We read in Genesis (Gen. 12:4) how Abraham left his country, and Lot went with him.

This prompts us to wonder whether God's word "leave your country" was not an invitation to leave the country of our body, rather than stay tied to it as lodgers. Certainly Paul had gone out of his body for he writes: "our abiding home is in heaven" (Phil. 3:20). In this sense, to leave one's family would be to free oneself from the ties and desires of the body: the soul is as it were a relation, for it cannot help but feel what the body feels, for as long as it clings to the ties which hold it here.

We should therefore leave this earthbound life and all its worldly attractions; yet it is not enough merely to change places, it is our very selves that must change. Would you cling to Christ? Then leave all worldly goods behind. Let us follow Abraham and leave behind the cares of a bad conscience: for if we are children of Abraham, we must accomplish the works of Abraham, that our works may shine before God and before men.

As for Abraham, he obeyed the command as soon as he heard it, without a moment's hesitation.

SAINT AMBROSE,

TREATISE ON ABRAHAM

Saturday

Peace of heart

The evening before Jacob was to meet his brother and attempt a reconciliation, he fell asleep beside a river. Such perfect virtue makes a soul quiet, peaceful, unchanging. This is what our Lord meant by his words: "I leave you peace, my peace I give you." And it was a gift he kept for the perfect. Men striving for perfection do not allow themselves to be moved easily by events of the world. They are not afraid whatever trouble comes their way, they are not constantly paralyzed with worry, they meet pain with courage. With their feet firmly planted on the shore, they watch without fear as the waves of human storms arise. It is Christ who gives this steadfastness to Christian souls: When the trial comes, a profound peace fills their hearts so that no room is left for disturbance or anxiety of spirit.

It was in this way that Jacob, who had cleansed his heart of resentment and so was a man of peace, went ahead of his family to be alone by himself; it was then that he wrestled with God. And the truth is that everyone who frees themself from worldly things draws near to the image and likeness of God. And this struggle with God means nothing less than to strive for perfection; to encounter him who is so much greater than ourselves is to gain a unique likeness to the Lord.

SAINT AMBROSE,

TREATISE ON ABRAHAM

Sunday

SAINT AUGUSTINE (354–430)

Late have I loved you

So late have I loved you, Beauty, ancient yet so new! I have come to love you now, yet so late in the day. You were within me, but I was in the world outside myself. I sought you outside myself, and, wantonly misguided, I wallowed in the beauty of those creatures you had made. You were still with me, but I was not with you. The very beauty of the world kept me far from you, and yet, unless each one of them had all not been in you, they could have had no being. You called out to me; you cried my name; and at last you burst through my deafness. You flashed forth upon me; your light surrounded me; I was blind no more. You breathed your sweetness and I drew breath; now I gasp for more. I tasted: now I hunger and thirst for you. Your finger touched me: I surrender to your loving peace.

SAINT AUGUSTINE, *THE CONFESSIONS*

Monday

On a certain day—Nebridius was away for some reason I cannot recall—there came to Alypius and me at our home one Ponticianus, a fellow countryman of ours, being from Africa, holder of an important post in the emperor's court. There was something or other he wanted of us and we sat down to discuss the matter. As it happened he noticed a book on a gaming table by which we were sitting. He picked it up, opened it, and found that it was the apostle Paul, which surprised him because he had expected that it would be one of the books I had grown out of teaching. Then he smiled a little and looked at me, and expressed pleasure but surprise too at having come suddenly upon that book and only that book, lying before me. For he was a Christian and a devout Christian; he knelt before You in church, O our God, in daily prayer and many times daily. I told him that I had given much care to these writings.

Whereupon he began to tell the story of the Egyptian monk Antony, whose name was held in high honor among Your servants, although Alypius and I had never heard it before that time. When he learned this, he was the more intent upon telling the story, anxious to introduce so great a man to men ignorant of him, and very much marvelling at our ignorance. But Alypius and I stood amazed to hear of Your wonderful works, done in the true faith and in the Catholic Church so recently, practically in our own times, and with such numbers of witnesses. All three of us were filled with wonder, we because the deeds we were now hearing were so great, and he because we had never heard them before.

SAINT AUGUSTINE,

THE CONFESSIONS, TRANS. FRANK SHEED

Christmas

Tuesday

My tongue will acclaim the righteousness of the Lord (Ps. 51:14), of the Lord through whom all things have been made and who himself has been made in the midst of all things:

who is revealer of his Father, Creator of his Mother; who is Son of God through his Father without mother, and Son of Man through his Mother without father. He is greatest day among the Angels, twilight among men: Word of God before all time, Word made flesh at the chosen time.

Maker of the sun, he himself is made under the sun. Disposing all Ages in the bosom of the Father, he consecrates this unique day in the womb of his mother: in Him he abides, from her he goes forth. Creator of heaven and earth, he was born on earth under the heaven. Wisdom too deep for utterance, wise now a baby asleep; filling all the world, he lies in his crib; ruler of the stars, he suckles his mother's breast.

Great in his divine nature, he is become small to be our servant (Phil. 2:6); yet his greatness is not belittled by this smallness, nor is his smallness overshadowed by his greatness. For when he took these tiny limbs, he did not set aside his divine workings (Wis. 8:1). Nor did he cease *to deploy his strength from one end of the earth to the other, ordering all things for good* (Wis. 8:1). And when, clothed in feeble flesh, he entered the Virgin's womb, he was not a prisoner. For the food of wisdom was not taken from the Angels, while we ourselves were tasting how good the Lord is.

SAINT AUGUSTINE,

SERMON FOR CHRISTMAS

Wednesday

Now we should not marvel when we hear this of the Word of God. For take my own, simple human words: they come into your minds quite easily and without in any way being detained by the fact that you hear them. Now unless the words I speak to you were received in this way, you would be none the wiser. And if—supposing—you kept them to yourself, they would not pass on to anyone else.

It is equally clear that this sermon of mine consists of words and syllables. But unlike food for the stomach, you do not take up this and that individual morsel, rather, you hear my words as a whole. Nor need I worry as I talk to you that someone will take on board all I have to say leaving nothing for anyone else. No, I know each of you is listening and that you hear everything yet still leave it all for another to hear. Nor is this happening at one time for one person and at another time for someone else; so that as I speak my sermon goes first to you and then out again so as to pass on to your neighbour. (No, this is not the way—even with human words.) Rather what I am saying comes to you all at the exactly same time, all of it in equal measure to each one of you. And, let us suppose, you were able to memorize it, word for word as it came to you, you would each of you take it home as a complete whole.

So how much more so might the Word of God, through whom all things were made and which, while remaining itself, renews all things, that is not hemmed in by place or stretched by time, nor even made up of varying syllables: not ended in silence. . . .

How much more could this great Word of God make fruitful the womb of his Mother, assuming a body without ever leaving the bosom of his Father. Going out from the one to appear before men's eyes and yet still remaining to illuminate the minds of angels. At once to come and be upon the earth, while still present to unfold the heavens. To be made Man, and to make men.

SAINT AUGUSTINE,

SERMON FOR CHRISTMAS

Thursday

Christ's passage to the Father

The Hebrew people spent forty years in the desert with Moses as their leader. It was at this time that the tent of the tabernacle, where God was worshipped with sacrifices that foreshadowed one still to come, received its name; the tent of meeting. The Law of God was announced on the mountain in the midst of terrifying portents; so that the people went in terror of signs and sounds that told them of the certain presence of God. And all this took place seven weeks after the paschal meal when the lamb had been sacrificed immediately after they had fled from Egypt to begin their sojourn in the desert.

The Hebrew people prefigured Christ: They stood for his passage from the world to the Father by means of the sacrifice of his Passion. For the Hebrew Pasch or Passover means passage. The reality is that once the new covenant was revealed after the sacrifice of Christ as our Pasch, the Holy Spirit came down from heaven after seven weeks. And the gospel names him "the finger of God" to remind us of that revelation in Sinai which foreshadowed all this. For in Exodus we are told that the tablets of the law were written by "the finger of God."

SAINT AUGUSTINE, *THE CITY OF GOD*

Friday

God made us in his own image, Three in One

This trinity of the mind is not really the image of God because the mind remembers and understands and loves itself, but because it is also able to remember and understand and love him by whom it was made. And when it does this it becomes wise. If it does not do it, then even though it remembers and understands and loves itself, it is foolish. Let it then remember its God to whose image it was made, and understand and love him. To put it in a word, let it worship the uncreated God, by whom it was created with a capacity for him and able to share in him. It is after all written, "Behold the worship of God is wisdom" (Jb 28:28). In this way it will be wise not with its own light but by sharing in that supreme light, and it will reign in happiness where it reigns eternal. For this is called man's wisdom in such a way that it is also God's. Only then is it true wisdom; if it is merely human it is hollow.

SAINT AUGUSTINE, DE TRINITATE

Saturday

Truth who is eternity

O Truth who is eternity: Love who is Truth: Eternity who is Love. You are my God: how could I not long for you day and night.

I knew you at once, when first you raised me up, so that I might begin to know that something was there to be seen, but knowing at the same time I was not yet ready to see. You confused my feeble sight even as you shone so bright within me; I trembled with love and with fear. For I knew then how far from you I was. I felt as though I was in a land quite different from your home land. But then I heard your voice calling me from high above:

"I am the food for grown-ups. Grow and you shall eat me. Yet you will not change me into yourself as when you eat ordinary meat: for I will change you into myself. . . ."

and again that far off voice speaks:
"I am who I am."

SAINT AUGUSTINE,

THE CONFESSIONS, BK 7:12

―――――――― *W e e k   F o u r t e e n* ――――――――

Sunday

SAINT BENEDICT OF NURSIA (C. 480–C. 547)

Achieving the goal

Are you making all haste on the way to your heavenly home? With
the help of Christ then, keep this little rule which we have written
down for beginners. Once you have done so, you can then set out
to gain the higher reaches of wisdom and virtues which we have already mentioned. Under God's guidance and care you will attain
them. Amen.

THE RULE OF SAINT BENEDICT

Monday

The lost virtue

Benedict couches his teachings on humility in six basic principles.
With these understandings it is clear that Benedict's definition of
humility and the use of the term in the twentieth century are light
years apart.

In the first place, Benedictine spirituality implies, the presence of God demands total response. If I really believe God is present in my life, here and now, then I have no choice but to deal with that. Life, in fact, will not be resolved for me until I do. No manner of other agendas will ever completely smother the insistency of the God one. No amount of noise will ever successfully drown out the need to discover what is most important among all the important things of life. No degree of success will ever feel like success until I am succeeding at the center point of life.

JOAN CHITTISTER, O.S.B.,

WISDOM DISTILLED FROM THE DAILY:

LIVING THE RULE OF SAINT BENEDICT TODAY

Tuesday

Monastic humility

Second, the Rule makes clear, the pride that is the opposite of humility is not the excitement that comes with doing well what I do best. The pride that is the opposite of monastic humility is the desire to be my own God and to control other people and other things. It is not pride to enjoy my achievements. That kind of awareness is the spirit of the *Magnificat* at its height. It is pride to want to wrench my world and all the people in it to my ends. It is arrogance to the utmost to insist that other people shape their lives to make mine comfortable. It is arrogance unabashed to think that God must do the same.

CONTINUES . . .

Wednesday

A process of always arriving

The third basic principle of monastic humility is that spiritual development is a process. If spirituality of the immediate past is tainted by anything at all, it is the notion that growth is an event. People who graduated from high school were considered grown-up. People who got married were said to be grown-up. People who went to monasteries were undoubtedly grown-up. We treated the spiritual life in the same way. We put people through a series of spiritual gymnastics and assumed if they did certain things certain ways, that in itself was proof of spiritual progress. But nothing is more insidious than spiritual pride; nothing more impervious to identification. No, the monastic mind-set says, spiritual development is not an event. Spiritual development is a process of continuing conversion. "What do you do in the monastery?" an ancient tale asks. "Oh, we fall and we get up. We fall and we get up," the monastic answers. In monastic spirituality, we never arrive; we are always arriving.

CONTINUES . . .

Thursday

Humility frees the spirit

In Benedictine spirituality, too, humility and humiliations are two distinct concepts, and they are not necessarily related. The Rule does not call for humiliations. The Rule calls for humility it would take to deal with the humiliating aspects of life and come out of them psychologically well and spiritually sound. It is possible, in other words, to live our whole life in a series of humiliations and know nothing about humility. Humiliation may teach us a lot about oppression, or a lot about underdevelopment or a great deal about anger, but it will not necessarily prove that we have learned anything about humility. Benedictine humility frees the spirit; it does not batter it.

CONTINUES . . .

Friday

My place in the universe

Humility, the Rule implies, is the glue of our relationships. Humility is the foundation of community and family and friendship and love. Humility comes from understanding my place in the universe.

CONTINUES . . .

Saturday

Ascend through yourself

Finally, the Rule shows us, self-love is destructive of self. In 1980, so corrosive had the effects of exaggerated self-importance become that the American Psychiatric Association began to identify narcissim as a personality disorder. Clearly, the cultural effects of rampant individualism have come home to haunt us.

To Benedict, this process [of humility] is clearly the work of a lifetime. He calls it "the ladder of humility," a climb with basic parts, a progression—not a leap—that involves the integration of both body and soul. "Our body and our souls are the two sides of the same ladder."

The tower and ladder symbols were favorites with the ancients, but it was left to Augustine to give us that marvellous line: "Do you seek God? Seek within yourself and ascend through yourself." If we are really seeking God, we have to start at the very core of our own hearts and motives and expectations. We can't blame the schedule or the finances or the work or the people in our lives for blocking our progress. We have to learn to seek from within ourselves. We have to stop waiting for the world around us to be perfect in order to be happy.

JOAN CHITTISTER, O.S.B.,

WISDOM DISTILLED FROM THE DAILY

---------------- *W e e k   F i f t e e n* ----------------

☜

Sunday

SAINT JOHN CLIMACUS (C. 579–C. 649)

On faith, hope, and love

And now at length, after all that has been said, there remains that triad, faith, hope, and love, binding and securing the union of all. "But the greatest of these is love" (I Cor. 13:13), since that is the very name of God himself (cf. I John 4:8). To me they appear, one as a ray, one as light, and one as a disk,[2] and all as a single radiance

---

[2]A common image among the Fathers to express the unity of the Trinity.

and a single splendor. The first can make and create all things, the mercy of God encircles the second and keeps it from confusion, while the third never fails, never halts on its way, never gives respite to the man wounded by its rapture.

The man who wants to talk about love is undertaking to speak about God. But it is risky to talk about God and could even be dangerous for the unwary. Angels know how to speak about love, but even they do so only in proportion to the light within them.

"God is love" (I John 4:16). But someone eager to define this is blindly striving to measure the sand in the ocean.

SAINT JOHN CLIMACUS

Monday

Love, by its nature, is a resemblance to God, insofar as this is humanly possible. In its activity it is inebriation of the soul. Its distinctive character is to be a fountain of faith, an abyss of patience, a sea of humility.

Love is the banishment of every sort of contrariness, for love thinks no evil.

Love, dispassion, and adoption are distinguished by name, and name only. Light, fire, and flame join to fashion one activity. So too with love, dispassion, and adoption.

Fear shows up if ever love departs, for the man with no fear is either filled with love or is dead in spirit.

There is nothing wrong about offering human analogies for longing, fear, concern, zeal, service, and love of God. Lucky the man who loves and longs for God as a smitten lover does for his beloved. Lucky the man whose fear of God is in no way less than the fear of the accused in front of a judge. Lucky the man who is caught up with the zeal of loyal slaves towards their owner. Lucky the man who is as passionately concerned with the virtues as a jealous husband watching over his wife. Lucky the man who prays before God like a courtier before the king. Lucky the man who strives without end to please the Lord as others try to please men.

Not even a nursing mother clings to her child as a loving son clings to the Lord at all times.

Someone truly in love keeps before his mind's eye the face of the beloved and embraces it there tenderly. Even during sleep the longing continues unappeased, and he murmurs to his beloved. That is how it is for the body. And that is how it is for the spirit. A man wounded by love had this to say about himself—and it really amazes me—"I sleep (because nature commands this) but my heart is awake (because of the abundance of my love)" (Song of Songs 5:2). You should take note, my brother, that the stag, which is the soul, destroys reptiles[3] and then, inflamed by love, as if struck by an arrow, it longs and grows faint for the love of God.

> As a hart longs for flowing streams,
> so longs my soul for you, my God.
>
> PS. 41:1

> SAINT JOHN CLIMACUS

---

[3]The stag, according to Origen, was able to kill its deadly foe first by flushing it from its hole with its breath and then trampling it underfoot.

Tuesday

AELRED OF RIEVAULX (1109–1167)

Bouts of acute pain from arthritis and the stone had compelled
Aelred reluctantly to submit to mitigations in his daily régime from
about 1157 onwards, and to find a way of being as little trouble as
possible to everyone else on these occasions. His solution had been
to erect an outbuilding near the common infirmary of the abbey,
where he could have a fire and be close enough to benefit from the
provisions normally made for the sick. There, at the same time, he
could conduct the business of the monastery and see members of his
community without disturbing anyone else. In this place, when he
was at home, he more and more worked and talked and prayed.

By Walter Daniel's account there must have been a good deal of
talking to be done. Rievaulx had been growing steadily all through
Aelred's life and, towards the end, on the greater feast days, when
the lay brothers came in from the granges, the church was crowded
with the brethren "like bees in a hive." There were, we are told, one
hundred and forty monks and five hundred lay brethren at the time
of Aelred's death. Inevitably the life of this large community con-
verged upon the abbot's simple lodging, where there was an atmosphere of freedom in which to talk about scripture and the problems
of monastic life and anything that was wholesome and interesting.
For Aelred, who had often had to be very firm with himself in his
search for the appropriate self-discipline, knew the importance of
allowing the immature their root-room. He understood, as his own
ascetic teaching makes clear, when to insist but, unlike disciplinari-
ans whom Walter Daniel calls "silly abbots," Aelred never crushed

the spontaneity of his young men. Twenty or thirty at a time could be found any day round his bed, or sitting on it, talking to him. Walter Daniel says that they felt able to be so open with him that they were rather like children with their mother.

AELRED OF RIEVAULX, AELRED SQUIRE, O.P.

Wednesday

Uncommon bravery of spirit

The summary and conclusion of Aelred's lengthy and painstaking inquiry is that their friendship and love must be sublimated into a spiritual—yet nonetheless passionate—movement of the soul that brings both monks into closer communion with Christ.

Let Aelred Squire sum up:

> The first thing is to purify oneself, allowing oneself nothing that is not right, withdrawing oneself from nothing that is profitable. Loving oneself thus, one must love one's neighbor too, according to the same rule. But because love has gathered so many together here in this place, one must choose from among them a man to admit to the secrets of friendship by the law of familiarity.
>
> These two can help each other, console each other, pray for each other. And so, praying to Christ for his friend, and longing to be heard by Christ for his friend's sake, he reaches out with devotion and desire to Christ himself. And suddenly and insensibly, affection passing into affection, as though touched by the gentleness of Christ close at hand, he begins to taste how sweet he is and to feel how lovely he is. Thus, from that holy love with which he

embraces his friend, he rises to that by which he embraces Christ.

It is, as it were, only a step to heaven where God is all in all.

All that lies behind the work on *Spiritual Friendship* can never be known to us, but its significance for Aelred's life must run through every year of it, giving a hidden meaning to all its eventualities. It is clearly linked to the deepest of his personal problems, and his stability in striving for their solution, and in helping others to do so too, is a mark of uncommon bravery of spirit.

AELRED OF RIEVAULX, AELRED SQUIRE, O.P.

Thursday

SAINT BRUNO (1032–1101)

Saint Bruno's Credo
I believe firmly in the Father, the Son and the Holy Spirit:
The Unbegotten Father,
the only-begotten Son
and the Holy Spirit who proceeds from them both.
I believe these three persons are one God.

I believe, moreover, that this Son of God was conceived by the Holy Spirit and born of the Virgin Mary, a virgin most pure, not only before giving birth, but also in the act and forever thereafter.

I believe the Son of God was conceived as a man among men, yet without sin; that he was arrested and treated with contempt; unjustly bound, spat upon and scourged; that he died, was buried and descended to the nether world to deliver the faithful who were captive there. He descended to set us free, then rose and ascended into heaven, and from there he will come to judge the living and the dead.

I believe in the sacraments, according to the faith and devotion of the Catholic church; in particular, that what is consecrated on the altar is the true body of our Lord Jesus Christ, his real Flesh and Blood, which we receive for the forgiveness of sins, and in the hope of eternal salvation. I believe in the resurrection of the body and life eternal. Amen.

I believe and confess that the holy and ineffable Trinity, Father, Son and Holy Spirit, is one only God, of one substance and nature, one dignity and power. We believe, moreover, that the Father is neither born nor created, but is unbegotten; that, whereas the Son is born from him, and the Spirit proceeds from him, he draws his origin from no one.

He is therefore the source and origin of the entire Divinity. Ineffable in his essence, ineffable also in the manner in which he begot the Son from his own substance, not as something different from himself, but as God from God, Light from Light.

From him comes all paternity, in heaven and on earth. Amen.

Friday

To my esteemed friend, Raoul, Dean of . . . Rheims . . . my greeting . . . I am living in the wilderness of Calabria, far removed from habitation. There are some brethren with me, some of whom are very well educated, and they are keeping assiduous watch for their Lord, so as to open to him at once when he knocks. I could never begin to tell you how charming and pleasant it is. The temperatures are mild, the air is healthful; a broad plain, delightful to behold, stretches between the mountains along their entire length, bursting with fragrant meadows and flowery fields. One could hardly describe the impression made by the gently rolling hills on all sides, with their cool and shady glens tucked away, and such an abundance of refreshing springs, brooks and streams. Besides all this, there are verdant gardens, and all sorts of fruit-bearing trees.

FROM *THE WOUND OF LOVE,* A CARTHUSIAN MISCELLANY

Saturday

A Carthusian Prayer

Increase for us your mercy, Lord, so that in silent seclusion we may acquire that placid glance that wounds your heart and that love through which its purity allows you to be seen.

This we ask through Christ your Son our Lord who with the Spirit reigns with you, Father, one God, now and forever. Amen.

W e e k   S i x t e e n

Sunday

WILLIAM OF ST.-THIERRY (C. 1085–C. 1148)

A letter to the Carthusians of God's Mount

The very name Mont Dieu affords grounds for fair hopes: Namely that, as the psalm says of the mountain of the Lord, there will come to dwell on it "the race of those who seek the Lord, seek the face of

Jacob's God; the man with unstained hands and clean heart, one who has not received his soul in vain" (Ps. 23:4ff.).

This piety is the continual remembrance of God, an unceasing effort of the mind to know him, an unwearied concern of the affections to love him, so that, I will not say every day, but every hour finds the servant of God occupied in the labor of ascesis and the effort to make progress, or in the sweetness of experience and the joy of fruition.

The habit you wear promises not only the outward form of piety but its substance, in all things and before all things, and that is what your vocation demands.

WILLIAM OF ST.-THIERRY, *THE GOLDEN EPISTLE*

Monday

The man who has God with him is never less alone than when he is alone. It is then he has undisturbed fruition of his joy, it is then that he is his own master and is free to enjoy God in himself and himself in God, it is then that in the light of truth and the serenity of a clean heart a pure soul stands revealed to itself without effort, and the memory enlivened by God freely pours itself out in itself. Then either the mind is enlightened and the will enjoys its good or human frailty freely weeps over its shortcomings.

Accordingly, as your vocation demands, dwelling in heaven rather than in cells, you have shut out the world, whole and entire, from yourselves and shut up yourselves, whole and entire, with God. For the cell *(cella)* and heaven *(coelum)* are akin to one another: The resemblance between the words *coelum* and *cella* is borne out by the devotion they both involve. For both *coelum* and *cella* appear to be derived from *celare*, to hide, and the same thing is hidden in cells as in heaven, the same occupation characterizes both the one and the other. What is this? Leisure devoted to God, the enjoyment of God.

CONTINUES . . .

Tuesday

Both in a church and in a cell the things of God are practiced, but more continually in the cell. In a church at certain times the sacraments of Christian religion are dispensed visibly and in figure, while in cells as in heaven the reality which underlies all the sacraments of our faith is constantly celebrated with as much truth, in the same order, although not yet with the same untarnished magnificence or the same security that marks eternity. Therefore, as has been said, the cell quickly expels as an abortion the man who does not belong to it, is not its true son: It vomits him forth like a useless and harmful food. The workshop of piety cannot long suffer such a one to remain in its bosom.

However, the wise man will be all the wiser for the punishment of the fool, and the just man will wash his hands in the blood of the sinner. Therefore, as the prophet says: "If you are converted, Israel, be converted" (Jer. 4:1), that is to say, attain to the summit of perfect conversion. For no one is allowed to remain long in the same condition. The servant of God must always either make progress or go back; either he struggles upwards or he is driven down into the depths.

But from all of you perfection is demanded, although not the same kind from each. If you are beginning begin perfectly; if you are already making progress be perfect also in your doing of that; if you have already achieved some measure of perfection measure yourselves by yourselves and say with the Apostle: "Not that I have already won the prize, already reached fulfilment. I only press on in the hope of winning the mastery, as Christ Jesus has won the mastery over me. This at least I do: forgetting what I have left behind, intent on what lies before me, I press on with the goal in view, eager for the prize, God's heavenly summons in Christ Jesus." And he adds: "All of us who are perfect must be of this mind" (Phil. 3:12ff.).

CONTINUES . . .

Wednesday

Animal man

As one star differs from another in brightness (I Cor. 15:41) so cell differs from cell in its way of life: There are beginners, those who are making progress and the perfect. The state of beginners may be called "animal," the state of those making progress "rational" and the state of the perfect "spiritual." Those who are still animal may on occasion claim forbearance in some respects in which no indulgence should be shown to those who are considered as already rational. Again certain things are tolerated in the rational which are not tolerated in the spiritual: everything in them must be perfect, calling for imitation and praise rather than for blame.

Every religious institute is made up of these three kinds of men. As each is marked by a name proper to it, so each is recognized by distinctive pursuits. All those who are born of the light should consider carefully in the light of the present day what is lacking to them, whence they have come, how far they have come, the progress of the day and of the hour.

There are the animal, who of themselves are not governed by reason nor led by affection, yet stimulated by authority or inspired by teaching or animated by good example they acquiesce in the good where they find it and like blind men, led by the hand, they follow, that is, imitate others. Then there are the rational, whom the judgement of their reason and the discernment that comes of natural learning endow with knowledge of the good and the desire for it, but as yet they are without love. There are also the perfect, who are led by the spirit and are more abundantly enlightened by the Holy Spirit; because they relish the good which draws them on they are called wise. They are also called spiritual because the Holy Spirit dwells in them as of old he dwelt in Gideon.[4]

WILLIAM OF ST.-THIERRY, THE GOLDEN EPISTLE

Thursday

SAINT BERNARD OF CLAIRVAUX (1090–1153)

On Loving God

. . . from the sole name of Christ thousands of thousands of believers are called Christians. . . . Hidden as in a vase, is this Name of Jesus, you my soul, possess a salutary remedy against which no spiritual illness will be proof. Carry it always to your heart, always in your hand and so insure that all your affections, all your actions, are directed to Jesus.

SAINT BERNARD, SERMONS ON THE SONG OF SONGS

---

[4]The Latin here literally reads: "because indeed the Holy Spirit puts them on just as of old he put on Gideon, as the clothes of the Holy Spirit they are called spiritual" (Judg. 6:34). "The Spirit of the Lord puts on Gideon," just as Paul tells the Galatians (3:27) "as many of you as were baptized into Christ have put on Christ." William found a deeper meaning: "Clothes of the Holy Spirit" tells of our being intimately filled with the Holy Spirit.

Jesu dulcis memoria

Jesu, the very thought of thee
with sweetness fills my breast;
but sweeter far thy face to see,
and in thy presence rest.

Nor voice can sing, nor heart can frame,
nor can the memory find,
a sweeter sound than thy blest name,
O Savior of mankind.

Friday

Saint Bernard attempts to correct a monk
Bernard to his beloved son THOMAS,[5] as being his son . . .

. . . How can you take unlimited pleasure in a love that
soon must end? But I ever love you, not your possessions;
let them go whence they were derived. I only require
you for one thing: that you would be mindful of your promise, and not deny us any longer the satisfaction of your
presence among us, who love you sincerely, and will love
you for ever.

In fact, if we love purely in our life, we shall also not
be divided in death. For those gifts which I wish for in your

---

[5]Thomas had taken his vows as a Cistercian monk at Clairvaux and subse-
quently was elected prior of Beverley, England. But he now seems to be faltering in his vocation, led astray and back to the world by his family's wealth
and position.

case, or rather for you, belong not to the body or to time only; and so they fail not with the body, nor pass away with time; for when the body is laid aside they delight still more, and last when time is gone. They have nothing in common with the gifts I have already mentioned, for it was not the Father who gave you them, but the world.

Woe to you, sons of this world, because of your empty wisdom which is foolishness. You do not know the spirit of salvation, you do not share in its intimacy, which the Father alone discloses only to his Son, and to those to whom the Father will reveal him. . . .

TO THOMAS, PRIOR OF BEVERLEY, LETTER XL

Saturday

Love leaves no room for fear

To understand the heart of Bernard we must turn to those pastoral writings which most clearly show him as a true monastic *abba*. In them we may find a picture of a Christian growth expressive of some of the major insights of monastic tradition, cast in language so rich in poignant imagery that it remains among the greatest achievements of medieval spirituality. Here Bernard is occupied with the analysis of Christian love—so much so that he merits the title *Doctor Caritatis*, teacher of charity, almost as much as does Augustine. Anthony the Great is recorded as claiming, "I no longer fear God, but I love him"; and Bernard brilliantly describes the advance in the Christian life from fearful distance to loving intimacy. Love is not born without a measure of self-regarding fear (Bernard is nothing if not a realist), but it must speedily be left behind. "Perhaps

we should say that we are called by fear and justified by love"
(Letter 109).

In the third sermon on the Song of Songs, he distinguishes between the successive stages of kissing Christ's feet, his hands and his mouth; and the kiss of the feet, with which we begin, is like the kiss of the sinful woman in the Gospel, the kiss of fear and penitence, as we wait prostrate for the Lord's words of forgiveness. And much later on (Sermon 58:2), commenting on the text, "For lo, winter is past . . . the time for pruning has come":

> For us, brothers, it is always a time for pruning, as it is always a job to be done. But one thing I am sure of: The winter is over for us. Do you see what I mean by "winter"? it is the fear for which love leaves no room. . . . Summer-time is love *(caritas)*.

ROWAN WILLIAMS, *THE WOUND OF KNOWLEDGE*

———————— *W e e k   S e v e n t e e n* ————————

Sunday

The Song of Songs

The meaning of the wall, and of the crannies in which the dove rests. How the soul makes these crannies for itself in the wall of the angels, and how it hollows out the rock which is Christ, as Paul and David did. The two kinds of heavenly contemplation; those searchers whom glory overwhelms, and those whom it does not.

"My dove in the clefts of the rock, in the crannies of the wall."

The dove finds safe refuge not only in the clefts of the rock, she also finds it in the crannies of the wall. Now if we interpret "wall" not as a conglomeration of stones but as the communion of saints, let us see if perhaps the crannies of the wall are the places of those angels who fell through pride leaving behind those empty spaces which are to be filled by men, like ruins repaired by men, like ruins repaired by living stones. Hence the apostle Peter says: "Come to him, to that living stone, and like living stones be yourselves built into spiritual houses" (I Peter 2:4–5). Nor do I think it irrelevant if we understand the guardianship of angels to represent a wall in the Lord's vineyard, in the Church of the predestined, since Paul says: "Are they not all ministering spirits sent forth to serve, for the sake of those who receive the inheritance of salvation?" (Heb. 1:14). And the prophet: "The angel of the Lord encamps around those who fear him" (Ps. 33:8).

SAINT BERNARD, SERMON 62

Monday

SAINT ANSELM (1033–1109)

A Prayer

Lord, teach me to seek you and show me yourself when I
    look for you.
I cannot seek you unless you show me how:
I cannot find you unless you reveal yourself.
So let me look for you in hope and with longing,
    let me long for you as I seek.
But let me find you in love and love you as I find you.

SAINT ANSELM

Tuesday

The mind images the Trinity[6]

The mind may most properly be said to be its own image in which it contemplates, as it were, the image of what it is unable to see face to face. Since the mind itself, alone among all creatures, is able to remember, understand and love itself, I cannot see how it may be denied that it is the true image of that being which, through its memory and intelligence and love, is united in that transcendent and indescribable Trinity. At the very least, it proves itself to be more truly the image of that Supreme Being by its capacity to remember, conceive of and love the Trinity that is one God. For the greater and more like that Being it is, the more truly may it be recognized to be its image.

But it is quite inconceivable that any rational creature can have been endowed naturally with a power of such excellence and so like the supreme Wisdom as this power of remembering, of conceiving and of loving the best and greatest of all beings. Therefore, no faculty has been given to any creature that is more truly the image of the Creator.

ANSELM'S *MONOLOGIUM*, C. 67

[6] In this passage, Anselm follows closely Augustine's argument in *De Trinitate* (see Friday, Week Thirteen, p. 79).

Wednesday

MEISTER ECKHART (1260–1327)

What we should do when God seems hidden

You ought to know that a man with good will can never lose God. Rather, it sometimes seems to his feelings that he loses him, and often he thinks that God has gone far away. What ought you to do then? Just what you did when you felt the greatest consolation; learn to do the same when you are in the greatest sorrow, and under all circumstances behave as you did then. There is no advice so good as to find God where one has left him; do so now, when you cannot find him, as you were doing when you had him; and in that way you will find him. But a good will never loses or seeks in vain for God. Many people say: "We have a good will," but they do not have God's will. They want to have their will and they want to teach our Lord that he should be doing this and that. That is not a good will. We ought to seek from God what is his very dearest will.

MEISTER ECKHART

Thursday

Ave Gratia Plena

"Greetings to you, full of grace, the Lord is with you" (Luke 1:35). The Holy Spirit will come down from above the highest throne, and will enter you from the light of the eternal Father (Wis. 18:15 and John 1:17).

There are three things here to understand. First, the lowliness of the angelic nature; second, that he acknowledged himself unworthy to name the mother of God; third, that he did not speak the word only to her, but that he spoke it to a great multitude, to every good soul that longs for God.

I say this: If Mary had not first given spiritual birth to God, he would never have been born bodily from her. A woman said to our Lord: "Blessed is the womb which bore you" (Luke 11:27). Then our Lord said: "It is not only the womb which bore me which is blessed; they are blessed who hear God's word and keep it" (Luke 11:28). It is more precious to God to be born spiritually from every such virgin or from every good soul than that he was bodily born of Mary.

In this we must understand that we must be an only son whom the Father has eternally begotten. When the Father begot all created things, then he begot me, and I flowed out with all created things, and yet I remained within, in the Father. In the same way, when the word that I am now speaking springs up in me, there is a second process as I rest upon the image, and a third when I pronounce it and you all receive it; and yet properly it remains within me. In the same way, I have remained within the Father. In the Father are the images of all created things. This piece of wood [pointing to the pulpit] has a rational image in God. It is not merely rational, but it is pure reason.

MEISTER ECKHART, SERMON PREACHED IN COLOGNE C. 1322

Friday

Our Lady said: "How should this happen?" Then the angel said: "The Holy Spirit will come down from above into you" (Luke 1:34–35), from the highest throne, from the Father of eternal light.

"In the beginning" (John 1:1). "A child is born to us, a son is given" (Isa. 9:6), a child in the smallness of its human nature, a Son in its everlasting divinity. Thomas Aquinas (*Summa* c. Gen. 3:21) tells us: "All created things behave as they do because they want to give birth and they want to resemble the Father." And I would add: "Every being which acts, acts for the sake of its end, that in its end it may find rest and repose." Someone else comments: "All created things act according to their first purity and according to their highest perfection." Fire as fire does not burn; it is so pure and so fine that it does not burn; but it is fire's nature that burns and pours its nature and its brightness according to its highest perfection into the dry wood. God has acted like this. He created the soul according to the highest perfection, and poured into it in its first purity all his brightness and yet he has remained unmixed.

Recently I said in another place: "When God created all things, even if God had not before begotten anything that was uncreated, that carried within itself the images of all created things: That is the spark"—as I said before in the Maccabees' church (as you would have heard, if you were listening)—"and this little spark is so closely akin to God that it is an undivided simple one, and bears within itself the images of all created things, images without images and images beyond images."

CONTINUES . . .

Saturday

Yesterday in the school among the important clerics there was a disputation. "What surprises me," I said, "is that scripture is so rich that no one can fathom the least word of it." But if you ask me, because

I am an only[7] son whom the heavenly Father has eternally borne, if then I have eternally been a son in God then I say: "Yes and no. Yes, a son, as the Father has eternally borne me, and not a son, as to being unborn."[8]

"In the beginning." Here we are given to understand that we are an only son whom the Father has eternally borne out of the concealed darkness of the eternal concealment,[9] remaining within in the first beginning of the first purity, which is a plenitude of all purity. Here I have my everlasting rest and sleep, in the eternal Father's hidden knowledge, remaining unspoken within. Out of the purity he everlastingly bore me, his only-born Son, into that same image of his eternal Fatherhood, that I may be Father and give birth to him of whom I am born. It is just as if someone were to stand before a high cliff and were to shout: "Are you there?" The echo of his voice would shout back: "Are you there?" If he were to say: "Come out of there!" the echo too would say: "Come out of there!" Yet, if someone saw a piece of wood in that same way, then it would become an angel, a rational being, and not just rational; it would become an angel, pure reason in primal purity, for there lies the plenitude of all purity.

---

[7] Eckhart is not seeking to blaspheme: We are each of us uniquely created by the Father from before time—that is to say, he always knew us before we were.

[8] In so far as the soul is "the little spark" it is at the same time eternally being born from the Father and eternally unborn as one with the Father. See Julian of Norwich following Meister Eckhart's sermon.

[9] That is to say: however long we live, and even in Eternity, we will never fully know God.

Now God acts like this: He gives birth to his Only-Begotten Son into me, so I give him birth again into the Father. And that was no different from when God gave birth {existence} to the angel while he was born of the Virgin.

EXTRACT FROM A SERMON
BY MEISTER ECKHART
PREACHED IN COLOGNE C. 1322

Week   Eighteen

Sunday

THE CLOUD OF UNKNOWING

A cloud of forgetting

Now you say, "How shall I proceed to think of God as he is in himself?" To this I can only reply, "I do not know."

With this question you bring me into the very darkness and *cloud of unknowing* that I want you to enter. A man may know completely and ponder thoroughly every created thing and its works, yes, and God's works, too, but not God himself. Thought cannot comprehend God. And so, I prefer to abandon all I can know, choosing rather to love him whom I cannot know. Though we cannot know him, we can love him. By love he may be touched and embraced, never by thought. Of course, we do well at all times to ponder God's majesty or kindness for the insight these meditations may bring. But in the real contemplative work you must set all this aside and cover it over with a *cloud of forgetting*. Then let your loving desire, gracious and devout, step bravely and joyfully beyond it and reach out to pierce the darkness above. Yes, beat upon that thick *cloud of unknowing* with the dart of your own loving desire and do not cease come what may.

THE CLOUD OF UNKNOWING, CHAP. 6

Monday

The mantra

If you want to gather all your desire into one simple word that the mind can easily retain, choose a short word rather than a long one. A one-syllable word such as "God" or "love" is best. But choose one that is meaningful to you. Then fix it in your mind so that it will remain there come what may. This word will be your defense in conflict and in peace. Use it to beat upon the cloud of darkness above you and to subdue all distractions, consigning them to the *cloud of forgetfulness* beneath you. Should some thought go on annoying you demanding to know what you are doing, answer with this one word alone. If your mind begins to intellectualize over the meaning and connotations of this little word, remind yourself that its value lies in its simplicity. Do this and I assure you these thoughts will vanish. Why? Because you have refused to develop them with arguing.

THE CLOUD OF UNKNOWING, CHAP. 7

Tuesday

THE ANCRENE RIWLE

Four chief kinds of love are known in this world: the love between good friends, between man and woman, between mother and child, between body and soul. The love which Jesus Christ has for his beloved goes beyond these four and surpasses them all.

Our Lord does not kiss with [the kiss of the mouth] any soul that loves anything but him or those things which help it to possess him for his sake.

Devotions for the Anchoress

At mass, when the priest elevates the Body of God, stand and say this verse: "Behold the salvation of the world, the Word of the Father, a true sacrifice, living flesh, the whole Godhead, true Man," and then fall to your knees with these greetings: "Hail, cause of our creation! Hail, price of our redemption! Hail, viaticum of our journey! Hail, reward of our hope! Hail, consolation of our time of waiting! Be thou our joy who art to be our reward; let our glory be in thee throughout all ages for ever. Amen."

C. 1190

Wednesday

JULIAN OF NORWICH (1342–1428?)

Such tender love

. . . he showed me further understanding of his intimate and homely love. I saw that he is the ground of all that is good and supporting for us. He is our clothing that lovingly wraps and folds us about; it embraces us and closes us all around as it hangs upon us with such tender love; for truly he can never leave us. This made me see that he is for us everything that is good.

REVELATION OF LOVE, TRANS. JOHN SKINNER

Thursday

Humanity's fair nature was first
prepared for his own Son

God, the blissful Trinity, is everlasting Being; as surely as he is endless and without beginning, so surely was it his endless purpose to make mankind. Yet man's fair nature was first prepared for his own Son, the second Person: Then, when the chosen time came, by full accord of all the Trinity, he made us all at once; and in our making, he knitted us and oned us to himself. And in this bond we are kept as clean and noble as at the time of our making. And, by the power of this same precious bond, we love our Maker and like him, praise him and thank him with a joy in him that has no end. This then is the task which he works continually in every soul that shall be saved all according to this said plan of God.

REVELATION OF LOVE, CHAP. 58

Friday

Our soul dwells in God

And because of the great, endless love God has for all humankind, he makes no distinction in the love he has for the blessed soul of Christ and the least soul that shall be saved. For it is very easy to believe and trust that the dwelling of the blessed soul of Christ is full high in the glorious Godhead. Yet in truth, as I understand our Lord to mean, where the blessed soul of Christ is, there too is the substance of all souls that are to be saved by Christ.

We ought to take great joy that God dwells in our soul, and even more joy that our soul dwells in God. Our soul is made to be God's dwelling place, and the dwelling place of the soul is God, that is unmade. And here is a high understanding inwardly to see and to know that God, who is our Maker, dwells in our soul. And a higher understanding yet is to see and know that our soul, which is made, dwells in God's substance: of which substance we are all that we are. And I saw no difference between God and our substance, but as it were all God, and yet my understanding took it that our substance is in God, that is to say, that God is God, and our substance is a creature in God.

For the almighty truth of the Trinity is our Father, for he made us and keeps us in him; and the deep wisdom of the Trinity is our Mother in whom we are all enclosed; and the high goodness of the Trinity is our Lord and in him we are enclosed and he in us. We are enclosed in the Father, and the Son is enclosed in us, and the Holy Spirit is enclosed in us: all might, all wisdom, all goodness, one God, one Lord.

REVELATION OF LOVE, CHAP. 54

Saturday

In us is his homeliest home

And then our Lord, opening my spiritual eye, showed me my soul in the middle of my heart. I saw the soul as large, as if it were an endless world and as if it were a blissful kingdom. And by the details I saw therein, I understood it to be a glorious city.

In the middle of that city sits our Lord Jesus, God and man, a fair person, large in stature, highest bishop, solemnest king, most honourable Lord. And I saw him clad solemnly, worshipfully. He sits in the soul of his own right in peace and rest. And the Godhead rules and cares over heaven and earth and all that there is; sovereign might, sovereign wisdom, sovereign goodness. The place that Jesus takes in our soul, he shall never remove from it without end—as I see it; for in us is his homeliest home and his endless dwelling.

And in this he showed the pleasure he takes in the making of our soul. For as well as the Father might make a creature, and as well as the Son could make a creature, so well did the Holy Spirit will that our soul was made; and so it was done. And therefore the blessed Trinity rejoices without end in the making of our soul; for he saw from without beginning what would please him without end.

REVELATION OF LOVE, CHAP. 67

Sunday

God is nearer to us than our own soul

And thus I saw most surely that we more readily come to the knowing of God than to that of our own soul; for our soul is so deeply grounded in God, and so endlessly treasured, that we may not come to know it until first we know God, which is the maker to whom it is oned. But notwithstanding, I saw that, for the fulfilling and perfecting of our nature, we must desire wisely and truly to know our own soul, by which we are taught to seek it where it is, that is in God. And so by the gracious leading of the Holy Spirit we shall know them both in one, whether we are stirred to know God or our own soul, both promptings are good and true.

God is nearer to us than our own soul; for he is the ground in whom our soul stands, and he is the mean that keeps the substance and sensuality together, so that they shall never part. For our soul sits in God in very rest and our soul stands in God for very strength and our soul is kindly rooted in God in endless love.[10] And therefore if we wish to know our soul and communing and having dalliance therewith, we will need to seek into our Lord God in whom it is enclosed.

REVELATION OF LOVE, CHAP. 56

[10] This single apophatic phrase might be the best sum of all that Julian has to tell.

Monday

We work his will always

Christian mystics have always recognized the intimate connection between the Trinity and the human soul. Julian ponders this mystery with peculiar affection: "Not only are we made in his image and likeness, but the whole workings of our redemption, the way we walk in and towards God is Trinitarian."

Time and again God showed in all these revelations that we work his will always and do him honor continually without stint. And the nature of this work was shown in the first revelation in marvellous ground, for it was shown in the working of the soul of our blissful lady Saint Mary, in all her truth and wisdom. And I hope, by the grace of God, to tell it just as I saw.

Truth sees God, and wisdom beholds God, and of these two comes the third: that is a holy marvellous delight in God, which is love. For where truth and wisdom truly are, there too is love flowing from them both, and all is of God's making; for he is the endless sovereign truth, endless sovereign wisdom, endless sovereign love—unmade. And the soul is a creature in[11] God, that has the same properties though they be made. And so now and evermore it does what it was made for: it sees God, it beholds God and it loves God. And because of this, God takes enjoyment in his creature, and the creature in God, both endlessly marvelling. In which marvelling

[11] In=of. That is, "creature of God." Yet to retain "in" stresses the indwelling of the Father as maker, a characteristically Julian insight.

we see our God, our Lord, our Maker, so high, so great and so good compared to that which is made so that of ourselves we seem nothing. But the brightness and the clearness of truth and wisdom makes us see and know that we are made for love: in which love God endlessly keeps us.

REVELATION OF LOVE, CHAP. 44

Tuesday

And so was my understanding led by God to see in him and understand, to learn and to know of him that our soul is a made trinity, like to the unmade blessed Trinity, known and loved from without any beginning; and in the making it is oned to the Maker, as has already been said. This was a most sweet sight and marvellous to behold, where there was peace and rest, certainty and much delight. And because of the worshipful oneing that was thus made by God, between the soul and the body, it follows that human nature must be restored from a double death. This restoring might never take place until the time the second Person of the Trinity had taken the lower part of our nature, to whom that higher part was oned in the first making. And both these parts were in Christ, the higher and the lower; which is but one soul. The higher part was one in peace with God in fullest joy and bliss; the lower part, which is sensuality, suffered for the salvation of mankind.

And these two parts were seen and felt in the eighth showing, in which my body was filled full of feeling and remembrance of Christ's passion and his death. And furthermore, with this came a subtle feeling and secret inner sight of the high part that I was shown at the time, where I might not, for I was offered no intermediary, look up to heaven. And that was because of that mighty beholding of the inner life; this inner life is that high being, that precious soul which is endlessly in its joying in the Godhead.[12]

REVELATION OF LOVE, CHAP. 44

Wednesday

MARGERY KEMPE (1373–1440)

I was told by our Lord to go to an anchoress in the same city (Dame Julian). She welcomed me; and I was able to tell her of the grace that God had put into my soul; of my compunction for past sins, of my contrition, the consolation I received in my devotions. I told her equally of my compassion for Christ when I meditated, how I had enjoyed the grace of contemplation. I also described some of my many conversations with our Lord and the words he had put into my soul. I also told her in detail of the numerous and wonderful revelations; for what I wanted to learn from this anchoress was if I had been deceived by them. For I knew she was an expert in this very field, so I knew she would offer me very good advice.

When she heard about our Lord's wonderful goodness, the anchoress thanked him with all her heart for visiting me like this. Her advice was that I should remain always obedient to God's will,

[12] Compare Julian's vision of the soul's interaction with the Trinity to that of Augustine (Friday of Week Thirteen, p. 79). Augustine, the man, is active and cerebral with his memory, understanding, and will; Julian, the woman, is receptive, acknowledging how we are "oned to our Maker" and how Christ's passion and death has restored—and is still restoring—our lower and higher nature.

carrying out with all my strength whatever prompting he put into my soul. But I must always be careful that these were not contrary to God's glory and to the benefit of my fellow Christians. Because, if this were the case, then such promptings were not those of a good spirit, but rather of an evil spirit.

THE BOOK OF MARGERY KEMPE, TRANS. JOHN SKINNER

Thursday

"The Holy Spirit can never urge us to do anything against charity; for if he did so, he would be acting against his own self, for he is the sum of all charity. And so it is that he leads a soul to chastity, for those who live chaste lives are named as temples of the Holy Spirit; and the Holy Spirit grounds a soul, making it steadfast in true faith and right belief.

"But the sort of person who is forever in two minds, dithering at every turn, he is full of doubts—just like a wave at sea, pitched up and thrown over by the wind. No one like this is likely to receive the gifts of God.

"Whatever creature who knows these signs should believe firmly that the Holy Spirit dwells in their soul. And moreover, when God gives a creature tears of contrition, compassion and devotion, they ought to know that the Holy Spirit is present in their soul. It is, as Saint Paul says, the Holy Spirit who prays for us, expressing our pleas in ways that we could never put into words. He means that the Holy Spirit makes us ask and pray, mourning and weeping with tears that are too plentiful even to count. No evil spirit could ever affect these signs: Saint Jerome tells us that human tears torment the devil even more than the pains of hell. God and the devil will always be at odds, they shall never be able to live in the same place together. And remember, the devil has no hold over our human soul."

CONTINUES . . .

Friday

"Holy Writ says as much: the soul of a just person is the seat of God: this is who I trust you are, my sister, and I will pray that God gives you perseverance. Put all your trust in God and don't be afraid of the world's chatterings. For the more contempt and shame and in-sults you have from the world, the more your rise in the eyes of God. Patience is all you need: remember our Lord's saying, 'your endurance shall win you your lives.' "

The anchoress and I had a great deal to say to each other about all these sacred and holy matters, dwelling on the love of our Lord Jesus kept us absorbed for the many days we spent together.[13]

THE BOOK OF MARGERY KEMPE, TRANS. JOHN SKINNER

Saturday

RICHARD METTHLEY, CARTHUSIAN (FIFTEENTH CENTURY)

God visited me in power
Ineffable is the yearning of love. But if naught were said of it haply

---

[13]Margery's account of her meeting Julian is the single historic witness we have firsthand of the hidden anchoress of Norwich.

some might say that it was a thing of naught; and so, following God's will, I will set out as best I can what I have experienced. And if I cannot tell it as it is, yet I do not doubt that what I am about to say is true. Since, then, one who has had experience bids thanksgiving be made to God, he who has not experienced it should not impugn it out of envy for the solitary.

On the feast of Saint Peter in Chains (August 1) I was in the church at Mount Grace, and after celebrating Mass was engaged upon thanksgiving in prayer and meditation, when God visited me in power, and I yearned with love so as almost to give up the ghost. How this could be I will tell you, my brethren, as best I can by the grace of God. Love and longing for the Beloved raised me in spirit into heaven, so that save for this mortal life nothing (so far as I know) would have been lacking to me of the glory of God Who sitteth on the throne. Then did I forget all pain and fear and deliberate thought of anything, and even of the Creator. And as men who fear the peril of fire do not cry "Fire hath come upon my house; come ye and help me," since in their strait and agony they can scarce speak a single word, but cry "Fire, Fire, Fire!" or, if their fear be greater they cry "Ah! Ah! Ah!" wishing to impart their peril in this single cry, so I, in my poor way. For first I oft commended my soul to God, saying: "Into thy hands," either in words or (as I think rather) in spirit. But as the pain of love grew more powerful I could scarce have thought at all, forming within my spirit these words: "Love! Love! Love!" And at last, ceasing from this, I deemed that I would wholly yield up my soul, singing, rather than crying, in spirit through joy: "Ah! Ah! Ah!"

HEAR OUR SILENCE,

A PORTRAIT OF THE CARTHUSIANS,

JOHN SKINNER

Sunday

MARTIN LUTHER (1483–1546)

*Martin Luther writes
to Pope Leo X*

Most Holy Father: . . ..

The honorable Sir Charles Miltitz, chamber secretary to Your August Holiness, has been with us. In the presence of the Most Illustrious Sovereign Frederick he very harshly accused me in the name of Your Holiness of lacking respect for and being rash toward the Roman Church and Your Holiness, and demanded satisfaction for this. Hearing this, I was deeply grieved that my most loyal service has had such an unhappy outcome and that what I had undertaken—to guard the honor of the Roman Church—had resulted in disgrace and was suspected of all wickedness, even so far as the head of the Church was concerned. . . .

The demand is made that I recant my theses. If such a revocation could accomplish what I was attempting to do with my theses, I would issue it without hesitation. Now, however, through the antagonism and pressure of enemies, my writings are spread farther than I ever had expected and are so deeply rooted in the hearts of so many people that I am not in the position to revoke them. In addition, since our Germany prospers wonderfully today with men of talent, learning, and judgment, I realize that I cannot, under any circumstances, recant anything if I want to honor the Roman Church—and this has to be my primary concern. Such a recanting would accomplish nothing but to defile the Roman Church more and more and bring it into the mouths of the people as something that should be accursed.

CONTINUES . . .

Monday

See, Father, those whom I have opposed have inflicted this injury and virtual ignominy on the Roman Church among us. With their most insipid sermons, preached in the name of Your Holiness, they have cultivated only the most shameful avarice and have substituted for sanctification the vile and abominable Egyptian scandal (Josh. 5:9). As if that had not been bad enough, they accuse me before Your Holiness—me, who opposed their tremendous monstrosities—of being the author of the temerity which is theirs.

Most Holy Father, before God and all his creation, I testify that I have never wanted, nor do I today want, to touch in any way the authority of the Roman Church and of Your Holiness or demolish it by any craftiness. On the contrary, I confess the authority of this Church to be supreme over all, and that nothing, be it in heaven or on earth, is to be preferred to it, save the one Jesus Christ who is Lord of all—nor should Your Holiness believe the schemers who claim otherwise, plotting evil against this Martin.

Since in this case I can do only one thing, I shall most willingly promise Your Holiness that in the future I shall leave this matter of indulgences alone, and will be completely silent concerning it (if [my enemies] also stop their vain and bombastic speeches). In addition I shall publish something[14] for the common people to make them understand that they should truly honor the Roman Church, and influence them to do so. [I shall tell them] not to blame the Church for the rashness of [those indulgence preachers], nor to imitate my sharp words against the Roman Church, which I have used—or rather misused—against those clowns,[15] and with which I have gone too far. Perhaps by the grace of God the discord which has arisen may finally by quieted by such an effort. . . .

SIGNED, FRIAR MARTIN LUTHER, D.

(I.E., DOCTOR OF THEOLOGY)

[14] Luther had already published *Zcedell* or "A little scrap of paper" a whole year before; the pamphlet sought to reassure ordinary folk that they should remain loyal to the Catholic Church while reminding them also of the all-important distinction between good works and indulgences.
[15] Preachers like the Dominican John Tetzel who were licensed to preach indulgences.

Tuesday

Latin	English
Anima Christi, sanctifica me	Soul of Christ, sanctify me
Corpus Christi, sana me	Body of Christ, make me whole
Sanguis Christi, inebria me	Blood of Christ, exhilarate me
Aqua lateris Christi, lava me	Water from the side of Christ, wash me
Passio Christi, conforta me	Passion of Christ, be my comfort
O bone Jesu, exaudi me.	Hear me, good Jesus.
Intra tua vulnera absconde me:	Hide me within your wounds:
Ne permittas me separari a te:	Never let me part from you:
Ab hoste maligno defende me:	From the evil enemy defend me:
In hora mortis meae voca me:	Call me at my dying hour:
Et jube me venire ad te:	Tell me to come to you:
Ut cum Sanctis tuis laudem te	So that with your Saints I may praise you
In saecula saeculorum.	For ever and ever.
Amen.	Amen.

TRADITIONAL PRAYER OF SAINT IGNATIUS LOYOLA

Wednesday

SAINT IGNATIUS LOYOLA (1491–1556)

Prayer to obtain God's love

Receive, Lord, all my liberty.

Accept too my memory, understanding and my
   whole will.

Whatever I have, all that I possess: it is you who gave
   them to me:

to you I return them—entirely;

rule them now with your will.

Only give me your love and your grace,

this is all I ask and need.

SPIRITUAL EXERCISES, FOURTH WEEK

Thursday

Meditation on the Two Standards

As a first prelude, consider how Christ for his part wishes and calls
everyone to come under his standard, while Satan would lure all
men to his side.

The second prelude is to imagine the place . . . visualize a wide
plain, stretching out all around Jerusalem; here stands our Lord Jesus Christ, leader and ruler over all that is good. While on another
field, somewhere near Babylon, stands our enemy, Satan. . . .

. . . . consider the message Christ our Lord makes to all his servants and friends; he sends them on a mission, telling them that they

should go out and help everyone. Firstly, they should invite them to perfect spiritual poverty, and, if it should please his divine majesty and if he chooses to call them, to physical poverty as well. Then there follows hatred and contempt of their sins. And finally this will lead to their being humble. So that there are three steps: the first is poverty as opposed to riches, the second shame and contempt as against worldly honor; and the third is humility as opposed to pride. From these three steps they may lead on to all other virtues. . . .

SPIRITUAL EXERCISES,

SECOND WEEK

Friday

Dedication

Behold, King of all and Lord of the universe, though totally unworthy yet trusting in your grace and your power, I make my spiritual offering to you and dedicate my entire will to yours. This I do in the presence of your own infinite goodness, in the sight of your glorious Virgin Mother and of all the court of heaven, making this my soul's true desire, this my deepest resolve (providing only that this is for your greater service and praise) to follow your example in bearing all injuries, all insults and poverty itself, as well as spiritual poverty, so long as your most holy majesty is pleased to call and receive me to such a state of life.

SPIRITUAL EXERCISES,

SECOND WEEK

Saturday

The Third Method of prayer

This has the body in harmony with the soul . . . it is when each breath and each prayer are made together so that one word from the Our Father takes the space of one breath. As you breathe in pay deliberate attention to the meaning of that word, or to the person to whom it is addressed, or to your own unworthiness, or to the distance between so high a person and yourself. . . .

Three Rules

The Second Rule is that if when you are meditating on the Our Father and you discover that one or two words give you spiritual delight or consolation, you should not be keen to move on but rest there. . . .

SPIRITUAL EXERCISES,

FOURTH WEEK

───────── *W e e k   T w e n t y - o n e* ─────────

Sunday

Visions of the Trinity

At Manresa, Ignatius had seen the Trinity in the form of three keys in a musical instrument; here in Rome on 6 March 1544, again at Mass, his understanding of the mystery was taken further:

At the *Te Igitur* I felt and saw, not obscurely but clearly, and very clearly, the very Being and Essence of God, under the figure of a sphere, slightly larger than the appearance of the sun, and from this Essence the Father seemed to go forth or derive, in such a way that on saying *Te,* that is, *Pater,* the Divine Essence was represented to me before the Father, and in this vision I saw represented the Being of the Most Holy Trinity without distinction or sight of the other Persons. . . .

and again at the end of Mass he saw the same.

These periods of illumination were punctuated at times with intervals of darkness and isolation. On 12 March he noted:

Finishing mass and afterwards in my room I found myself alone and without help of any kind . . . so remote and separated from the divine Persons as if I had never felt anything of them or would never feel anything of them again. Rather thoughts came to me against Jesus, sometimes against another.

In this darkness and desolation he recalled his trials at Manresa when he was tempted to suicide and applied to himself the rules [of discernment of spirits] he had then conceived, recognizing the devil at work.

EXCERPTS FROM

IGNATIUS'S SPIRITUAL DIARY

PHILIP CARAMAN, *IGNATIUS LOYOLA*

Monday

The Beauty within

Let us consider our soul to be like a castle made entirely out of a diamond or of very clear crystal, in which there are many rooms, just as in heaven there are many dwelling places. For in reflecting upon it carefully, Sisters, we realize that the soul of the just person is nothing else but a paradise where the Lord says he finds his delight. So, then, what do you think that abode will be like where a King so powerful, so wise, so pure, so full of all good things takes his delight? I don't find anything comparable to the magnificent beauty of a soul and its marvellous capacity. Indeed, our intellects, however keen, can hardly comprehend it, just as they cannot comprehend God; but he himself says that he created us in his own image and likeness.

Well, if this is true, as it is, there is no reason to tire ourselves in trying to comprehend the beauty of this castle.

THERESA OF AVILA,

THE INTERIOR CASTLE

Tuesday

The journey inward

What we have to do is see what Teresa is really saying about the soul. She is saying that it is *for God*; it is a capacity for God; he is its centre and all its beauty is because of him. This soul, this castle of immeasurable beauty and capacity, is ourselves. It is there, this wonder, inviting exploration and possession even to the innermost room where the most secret things pass between God and the soul and we are content to stay in the outer courts, if we choose to enter at all! For her, spiritual growth is seen as a journey inwards, a penetration of this interior castle. In her understanding, the castle is *already there*, our souls are, so to speak, *ready made,* we have only to get to know them by entering in. There is a problem but she avoids it by not seeing it! But to say that we are not yet in our castle, at least not in any but the outer-most court, is really saying the mansions are *not there yet*, they come into existence. So important is this insight, which Teresa grasped *practically* but did not express clearly in her use of a static image, for understanding what she calls the 'supernatural work' of God and later calls infused or mystical contemplation, to expound which is her reason for writing her book.

RUTH BURROUGHS,

INTERIOR CASTLE EXPLORED

Wednesday

What makes us human

By this time she had reached full spiritual growth. What, in her as in us all, has at the outset been mere potentiality, has now become reality under the constant action of God and her own surrender to this action.

We would be totally mistaken, however, were we to conclude from this that until we reach the seventh mansion we cannot think of God and pray to him as within us or close to us. It can never be said too often that God is always present, always bestowing himself in the measure that he can be received. On his side it is total gift, it is on our side that the check lies. Teresa is aware of this. She expresses the initial lack of intimacy between ourselves and God as due to the noise, the junk and the pernicious reptiles invading the outer courts of the castle where we are. Thus it is that we can't hear the voice of the king within nor can we catch his radiant light which is ever streaming. We would express it by saying that we are too small to receive much of God, too underdeveloped to be intimate with him. God continually offers intimacy, permeating our being as he permeates all that is. It is his most passionate desire that this constant, caring, nurturing become an indwelling of intimacy. At any moment, therefore, we can turn to our loving God who is closer to us than we are to ourselves. From the very outset, in our embryonic state, we are so richly endowed as to have the power to hold converse with none other than God himself. This is what makes us human beings.

CONTINUES . . .

Thursday

Second mansion

It is often the case with lay people, who have not been called to change their state of life, and they can easily feel "left out," that something has been denied them which has been given to others, who are very special to God. Lacking any marked experience they can settle for a mediocre life, it is true, yet some, unknown to themselves, are far from mediocre. Imperceptibly, they have become more faithful as the years have passed, more charitable, more truthful, more reliable. What they would call "saying their prayers" has become a much deeper reality, though the outward form may have changed little, and the same goes for their participation in the Mass. One of the principal objectives of this commentary is precisely to dissipate the almost universally held conviction—and it *is* almost universal in practice though there are those who would verbally subscribe to the opposite—that the sensible grace is the *real* thing and the non-sensible a second rate product. It seems to me that it is often those whose lives bear none of these supposedly authenticating experiences who are the closest to God.

CONTINUES . . .

Friday

There is enormous danger of secret vanity and illusion in spiritual impressions. Alas though, because of the ingrained conviction to the contrary, people feel discouraged and "left out" and therefore don't pray, don't surrender to God as he wants each of them to do. I hope this book of mine convinces them of their own call, as unique and beautiful as they can possibly imagine.

The other distinguishing characteristic of those in this mansion is the nature of their prayer. Prayer must be understood as a state of being, not just a particular activity. Our prayer is precisely our relation to God, what we are face to face with him. It is our stage of growth as a person. God is always calling, always summoning us into being; he is never inactive, never uninvolved, but the capacity to receive him is of varying depths. In this mansion there is relatively little; it will increase by active love. It isn't really true to say we pray because we have a soul or are a soul, we pray to become a soul.

RUTH BURROUGHS,

INTERIOR CASTLE EXPLORED

Saturday

from the convent of the Incarnation,
Avila, 1560

My present method of procedure in prayer is this. Only seldom, when I am in prayer, can I reason with the understanding, because my soul at once becomes recollected and I enter the state of quiet or that of rapture, so that I can use none of my faculties and senses. Of these last only the sense of hearing is of any help to me; and even then, although I can hear, I cannot understand anything.

It often happens that when I am not trying to think of the things of God, but am occupied in other things, and when, however much I endeavor to pray, I seem unable to do so because of great aridity, together with bodily pains, this recollection and elevation of spirit comes upon me so quickly that I can do nothing to check it, and in a moment I find myself experiencing the effects and benefits which it brings with it. And this happens without my having had any vision, or taken in anything with the mind, or realized where I am, save that, when I have thought the soul to be lost, I have found that it is enjoying great benefits. And such are these that, even if I tried for a whole year, I do not think that I could possibly produce them by my own efforts.

SAINT THERESA OF AVILA,

RELATION I

Sunday

Sometimes, though not often, for perhaps three, four or five days on end, I feel as if all good thoughts and fervent impulses and visions are leaving me, and are even vanishing from my memory, so that I cannot recall anything good that there has ever been in me even if I wish. Everything seems like a dream—or, at least, I can remember nothing of it. And in addition to all this I am oppressed by bodily pains: My understanding is troubled, so that I cannot think in the very least about God and have no idea under what law I am living. If I read, I cannot understand what I am reading; I seem to be full of faults and am not courageous enough to be virtuous, and the courage which I used to have in plenty has sunk so low that I feel I should be unable to resist the smallest of the temptations or slanders of the world. At such a time I get the idea that if I am to be employed for anything beyond the most ordinary tasks I shall be useless. I grow sad, thinking I have deceived everyone who has any belief in me; I want to be able to hide myself where nobody can see me; and my desire for solitude is the result, no longer of virtue, but of pusillanimity. I feel that I should like to quarrel with all who oppose me; and I cannot escape from this conflict, but God grants me the favor of preserving me from offending him more than usual, and from asking him to take this trial from me, if it is his will lest I offend him. With my whole heart I resign myself to his will, and I believe he is bestowing the greatest of favors upon me in not keeping me in this state forever.

SAINT THERESA OF AVILA, RELATION I

Monday

JOHN OF THE CROSS (1542–1591)

John of the Cross speaks to people who feel unable to change. We may have sensed in our lives a call to freedom, to wholeness, to more than what we are now. John felt this as a call to reach out for God. But within us, an unvoiced fear can make change impossible. It is the fear that when we reach, we may not find. It begs the question: If I give myself, will God fill me in my life?

Our being naturally hesistates to say 'yes' to a one-way track that may end only in wasteland. This is the undermining fear, and while we may not opt for a different track, we may never fully choose this one.

Here John of the Cross has something helpful to say. Poet, pastor, mystic, John is first a witness to the impact of God in his life. He has taken the risk of surrender, and can speak with the authority of one who has been there. He testifies to a God who, precisely, is pressing in to meet, to change, and to fill us in our deepest need.

IAIN MATTHEW, *THE IMPACT OF GOD*

Tuesday

Oh llama de amor viva . . .
Flame, alive, compelling,
yet tender past all telling,
reaching the secret centre of my soul!

Since now evasion's over,
finish your work, my Lover,
break the last thread, wound me and make me whole!

Burn that is for my healing!
Wound of delight past feeling!
Ah, gentle hand whose touch is a caress,
foretaste of heaven conveying
and every debt repaying:
slaying, you give me life for death's distress.

Ah! gentle and so loving
you wake within me, proving
that you are there in secret and alone;
your fragrant breathing stills me,
your grace, your glory fills me
so tenderly your love becomes my own.

. . . one feature pervades the poem, almost so obvious that it could be missed. It is this: all the initiative belongs to the other. That is John's most authentic witness to God. When John is most himself, what we find filling his mind is a God who is, supremely, active.

CONTINUES . . .

Wednesday

Imagine sitting on a quiet bench in the park, composing a quite personal letter, absorbed and writing. Someone is there—you notice out of the corner of your eye—someone is there looking at you; and has been for some time. . . . What a moment of exposure!

The gospel has eyes—"the eyes I long for so," John calls them and the point comes on the journey where the bride meets those eyes which had long been looking on: "It seems to her that he is now always gazing upon her." In the "Flame," John has captured that moment, and delivered it to us.

[Henri de Lubac writes] that "a person is enlightened," not "when they get an idea," but "when someone looks at them." A person is enlightened when another loves them.

So the gospel has eyes which are not dispassionate, nor merely passive. Their gaze engages what they see and affects it: "For God, to gaze is to love, and to work favors." These eyes [John continues] are effective: "God's gaze works four blessings in the soul: it cleanses the person, makes her beautiful, enriches and enlightens her."

This statement comes towards the end of the *Canticle* where the author is reviewing his whole journey and thanking God that it was possible at all (stanzas 32–33). It implies a whole way of looking at Christian life. Christianity is an effect, the effect of a God who is constantly gazing at us, whose eyes anticipate, radiate, penetrate and elicit beauty.

> You looked with love upon me
> and deep within your eyes imprinted grace;
> this mercy set me free,
> held in your love's embrace,
> to lift my eyes adoring to your face.

CONTINUES . . .

Thursday

These gospel eyes are traditionally called "grace": a God who gives, and whose gift makes us able to respond. John puts the doctrine neatly: "For God to set his grace in the soul is to make her worthy and capable of his love." This divine gazing is the foundation of any Christian endeavor—"without his grace, his grace cannot be merited." The trouble is that, because it is foundational, because it is as pervasive as the air, this divine initiative can be forgotten, and our religion becomes one more human enterprise, knotty, petty and ultimately suffocating. "Outside of God," John says, "everything is narrow."

The mystics keep alive the sense that the enterprise belongs to God, and so help the air to circulate. The "Living Flame" does this. As a hymn to God's initiative, it reminds us, not of a chance phenomenon, but of a state of affairs. "I am yours and for you . . ."—this is grace unfolded and writ large. John experienced God's self-giving with "most enlightened faith" and with the veil "drawn back." Yet, he says, "God is always like this, as the soul now sees him to be: stimulating, guiding, and giving being and strength and graces and gifts to all creatures, holding them all to himself."

The *"Flame"* tapped into an "always" rooted in God himself: in an eternal bestowing, Father to Son, Son to Father, rapt in the Spirit, and guaranteeing us infinite room to breathe: "The Father spoke one word, who was his Son, and this word he *is always speaking* in eternal silence. It is in silence that the soul must hear it."

CONTINUES . . .

Friday

"A person is enlightened when someone looks at them." Chaos is enlightened when God looks at it. The "Bridegroom" casts his gaze across the face of the abyss and sprays life across it. That is John's amazing understanding of creation: the universe, each element in it, each event in it, and the web of those events held together—all thought, all friendship, all history—are given by the eyes of Another, eyes "communicating" being to the world. Such a creation is flamboyant in its beauty, as the Word of God, glancing kindly but wildly, "scatters a thousand graces" and floods the cosmos with traces of who he is.

There is a marvellous sense here of God's creative act being, not just a primeval beginning, but a present event. The event is as gentle, in a sense as precarious, but also as loving as the gaze of one who cares.

There is a marvellous sense too that the universe has a character to it. John says that when the Father gazes, he gazes through his Son. The Son is his face, smiling upon the world. "God saw that they were good," which was to make them good by "seeing them" in his Son. Creation has a Son-like colour, a Son-like shape which the Son alone could fill.

That is John's real interest: the Son does undertake to fill us. His eyes not only hold us in being; they hold us in friendship, a friendship made possible when he meets us with human eyes. Humanity is enlightened when the Son becomes flesh, looks at us, draws us out of ourselves, raises us up to himself. In this the whole cosmos is renewed.

"This he did when he became man, lifting man up in the beauty

of God, and so lifting up all creatures in him. . . . In this raising up
in the Son's incarnation and in the glory of his resurrection according to the flesh, the Father gave creatures not just a partial beauty;
we can say that he entirely clothed them in beauty and dignity."

IAIN MATTHEW, *THE IMPACT OF GOD*

Saturday

GEORGE HERBERT (1593–1633)

Love bade me welcome

Love bade me welcome; yet my soul drew back,
    Guiltie of dust and sinne.
But quick-ey'd Love, observing me grow slack
    From my first entrance in,
Drew nearer to me, sweetly questioning,
    If I lacked anything.

A guest, I answer'd, worthy to be here.
    Love said, You shall be he.
I, the unkind, ungratefull? Ah, my deare,
    I cannot look on thee.
Love took my hand, and smiling did reply,
    Who made thee eyes but I?

Truth, Lord, but I have marr'd them: let my shame
    Go where it doth deserve.
And know you not, sayes Love, who bore the blame?
    My deare, then I will serve.

You must sit down, sayes Love, and taste my meat:
So I did sit and eat.

—— *Week   Twenty-three* ——

Sunday

MARY WARD (1585–1645)

Already leading a devout life, in the midst of the dangers and dis-
comforts of Penal times, Mary Ward has a spiritual experience that
intimates she is to do something further:

> there happened a thing of such nature that I knew not, nor
> ever did know, how to explain [it]. It appeared wholly di-
> vine and came with such force that it annihilated and re-
> duced me to nothing. My strength was extinguished and
> there was no other operation in me but that which God
> caused. The sight intellectually of what was done and what
> was to be fulfilled in me, I willing, of this only was I con-
> scious. Here it was shown me that I was not to be of the
> Order of Saint Clare; some other thing I was to do. What
> or of what nature I did not see, nor could I guess, only that
> it was to be a good thing and what God willed.

Monday

Following a trip to England, she returned to Saint Omer in 1609 accompanied by a small group of women, all determined to live some kind of religious life under her guidance. She bought a house which she furnished sparsely and set up a strict rule not too dissimilar to that of her Poor Clares. Slowly her purpose became clearer to her:

> About this time, in the year 1611, I fell sick in great extremity but being somewhat recovered, I went according to a vow made, in pilgrimage to our Blessed Lady of Sichem. Being alone in some extraordinary repose of mind I heard distinctly, not by sound of voice, but intellectually understood, these words: TAKE THE SAME OF THE SOCIETY— so understood as that we were to take the same of both in matter and manner, that only excepted which God, by diversity of sex, hath prohibited. These few words gave so great strength, and so changed the whole soul that it was impossible for me to doubt but that they came from him whose words are works. . . .

Ward's community was approved by Pope Paul V and growth was rapid, even dramatic, over the next sixteen years. But there was a continual opposition, especially from other religious Orders, until Pope Urban VIII finally confirmed the Institute's status.

Tuesday

In February 1631, Mary Ward was imprisoned and accused of being a "heretic, schismatic and rebel to Holy Church." On her release she maintained her innocence and determined to go to Rome to clear her name. To prepare the ground, she writes to the pope:

Most Blessed Father,

If no other aim or interest in mind than to direct and devote my efforts entirely to the better service of the Holy Church and the Apostolic See, I have, in any way, through my unworthy labor, met with your Holiness' displeasure, I most humbly ask for your forgiveness, lying prostrate at your feet. . . .

I have been publicly accused and declared a heretic, schismatic, obstinate and rebellious by Holy Church. . . . I have endured the denial of the Holy Sacraments between February 7, the day of my arrest, and March 28, the day on which I was given my Viaticum [Communion for the dying], followed two days later by the holy Oils of Extreme Unction. . . .

The infamy of being marked out in every place as guilty of such wickedness, and of being thrown into the jaws of death by order of Holy Church for supposedly having committed such attrocities . . . Our members have been mocked by the heretics for having abandoned their fatherland and families; they have been despised by their closest relations; their annual income has been unjustly seized, so that in four of our colleges, it has been necessary to ask for alms.

On arriving in Rome, ostensibly to be grilled by a commission of cardinals, Mary Ward was received warmly by the pope, who immediately exonerated her of all charges. She later learned that her imprisonment had been due to the powerful Cardinal Bentivoglio, papal Nuncio in the Spanish Netherlands, who had acted without the pope's knowledge.

Wednesday

THOMAS TRAHERNE (1637–1674)

These little limbs,
These eyes and hands which here I find,
These rosy cheeks wherewith my life begins,
Where have ye been? Behind
What curtain were ye from me hid so long!
Where was, in what abyss, my speaking tongue?

When silent, I,
So many thousand thousand years,
Beneath the dust did in a chaos lie,
How could I smiles or tears,
Or lips or hands or eyes or ears perceive?
Welcome, ye treasures which I now receive.

I that so long
Was nothing from eternity,

Did little think such joys as ear or tongue,
To celebrate or see:
Such sounds to hear, such hands to feel, such feet,
Beneath the skies, on such a ground to meet.

THOMAS TRAHERNE, "THE SALUTATION"

Thursday

SAINT THÉRÈSE OF LISIEUX (1873–1897)

Folly of a Little Flower

Having got Daddy's consent, I thought I could run to Carmel without delay, but many sore trials lay ahead to test my vocation. In fear and trembling I told my uncle what I have decided. He showed me every possible love and affection, but he withheld his permission for me to enter Carmel. He declared that he would not listen to one word of my vocation until I was seventeen. It was against all common sense, he said, to allow a mere child of fifteen to enter Carmel. Indeed, for an inexperienced child to enter such a place would be against religion. He added that it would need a miracle to change his mind. I knew then that all argument was useless, so I let the matter rest. But my heart was in a black pit. Prayer was my only comfort. I begged Jesus to perform this miracle, because that was the one obstacle in the way of my answering his call. It was some time before I dared to speak to my uncle again. I was in a panic as I forced myself to go to his house. But suddenly, it seemed that he had forgotten all about my vocation. I heard a long time afterwards that my distress had upset him a good deal so that he began to look at it from my point of view.

SAINT THÉRÈSE OF LISIEUX, *THE STORY OF A SOUL*

Friday

At the time, I could not understand what was happening. Instead of my recognizing this as a hopeful sign, God afforded me a grim martyrdom which lasted three days. Now I knew what bitter grief our Blessed Lady felt when she and Joseph searched for their boy Jesus when he was lost. I was alone in an empty desert—or perhaps I could describe my soul as a tiny rowing boat tossing without pilot in a great stormy sea. I knew that Jesus was with me, asleep in my boat, yet the night was black and I could not see him. Utter darkness. No flash of lightning to cut the clouds. Not that lightning is very nice, but, at least, if such a storm had burst, I might at least have had a glimpse of Jesus. No: It was night, dark night of the soul. Just like Jesus during his agony in the garden, I felt that I was abandoned—there was no help for me from heaven or earth. God had left me utterly alone. Nature too seemed to share my misery. The sun never shone once during those three terrible days; instead, rain teemed down. I have to say that in every crisis in my life, nature seems to share my soul. When I was crying, the sky also wept: When I was full of joy, there was the sun, with not a cloud in the sky.

On the fourth day, a Saturday, I went to see my uncle. I was very surprised when he took me straight into his study. I hadn't asked to see him on his own. He began very gently by saying that I shouldn't be afraid of him and then said there was no need for a miracle. He told me he had prayed to God asking him to set his heart right and his prayer had been answered. My uncle was a changed man. He said nothing more about common sense: He said

I was a little flower whom God wanted to pick. He would be the last man to stand in the way.

CONTINUES . . .

Saturday

Complete spiritual dryness

Now I'll tell you of the retreat before my Profession.

I was far from getting any consolation from it. Instead, I suffered complete spiritual dryness, almost as if I were quite forsaken. As usual, Jesus slept in my little boat. I know that other souls rarely let him sleep peacefully, and he is so wearied by the advances he is always making that he hastens to take advantage of the rest I offer him. It's likely that as far as I'm concerned, he will stay asleep until the great final retreat of eternity. But that doesn't upset me. It fills me with great joy. It's true that I'm a long way from being a saint, and this attitude of mine proves it. Instead of delighting in my spiritual aridity, I ought to blame my lack of faith and fervor for it. I should be distressed that I drop off to sleep during my prayers and during my thanksgiving after Holy Communion. But I don't feel at all distressed. I know that children are just as dear to their parents whether they are asleep or awake and I know that doctors put their patients to sleep before they operate. So I just think that God "knoweth our frame. He remembereth that we are dust."

So this retreat before my Profession was quite barren—like those afterwards. Yet, even though I didn't realize it, I was then being clearly shown how to please God and be good. I have often noticed that Jesus will never give me a store of provisions. He supplies me continually with fresh food and I find myself fed without knowing how. I believe quite simply that it is Jesus himself hidden deep within my poor little heart, who works within me in a mysterious manner and inspires all my daily actions.

SAINT THÉRÈSE OF LISIEUX,

THE STORY OF A SOUL

─────── W e e k   T w e n t y - f o u r ───────

Sunday

In her spiritual autobiography, Before the Living God, *Ruth Burroughs, now a Carmelite sister in Norwich, seems to share a similar experience.*

All at sea

Often the image would spring to my mind of myself in a little boat without oar or sail, on the vast expanse of ocean beneath a midnight sky. There was a sense of terror at the loneliness, at the dreadful depth below, at the utter helplessness of my state, but also the glorious security, unfelt though it was, of being held and controlled by the unseen God. I knew that I would rather be in that little boat with "nothing" than enjoy all that the world could offer me. I was wrapped around, clasped in mystery. Looking back I see great significance in this image. My sea was vast, swelling, full but it was calm. In spite of sensible sufferings there was, in my depths, a serenity—call it citadel. The time was to come when I was to be engulfed by storms, storms which threatened the citadel itself, but in the earlier part of my life the depths were serene.

RUTH BURROWS, *BEFORE THE LIVING GOD*

Monday

Thérèse, a victim of consumption, awaits her death
A Sister prophesied that a company of radiant white angels would be present at her deathbed. Her answer: "All such imaginings mean nothing to me. I can only nourish myself upon the truth." But just as she recoiled from prettifying the truth she also refused to have it made hateful. "Death will carry you off," someone said. "No, not death. The good God will come to take me. Death is not a ghost, a frightening figure like you see in pictures. The catechism says death is the separation of soul and body—nothing more." It is almost as if she had a gift for stripping everything of the trappings in which they were handed her, in order to see what things are really like.

Truth is humility. Thérèse holds to that, especially when it affects the truth about her own life. The distinction between her own nothingness and God's fulness in her is crystal-clear. "You really are a saint!" "No: I'm no saint. I've never done any holy deeds. I'm simply a quiet little soul upon whom God has heaped his graces. I'm only telling the truth. You'll know one day in heaven." Although truth is humility there still remains the one difference, one can see the truth but not humility. Which accounts for her astonishing statement: "It seems to me that humility is truth. I do not know whether I am humble. But I do know that I see the truth in everything."

HANS URS VON BALTHASAR, *THÉRÈSE OF LISIEUX*

Tuesday

And on the day she died: "Yes, I believe I have always searched for truth. Yes, I have always understood how to keep my heart quiet." Such is humility, which holds her on the narrow ledge between the abyss of truth on one side and that of lying on the other. Such humility is no virtue, but the sign that one possesses no virtue, since "it all flows from him." This is the point at which Thérèse fights her desperate battle against the great and even more pernicious misunderstanding of her virtue and sanctity. "No: I'm no saint. I've never done any holy deeds. . . ." She does not produce this light, she reflects it.

"I leaned forward, and looking through the open window saw the dying sun casting its last rays upon nature; the tops of the trees appeared transformed into gold. Then I said to myself: My soul also appears to be radiant and golden because it is exposed to the rays of love. If the divine sun were to refuse me its fire I too would immediately become dark and gloomy." There is only One who is light. Others may only stand in the light of the One and bear witness to the light.

People praised her patience. "I've never been patient for a moment. That's something I could never claim. People are always pretending to themselves." And the doctor joined in this hymn of praise: "How can *he* say such a thing. Me patient? It's a lie!"

And the brighter the truth about her humility the darker grew misunderstanding about her. "I promised her that I would get the true value of her virtues properly recognized." "I'd sooner you got the real love of God properly recognized. My poor nothing has nothing left to offer."

HANS URS VON BALTHASAR, *THÉRÈSE OF LISIEUX*

Wednesday

Demolition

By going directly to the gospel sources Thérèse joins with all her force in our Lord's initial movement: The demolition of religious façades. The blazing passion with which John the Baptist, in the spirit of Elijah, clears the ground to give the approaching Messiah room and air is itself only a preparation for the absolute passion with which the Son flattens every obstacle to the Father's glory. "Whoever draws near me, draws near to fire," runs one of Christ's apocryphal sayings, and each of his words, his actions and his miracles is fire—a fire all the more consuming since it is not the fire of justice but of love. And once God has cast this fire upon earth, he sends his saints to fan it into flame so that it cannot be damped down in the hearths of a "bourgeois" Christianity.

Thérèse of Lisieux also cleanses the Temple with a whip. She is fearless and aggressive. She loves *war*. She is a fighter by nature, "God wanted to make me conquer the fortress of Carmel at the sword's point." "Our Lord has granted me the grace of being totally unafraid of war: I must do my duty, whatever the cost." "Let us always grasp the sword of the spirit . . . let us never simply allow matters to take their course for the sake of our own peace; let us fight without ceasing, even without hope of winning the battle. What does success matter! Let us keep going, however exhausting the struggle may be. . . . One must do one's duty to the end."

MICHAEL HOLLINGS, *THÉRÈSE OF LISIEUX*

Thursday

THE BASILIAN NUNS OF MINSK

Persecuted by the State for remaining loyal to the Rule of Saint Basil while remaining in communion with Rome.

During the year 1838, Siemaszko, an apostate bishop, invited us three different times, and in writing, to embrace the schism. In his impious diatribes, he called Saint Basil a schismatic, pretending that the rule of the Basilians was nothing but a gross error, which he had adjured through the grace of God; and that after finding that truth was in the sole orthodox (Greek) religion, he exhorted us, as a pastor to his flock, to abandon the Roman Church, together with the Basilian rule.

Siemaszko required that at the bottom of the fatal invitation he had sent us we should write, *We have read it;* words equivalent in his mind to these: *We have accepted it.* After a first and second refusal on our part, he insisted very strongly; after a third, he began to threaten.

[A mock trial ensues, presided over by the bullying bishop; it concludes with a choice of sentences: freedom to retain their way of life and embrace the Orthodox religion or hard labor in Siberia.]

Of these two things, we chose the best, or convicts' labor with a hundred Siberias, rather than abandon Jesus Christ and his Vicar.

"We shall see that in time, when I shall have whipped you out of your skins in which you were born, and a new one will have grown over your bones, you will then become more tractable."

All my sisters uttered a general cry of indignation, and I distinctly heard my sister Wawrzecka say: "Flay us alive, cut our flesh to pieces, break our bones—we shall for ever remain faithful to Jesus Christ and his Vicar."

RECORD OF THE BASILIAN NUNS . . .

Friday

On hearing these words, Siemaszko ordered the soldiers to expel us from the house. He swore in a most horrid manner; and, infuriated against me, he exclaimed: "O blood of a Polish bitch! Blood of a Warsaw hound! I'll pull your tongue out of your throat!"

When we were near the church door, I threw myself at the feet, not indeed of Siemaszko, but of the Governor, asking him in a tone of ineffable grief for the permission to bid farewell to our Lord Jesus Christ in the Holy Sacrament. Siemaszko taunted me with some new insult, but the Governor granted my request. We all rushed into the church sobbing, and bathed in tears; for a few minutes we remained prostrate before the Sacrament and wrapped in prayer. O Lord! did we say, thy will is our will: Accompany us, strengthen us, teach us the mysteries of thy Passion, that we may have both desire and courage to die for thee.

We were thirty-five nuns, and when the soldiers were ordered to expel us from the church, only thirty-four arose; the thirty-fifth had remained a corpse before the Blessed Sacrament; her very heart had burst with grief and divine love. This good sister was named Rosalia Lauszecka; she had been a nun for thirty years, and was fifty-seven years old.

As soon as we came out of the church, I once more threw myself at the Governor's feet, begging him to let us carry away with us a crucifix, that the sight of our crucified Savior might teach us to bear our own cross. Siemaszko contended for not giving the permission; and a silver crucifix, containing the relics of Saint Basil, was even taken from us through violence: However, the Governor allowed us to take a wooden crucifix which used to serve for our processions. I bore it all along the road, resting it on my left shoulder. What consolation we derived from its presence during our forced march from Minsk to Witebsk! To be sure, I found it very heavy, but even so it was more kind than heavy: In this way we had constantly before our eyes the entire passion of Christ.

CONTINUES . . .

Saturday

We were hardly out of the church, when our children awoke and ran after us in tears, crying: "They have taken away our dear mothers! our dear mothers!" These children were orphans, forty-seven all told, and our other pupils amounting to about sixty. Their cries awoke the inhabitants of the city, amongst whom the most zealous and courageous joined the children.

All these good people overtook us at our first halt, near an inn called Wygodka, about three miles distant, where we stopped to be tied two by two together, with irons on our feet and hands.

We were thus chained together, each of us received the value of five shillings, with the promise of a similar sum every month for our food; but from that time we never received either money or food, and the five shillings had been hardly distributed, when they were taken by the commanding officer, who volunteered to become our steward, though he only ever bought us one small quantity of bread, milk and beer.

The most zealous amongst the inhabitants of Minsk followed us closely for several hours; but they were allowed to offer us neither help nor alms of any kind.

On that first day we were forced to walk about fifteen leagues [forty-five miles]; we passed the night in a village, where we were lodged in the huts of peasants, of whom some insulted us, whilst others were compassionate enough to offer us a part of their supper; but each of us had by our side two soldiers, who allowed nothing cooked to be offered us.

We arrived at Witebsk after a seven days' journey. The Cross of Jesus Christ was all along our strength and support. That dear crucifix I bore upon my shoulder both by day and by night; and my head rested continually on the feet of my Divine Master. Oh! how truly benign is that master. . . .

RECORD OF THE BASILIAN NUNS

—————— *Week Twenty - five* ——————

Sunday

Following Christ

Jesus said, "If you wish to be perfect, go and sell what you own and give the money to the poor . . . then come, follow me" (Mt. 19:21).

These words from the gospel seized the heart of Saint Antony, the first monk, and transformed his life forever. Jesus makes the same invitation today to follow him into the desert of monastic life. The monk, touched by grace and seized by the love of Christ, slowly turns away from the ways of the world and wholeheartedly gives himself to following the Lord.

The monastic life, consecrated exclusively to following Christ, is lived in a spirit of great simplicity, humility, and poverty according to the Gospel. The monk wishes to follow the poor, the oppressed, and the underprivileged people of the world. In his daily life, the monk has concrete ways of living out this identification with the poor, as through his humble manual work. His diet, which includes fasting and abstinence from meat, he joyfully accepts for Christ's sake, mindful that a great many people of the world are starving and are often exploited because of the affluence and waste embraced by society. When he can he gives individual assistance to those in need. The spirit of the Beatitudes remains always the ideal for all monks.

BROTHER VICTOR-ANTOINE, *A MONASTIC YEAR*

Monday

The Rule of Saint Benedict

The Rule is always more than a code of life or a manual of doctrine, although it is both of these. It is above all a résumé of a spiritual experience that lies at the heart of the monastic life. The principles of doctrines it evokes, or the details of obedience which are recommended or even imposed by it, have an inner power. This power is an experience of the very life of God in Christ Jesus and his Holy Spirit.

The letter of the Rule contains life within itself, and this life

can be awakened in the heart of the disciple. Hence the importance
of the very opening words of the Rule: "Listen my son."

DOM ANDRÉ LOUF, *THE CISTERCIAN WAY*

Saint Benedict tells us in Chapter 73, the last chapter of the Rule, that he wrote "this little Rule for beginners." Since the sixth century, innumerable monks and nuns have lived by it, and we are still doing so in diverse cultural settings and across all continents. The Rule has survived the passing of time and has inspired monks and nuns throughout the ages—proof of its universal appeal, its wisdom and certainly its timeless validity.

Many young students come to our monastery and show interest in monasticism. Some ask me why the Rule appeals to persons in this technological twentieth century. What does a sixth-century document have to say to people so removed in culture and time from St Benedict?

A MONASTIC YEAR CONTINUES

Tuesday

The Rule can be appreciated for various aspects, but one that particularly appeals to me is its wise latitude in the way it encourages us monks to walk in the footsteps of the Gospel. The Rule tacitly acknowledges a certain pluralism, making general points instead of specific ones about many observances, allowing for creativity and improvement, where this is possible. The Rule is not limited to its original place and time; like the Gospels, from which it draws its inspiration, it has wisdom as alive and full of meaningful implications today as it was at the time the Rule was composed.

A second reason for the Rule's continuing appeal is its deep sense of personalism. Beginning with the first words of the Prologue, "Listen my son," Saint Benedict's great love for the reader is evident. It is to him that Saint Benedict addresses the words of life of the Rule, thus passing on the grace, the wisdom, and the richness of his own experience. It is then up to the individual monk to embrace the Rule as a way of life, distilling wisdom day by day from it.

A third element that retains a timeless appeal to monks is the perfect pattern it creates for the monastic day. The Rule prescribes an equal distribution of time among prayer, sacred reading and intellectual work, manual work, a rest, thus bringing into balance all the activities of the monastic day. Saint Benedict was a genius in establishing through the Rule a way of life where the seasons of the earth, with their sequences of darkness and light, and the seasons of the Christian liturgy come into harmonious consonance, thus giving a dynamic balance and a healing rhythm to the monk's daily life.

CONTINUES . . .

L e n t

Wednesday

The Lenten spring has come.
The light of repentance is being offered to us.
Let us enter the season of Lent with joy,
Giving ourselves to spiritual strife, cleansing our soul
    and body,
Controlling our passions as we limit our food,
And striving to live by the virtues inspired by the Spirit.

Let us persevere in our longing for God
So as to be worthy upon the completion of the forty days
To behold the most solemn passion of Christ,
And to feast with spiritual joy
In the most holy Passover of the Lord.

At the beginning of Chapter 49 of the Rule, Saint Benedict states in strong, clear terms that "the life of a monk ought always to have the character of Lenten observance," thus emphasizing that for him Lent is not just one more liturgical season among many, but one that mirrors preeminently what the monk's life should be like at all times. He goes on to say that during Lent the monk should conduct his life with the greatest possible purity, avoiding the faults and negligence of the past. The monk will be able to accomplish this, Saint Benedict tells him, by refraining from sin and devoting himself to prayer, with tears, to holy reading, to repentance, and to abstinence. Saint Benedict takes the Lenten observance so seriously that he bids his monks to see it as a program and model for all of their monastic life.

CONTINUES . . .

Thursday

The first principle that Saint Benedict mentions, and this should be an obvious one, is "refraining from sin." Lent recalls for us, in particular, the forty days that Jesus spent in the desert doing battle with Satan, the tempter. Lent should be a similar time for us, too, to do battle, a time to fight not only the great temptations but, perhaps more importantly, our subtle faults, the seemingly small, habitual sins we consent to every day. Sometimes when we examine our consciences, we tend to look only for grave, serious sins and over-look the small ones that have become so encrusted in our personalities that we no longer recognize them for what they are. Lent is a propitious time to take inventory and a close look at our bare selves, to see the obstacles on our journey to God, things which should be eliminated from our lives. Lent provides us the occasion to work toward making radical changes in ourselves.

CONTINUES . . .

Friday

The second principle that Saint Benedict proposes is for us to apply ourselves to prayer with tears. During the early days of Lent, the Gospel parable of the Pharisee and the publican (Luke 18:9–14) is read to us in church. Jesus teaches that the Pharisee's prayer, filled with arrogance and pride, is not pleasing to God. In contrast, the humble prayer of the publican, a tax collector, who recognizes his sinfulness and makes appeal to God's mercy with inner tears, is the kind of prayer that touches the heart of God. Our Lenten prayer, like the publican's, ought then to be a humble and tearful prayer of compunction, a prayer of simplicity and trust, not in ourselves, but in the loving-kindness and tenderness of our God. This is the only form of prayer that can indeed bring us closer to God.

The third principle that Saint Benedict mentions is holy reading. Lent is a season when the reading of the Sacred Scriptures, both the Old and New Testaments, occupies a most important place in the monk's worship. He must not only apply himself to reading the Scriptures during his formal hours of prayer, but also to make room for continuing its reading at other times and intervals. The monk, just as any other Christian, should develop a continual hunger, almost addiction, for the Word of God, for through the Scriptures the Holy Spirit never ceases to speak to and educate us. As one of the early fathers poignantly said, "In the Scriptures Christ prays, weeps, and speaks directly to us." Lent is this wonderful, particularly well-suited time for reading and listening to the voice of God in his Word, thus entering into vital direct contact with him.

CONTINUES . . .

Saturday

The fourth principle that Saint Benedict emphasizes is at the heart of the Christian and, consequently, monastic life. He speaks of repentance. At the threshold of Lent, when placing the ashes on our foreheads, the priest repeats the Gospel words, "Repent and believe in the Gospel" (Mark 1:15). Repentance, undertaken with humble sincerity and joy, symbolizes the beginning of a new life and is the necessary requirement for making progress in this new life in Christ. Repentance, the work of the Holy Spirit in the innermost part of our hearts, implies a long, sustained spiritual effort. It is true that conversion and repentance are lifelong tasks, but Lent provides us with an exclusive period to work at it intensely. Lent is indeed "a school of repentance," as Father Schememann beautifully wrote, and we receive it every year as a gift from God, a time to deepen our faith and to reevaluate and change our lives.

The last principle mentioned by Saint Benedict, abstinence from food, long associated with Lent, is not solely a Christian or monastic practice. For the Christian, however, fasting bears a special connotation, being rooted in the example of Christ, who fasted forty days and forty nights (Matt. 4:2). Christ used fasting, and encouraged his followers to practice fasting, as a way of learning self-control and personal restraint. Through the painful experience of hunger, we come to the realization of our human limitations and of our utter dependence on God. Fasting is not only a physical activity but primarily a spiritual one.

> Lent is a journey, a pilgrimage! Yet, as we begin it, as we make the first step into the "bright sadness" of Lent, we see—far away—the destination. It is the joy of Easter; it is the entrance into the glory of the Kingdom. And it is the vision, the foretaste of Easter, that makes Lent's sadness bright and our Lenten effort a "spiritual spring."

ALEXANDER SCHEMEMANN, *GREAT LENT.*

BROTHER VICTOR-ANTOINE, *A MONASTIC YEAR*

W e e k　　T w e n t y - s i x

Sunday

CHARLES EUGÈNE DE FOUCAULD (1858–1916)

At the age of seventeen I began my second year [with the Jesuits] at the Rue des Postes. I think I never was in a worse state of mind. In certain ways I have done more actual evil at other times, but then the ground produced good as well as evil fruit; at seventeen I was all egotism, vanity and impiety. I was as it were made with desire for evil. . . .

Instead of a career in the army, which given his independent spirit was out of the question, De Foucauld became an explorer and map-maker. It was following his second geographical expedition to North Africa that he met the Abbé Huvelin. Charles was thirty years of age and ostensibly engaged in writing his great book, *Reconnaissance au Maroc*.

This remarkably humble priest had spent all his priestly life as vicar of Saint Augustine's church in Paris; yet he was a cultivated humanist, a fine Greek scholar, a wit, and by all accounts a saint. Baron Von Hügel described him as "a truly masculine saint who won and trained many a soul. . . . There sanctity stood before me in the flesh and this as the deepest effect and reason of the Catholic Church" (Letter to *The Times Literary Supplement*, May 25, 1922).

He was hearing confessions shortly after this first encounter between priest and geographer when Charles came to him and said simply: "Monsieur l'Abbé, I have no faith, I come to ask for instruction."

Monday

The penitent never made much of his conversion, but when his book was written, he went on pilgrimage to the Holy Land. On his return in 1890, he made more than one retreat before joining the Trappists at Notre Dame des Neiges in the department of Lozère. He was not to stay. After profession he was transferred at his own request to Akbès in Syria where the Trappists had an impoverished and run-down house. De Foucauld's hunger for the desert was growing. After spending three years in Rome studying for the priesthood, he was dispensed from his monastic vows as a Cistercian and found his way to the Holy Land once more where for three years he was gardener and "odd job" man for the Poor Clares at Nazareth, living in a shed at the bottom of their garden. But he was persuaded by the Abbé Huvelin to be ordained and he returned to Notre Dame des Neiges for this purpose and was priested in the summer of 1901. And then he left for his desert once more. After a short visit to the Trappist monastery of Staoüeli, he settled in Béni-Abbè, an oasis deep in the Sahara Desert. But after some years he moved again: It was his ambition to found an order of apostolic hermits who as well as being contemplative men should also combine this with an active and caring evangelization of the Tuaregs. He was joined by one or two companions but none persevered in the appalling austerity of life that he led; he made no converts.

On December 1, 1916 he was savagely murdered by the Senoussi, a local tribe he prayed to have helped: They cut him down, terrified of the hidden power of this silent Frenchman living among them yet alone in utter poverty.

JOHN SKINNER

Tuesday

Letter to a Trappist, studying theology in Rome:

Nazareth, June 21, 1898

I hope your life goes on being more and more buried, lost, drowned in Jesus, with Mary and Joseph. You are now passing through a time that can be compared to the early childhood of Jesus. He was learning to read at the knees of his holy priests; he was not yet working for the salvation of men—except by the inner impulses of his Sacred Heart, which was always praying for them to God, he was not working for any soul in particular. He was a little child. He did not help Saint Joseph in his work. He could not yet.

He was learning to read at Mary's knee. He sat at her

feet, smiled at her and kept good and quiet with his eyes fixed on her. This life was enough for him, the Son of God, for many years: it is as though you were five years old and were learning to read, like a child, and humbly and obediently do all you are told, just as Jesus at five years old did all that his parents told him.

Later he will take you to the desert . . . from there to Gethsemani . . . then to Calvary. But for now live with Jesus, Mary and Joseph as if you were alone in the world with them in their little home at Nazareth.

CHARLES DE FOUCAULD

Wednesday

To his married sister:

Jerusalem, November 19, 1898

When one is very sure that something is the will of God, it is so sweet to do the will of the Beloved that nothing else counts. He is here as he was at Nazareth. He is everywhere. What does it matter where I am? One thing only matters and that is to be where he wishes me to be, to do what pleases him most. Oh let us forget ourselves, forget ourselves, and live in Jesus, loving him with all our hearts; for you know when one loves one lives less for oneself than for the Beloved, and the more one loves the more one directs one's life outward towards him one loves.

If we love Jesus we live much more in him than in ourselves. We forget our concerns so as to think only of what concerns him, and since he is in peace and ineffable blessedness, seated at the right hand of the Father, we participate, according to the measure of our love, in the peace and beatitude of our divine Beloved.

You ask me to pray for peace for you, my dear; the secret of peace is to love, love, love.

Yes, I will pray for peace for you, or rather I will pray for the love of Jesus, who alone can be peace, and who gives it of necessity because he always brings it with him. Do you ask this too, ask for love, say "I love you and let me love you more." And think, say, do everything in the spirit of love. Do all that can rouse love in you, all that can lead others to love this divine spouse in our souls.

CHARLES DE FOUCAULD

Thursday

To a Trappist:

Notre Dame des Neiges [where he had been ordained]
July 17, 1901

I have thought constantly of you all through this my silence. Silence, you know, is quite the contrary of forgetfulness and coldness. In silence, one loves most ardently; words and talk often extinguish the inward fire. Let us keep silence, dear Father, like Mary Magdalene and Saint John the Baptist, and let us beg Jesus to light within us that great fire of love that made their solitude and silence so blessed. They knew indeed how to love. My first act on landing from the Holy Land was to go up to Saint Baume. May Mary Magdalene, the beloved and blessed, teach us to love, and love ourselves in Jesus, our All, and to be lost to all that is not he.

If I trusted to myself I should think my ideas crazy, but I trust to God who said, "If you would serve me, follow me," and again and again he said, "Follow me," and "Love your neighbour as yourself, and do to others as you would they should do to you." My idea of practicing this brotherly charity is to consecrate my life to helping those *brothers of Jesus* who lack everything, since they lack Jesus.

If I were one of those unhappy Mussulmans who know neither Jesus nor his Sacred Heart, nor Mary, our Mother, nor the Holy Eucharist, nor any of the things that make our happiness in this life and our hope in the next, and knew my sad state, how grateful I should be if someone would come and save me from it. . . .

CHARLES DE FOUCAULD

Friday

SEVEN CISTERCIAN MARTYRS OF TODAY:
BROTHER CHRISTIAN, BROTHER LUC, BROTHER CHRISTOPHE,
BROTHER MICHEL, BROTHER BRUNO, BROTHER CÉLESTIN,
BROTHER PAUL

Dom Christian, Prior of Notre-Dame de l'Atlas, Tiberine, Algeria, was abducted with his six brothers in the middle of the night by terrorists. Having been held prisoners for eight weeks, they were murdered on May 21, 1996. They are buried in the grounds of their monastery where they prayed and labored for reconciliation, peace and understanding between Christian and Muslim. Two years before his death, knowing certain death lay ahead, Christian de Chergé put down in writing his Testament of witness and love:

When we must face an A-Dieu

If it should happen one day—and it could be today—that I become a victim of the terrorism which now seems ready to engulf all the foreigners living in Algeria, I would like my community, my Church, my family, to remember that my life was GIVEN to God and to this country.

I ask them to accept that the Sole Master of all life was not a stranger to this brutal departure. . . . I would ask them to pray for me: for how could I be found worthy of such an offering?

I ask them to be able to link this death with the many other deaths which were just as violent, but forgotten through indifference and anonymity.

My life has no more value than any other. Nor any less value. In any case, it has not the innocence of childhood. I have lived long enough to know that I am an accomplice in the evil which seems, alas, to prevail in the world, even in that which would strike me blindly.

I should like, when the time comes, to have the moment of lucidity which would allow me to beg forgiveness of God and all my fellow human beings, and at the same time to forgive with all my heart the one who would strike me down.

CONTINUES . . .

Saturday

I could not desire such a death.

It seems to me important to state this.

I do not see, in fact, how I could rejoice if this people I love were to be accused indiscriminately of my murder. To owe it to an Algerian, whoever he may be, would be too high a price to pay for what will, perhaps, be called "the grace of martyrdom," especially if he says he is acting in fidelity to what he believes to be Islam.

I am aware of the scorn which can be heaped on Algerians indiscriminately.

I am also aware of the caricatures of Islam which a certain islamism encourages. It is too easy to salve one's conscience by identifying this religious way with the fundamentalist ideologies of the extremists.

For me, Algeria and Islam are something different: they are a body and a soul. I have proclaimed this often enough, I believe, in the sure knowledge of what I have received from it, finding there so often that true strand of the Gospel learnt at my mother's knee, my very first Church, in Algeria itself, and already inspired with respect for Muslim believers.

My death, clearly, will appear to justify those who hastily judged me naïve or idealistic: "Let him tell us now what he thinks of it!"

CONTINUES . . .

—— *W e e k   T w e n t y - s e v e n* ——

Sunday

But these people must realise that my most avid curiosity will then be satisfied. This is what I shall be able to do, if God wills— immerse my gaze in that of the Father, and contemplate with him his children of Islam just as he sees them, all shining with the glory of

Christ, the fruit of his Passion, and filled with the Gift of the Spirit, whose secret joy will always be to establish communion and to re-fashion the likeness, playfully delighting in the differences.

For this life lost, totally mine and totally theirs, I thank God who seems to have willed it entirely for the sake of that JOY in everything and in spite of everything.

In this THANK YOU, which sums up my whole life from now on, I certainly include you, friends of yesterday and today, and you, my friends in this place, along with my mother and father, my sisters and brothers and their families—the hundredfold granted as was promised!

And also you, the friend of my final moment, who would not be aware of what you were doing. Yes, I also say this THANK YOU and this A-DIEU to you, in whom I see the face of God. And may we find each other, happy *good thieves*, in Paradise, if it pleases God, the Father of us both.

AMEN. IN SHA'ALLAH.

Algiers, December 1, 1993

Tiberine, January 1, 1994

CHRISTIAN

Monday

A pope's first Christmas
Thursday, December 12, 1958

Nativity of our Lord Jesus Christ. First Christmas as Pope.

Midnight mass in the Pauline Chapel for the diplomats ac-credited to the Holy See. About 200 people. Numerous Communions, devout beyond all expectations. Excellent singing directed by Bartolucci. At 11 A.M. mass in St Peter's: Crowd impressive and devout. My third mass. More suitable music, in the presence of the archpriest, Card. Tedeschini. A simple mass but followed with great participation: It seemed to me to be more alive than in the past.

After mass gave solemn benediction to the vast crowd in the square. Appeared in tiara. Good order and great joy and peace. Afterwards went to the Bambin'Gesù hospital for children suffering from polio: Then to the S.Spirito hospital, welcomed by the Prime Minister Fanfani and other dignitaries. Two hours of spiritual joy and, I think, genuinely edifying emotion. *Laus Deo.* For lunch I wanted to have with me Mgr Angelo Rotta, my predecessor in Istanbul and friend for over forty years. I was alone with him and Don Loris, who wore the robes of a domestic prelate for the first time.

Friday 26

My visit to the Regina Coeli prison. Much calm on my side, but great astonishment in the Roman, Italian and international press. I was hemmed in on all sides: Authorities, photographers, prisoners, warders—but the Lord was close. These are the consolations of the Pope: The exercise of the fourteen works of mercy. *Soli Deo honor et gloria.*

PETER HEBBLETHWAITE,

JOHN XXIII, POPE OF THE COUNCIL

Tuesday

BEDE GRIFFITHS (1906–1993)

Enlarging the vision

A Catholic may believe that the development of episcopacy and papacy and the elaboration of the doctrine and sacramental life of the

Church in later times has been the work of the Holy Spirit, but he need not deny that other Churches have also been guided by the same Spirit and he will always be conscious that the Church is a living and growing organism so that its discipline and doctrine are always capable of reform and renewal. What remains fundamental to all Christian Churches is a common faith in Jesus Christ as Lord and Savior, which was expressed in the early Church in the simple formula, "Jesus is the Lord" (I Cor. 12:3), and a common baptism by which all alike receive forgiveness of sins through the gift of the Holy Spirit and are made members of the one Body of Christ. This common basis of faith for all Christians was summed up by Saint Paul in the formula: "One Lord, one faith, one baptism, one God and Father of all." (Eph. 4:5–6.) This alone is sufficient basis for Christian unity.

But beyond this we have to enlarge our vision of the Church to include not only all Christians but also all those who sincerely seek God. As we have seen, God is revealing himself at all times to all men in all circumstances. There is no limit to the grace of God revealed in Christ. Christ died for all men from the beginning to the end of time, to bring all men to that state of communion with God, with the eternal Truth and Reality, for which they were created. This gift of eternal life is offered in some way to all men without exception.

Wherever man encounters God, or Truth, or Reality, or Love, or whatever name we give to the transcendent mystery of existence, even if he is formally an atheist or an agnostic, he encounters the grace of God in Christ. For Christ is the Word of God, the expression of God's saving purpose for all mankind. That Word "enlightens every man coming into the world." (John1.)

CONTINUES . . .

Wednesday

Through death to new life

Perhaps we can best approach this inner mystery of the Upanishads by way of Katha Upanishad. It is a short Upanishad belonging to the middle period (about 500 B.C.), coming after the early period of the long prose Upanishads (the Brihadaranyaka and the Chandogya), written in verse and forming a real initiation into the secret doctrine of the Upanishads.

It begins significantly with the descent of the young man, Nachiketas, to the realm of the dead to receive instructions from Yama, the god of death. In every great religious tradition, it has been recognized that to reach the final truth one must pass through death. It is the meaning behind Aeneas's descent into the underworld in Virgil, and of Dante's descent into hell in the *Divine Comedy*. It is, of course, the meaning of Christian baptism. "You who were baptized were baptized into the death of Christ." (Rom. 6:3.) We have to die to this world and to ourselves, if we are to find the truth. What Nachiketas asks of Yama is "What lies beyond death?" This is the question that man has asked from the beginning of history and which people are still asking. But an answer cannot be given on the level of rational discourse. "This doctrine is not to be obtained by argument," says Yama. It can only be learned from one who has had experience of the mystery, who has passed through death into a new life.

BEDE GRIFFITHS,

THE MARRIAGE OF EAST AND WEST

Thursday

The Ashram and Monastic Life

The ashram is one of the oldest institutions in India, though it cannot properly be called an institution; it is rather a way of life. Its origin is to be sought in the time of the Aranyakas, the Forest-Books in the first millenium before Christ, when the Rishis retired into the forest to meditate and disciples gathered around them to share their meditation and to learn the way to experience God. This remains the essential character of an ashram. It is a place where disciples gather round a master or guru to learn his way of prayer and meditation and to seek for God. Ashrams have existed in India from the earliest times to the present day, but it is only recently that Christian ashrams have come into being.

Contemplation at the centre

What then is the significance of this way of life for monasticism as a whole and for Christian life in general? The first thing, I would say, is that it centers the whole life on contemplation or the experience of God. We have a long tradition of contemplation and contemplative life in the Church, but its meaning and significance have been obscured in recent times. The contact with Hindu spirituality enables us to discover its meaning for the Church today. In the first place we have to be clear what we mean by contemplation. The word is Latin, translating the Greek *theoria*, neither of which words convey its real significance. In the early Church, following Saint Paul, the human being was said to be composed of body, soul and spirit. In later times the body-soul psychology of Aristotle was introduced and the significance of the spirit was largely lost. Now the spirit or *pneuma* in Saint Paul corresponds very closely with the *atman* in Sanskrit, and this is the key concept of all Indian spirituality. The spirit transcends both body and soul or "psyche" and is the point of human transcendence or contact with the divine. It is a "capacity" for God, an "obediential" power in the old scholastic language, which enables the human being to receive the Spirit of God.

BEDE GRIFFITHS, EXTRACT OF

AN ARTICLE PUBLISHED BY *IN CHRISTO*

Friday

The role of contemplation

Now it is at this point of the spirit that contemplation takes place. Contemplation is the experience of God in the spirit. It is what Saint Paul means by living "in the spirit" or living "in Christ." It is thus the fundamental Christian experience. By saying, therefore, that an ashram is a place of contemplation we mean that it is a place where people come to experience God in the spirit; not in the ordinary way of indirect experience through the senses and the mind but in the depth of the spirit. It is precisely this transcendence, not only of the senses but also of the mind, which is the mark of Hindu spirituality and this is likewise the goal of Christian contemplation.

The consequences of this for monastic life are considerable. It means that monastic life will centre not so much on the liturgy or *lectio divina*, though these, of course, have an essential place, but in contemplative prayer. In the Benedictine tradition, the liturgy has always the central place and there is no doubt that accompanied by *lectio divina* it can lead effectively to contemplation. Cassian has described how in the midst of chanting the psalms one may be led to a sudden ecstasy when one is taken up to God. But contemplative prayer in the Yoga tradition is a method of arriving more directly at the prayer of contemplation. It consists precisely in seeking first of all to harmonize the senses and the mind, so as to bring them into a state of quiet and then to allow the spirit to become totally open to the action of the Spirit of God. This means in practise that personal prayer becomes more central than the common prayer of the liturgy. In an ashram it is normal to give a central place to the times of meditation in the eastern sense of contemplative prayer for an hour in the morning and an hour in the evening. The prayer of the liturgy then becomes an overflow from this contemplative prayer and also a means of nourishing it. In this way the whole life becomes really centred on contemplation.

CONTINUES . . .

⌒

Saturday

Freedom of spirit

I began by saying that an ashram is not an institution but a way of life. In the course of time, monastic life in the West has become highly institutionalized. This has its value and leads to a greater degree of stability. But if a monastery seeks to be a centre of contemplative life, it would seem that it needs to be more free of structures. Thomas Merton complained towards the end of his life, that the monastic life often tended to frustrate the very vocations for which it existed. A monastery can be so highly organized with its liturgy, its study and its work that there is no freedom to develop the contemplative gift which is unique in each person. A Hindu ashram on the other hand has no definite structure. Originally, it was a group of disciples gathered round a Guru. The Guru normally is not responsible for the organization of the ashram. This is the work of the "devotees." It is they who provide the necessary funds, erect the building and manage the affairs of the ashram. The Guru is responsible for the spiritual development of each devotee. This gives great freedom for each aspirant to develop his own inner life. The relation of devotees is essentially not to one another but to the Guru. This has its own value, but it also has its weakness. It can lead to great instability and to a lack of any real community life. In a Christian ashram the aim should rather be to allow as much liberty as possible but to create a genuine community with fraternal bonds with one another. For the Christian the Guru is Christ and the spiritual father can never be more than one who leads others to Christ.

CONTINUES . . .

———— *W e e k   T w e n t y - e i g h t* ————

Sunday

Yet this need for greater freedom seems to be of great importance today. There are many people who are seeking a contemplative way of life, who want to live a dedicated life "in the Spirit." But they are not prepared for the organized life of the ordinary monastic community. There is a growing need for freer communities, of both men and women, married and single, who can lead a dedicated life of prayer but with the freedom to develop their own way. Yet at the same time they need a spiritual guide, who can direct them on the path; perhaps a group of "oblates" attached to a monastery but retaining their own independence would answer the need. Some might live at home, earning their living but coming together regularly for prayer and meditation. Others might be living in community, but again with freedom to follow their own way. We have had people coming to our ashram from all over the world in recent years, all of them in search of God, that is, living in the presence of God, so as to give meaning and purpose to their lives. They do not want the discipline of monastic life, but the freedom to follow the call of God and to discover a way of prayer and meditation which will lead to personal fulfilment.

I believe the community founded by Father John Main in Canada has found a way to answer the need of such people and an ashram may also be a way of responding to their need. But we must be open to the call of God today. There is a movement of the Spirit throughout the world and we have all to find how to respond to this movement. The old monastic institutions have still their validity, but it seems that new developments are called for and we need to be open to the Spirit wherever he is leading us.

Where the Church has newly taken root, special attention should be given to the establishment and development of fresh forms of religious life. These should take into account the natural endowments and manners of the people, and also local customs and circumstances.

VATICAN II: P.C. 17

DOM BEDE GRIFFITHS,
EXTRACT OF AN ARTICLE
PUBLISHED BY *IN CHRISTO*

Monday

JOHN MAIN O.S.B. (1926–1982)

Maranatha

Come Lord Jesus

All Christian prayer is a growing awareness of God in Jesus. . . . And for that growing awareness we need to come to a state of undistraction, to a state of attention and concentration—that is to a state of awareness . . . the only way I have been able to find to come to that quiet, to that undistractedness, to that concentration, is the way of the mantra.

CONTINUES . . .

Tuesday

Only Presence

Throughout the *Cloud of Unknowing* the author urges us to choose a word that is full of meaning; but that once you have chosen it, to turn from the meaning and associations and to listen to it as a sound. "Maranatha" is a perfect mantra from that point of view.

Most people say it in rhythm with their breathing. The important thing is to articulate it clearly in the silence of your mind, a silence that is itself deepening and spreading all the time, and to concentrate on it to the exclusion of all other thoughts . . . you begin by saying it, you then sound it in your heart and finally you come to listen to it with total attention.

Saying the mantra is as easy as falling off a wall: All you do is to begin to say it in your mind—then sound it—next is to listen to the sound of it. The only quality you then require is simplicity—to keep saying it. "Unless you become as little children." What word does a child keep repeating: "Abba, Father." Each repetition is a new confidence established—not because the child *thinks* about it, but because the child experiences the relationship as *real*. That is what the mantra is about—no thought, no imagination: Only PRESENCE.

DOM JOHN MAIN, O.S.B.

Wednesday

THOMAS MERTON (1915–68)

The meaning of the Cross

In the first two chapters of the first Epistle to the Corinthians, Saint Paul distinguishes between two kinds of wisdom: One which consists in the knowledge of words and statements, a rational, dialectical wisdom, and another which is at once a matter of paradox and experience, and goes beyond the reach of reason. To attain to this spiritual wisdom, one must first be liberated from servile dependence on the "wisdom of speech" (I Cor. 1:17). This liberation is effected by the "word of the Cross" which makes no sense to those who cling to their own familiar views and habits of thought and is a means by which God "destroys the wisdom of the wise" (I Cor. 1:18–23).

THOMAS MERTON,

ZEN AND THE BIRDS OF APPETITE

Thursday

The Cross is completely baffling both to the Greeks with their philosophy and to the Jews with their well-interpreted Law. But when one has been freed from dependence on verbal formulas and conceptual structures, the Cross becomes a source of "power." This power emanates from the "foolishness of God" and it also makes of us "foolish instruments" (the Apostles: I Cor. 1:27ff). On the other hand, he who can accept this paradoxical "foolishness" experiences in himself a secret and mysterious power, the power of Christ living in him as the ground of a totally new life (I Cor. 2:1–4).

Here it is essential to remember that for a Christian "the word of the Cross" is nothing theoretical, but a stark and existential union with Christ in his death in order to share in his resurrection. To fully "hear" and "receive" the word of the Cross means much more than simple assent to the dogmatic proposition that Christ died for our sins. It means to be "nailed to the Cross with Christ," so that the ego-self is no longer the principle of our deepest actions, which now proceed from Christ living in us: "I live, now not I, but Christ lives in me" (Gal. 2:19–20). To receive the word of the Cross means the acceptance of a complete self-emptying, a *kenosis*, in union with the self-emptying of Christ "obedient unto death" (Phil. 2:5–11). It is essential to true Christianity that this experience of the Cross and of self-emptying be central in the life of the Christian so that he may fully receive the Holy Spirit and know (again *by experience*) all the riches of God in and through Christ (John 14:16–17).

As Gabriel Marcel puts it: "There are thresholds which thought

alone, left to itself, can never permit us to cross. An experience is
required—of poverty and sickness."

THOMAS MERTON,

ZEN AND THE BIRDS OF APPETITE

Friday

The humanity of Christ in prayer

Readers of Saint Theresa are familiar with a problem (or pseudo-
problem) that was raised by illuminism and quietism in the
sixteenth and seventeenth centuries. Mental prayer grows progres-
sively simpler until it becomes "contemplation" in which there
are few ideas or even none at all, and in which images play little
or no part. But Christian prayer is obviously centred on the Person
of Jesus Christ. Should contemplative prayer be understood as
directed only to Christ as God, not as man? In other words, is there
a time when the humanity of Christ no longer has any place in
mental prayer? Or is there even a time when it becomes right and
proper to deliberately *exclude* Christ the man from prayer, in order
to be able to lose oneself entirely in his Divinity? Saint Theresa, with
a healthy Catholic instinct, rejected the idea that the "one mediator"
between God and men, the Man-God, should somehow become
an obstacle instead of a mediator. She doubtless sensed the inner confusions and contradictions inherent in this abstract and
arbitrary separation between the humanity and divinity of Christ.
Let us recall briefly what she tells us of the "problem" as she experienced it.

First she refers to writers "who advise us earnestly to put aside
all corporeal imagination and to approach the contemplation of the
divinity. For they say that anything else, even Christ's humanity, will

hinder or impede those who have arrived so far from attaining to the most perfect contemplation. They quote the words of the Lord on this subject to the Apostles with regard to the coming of the Holy Spirit" (*Life,* Chapter 22).

THOMAS MERTON,

THE MONASTIC JOURNEY

Saturday

Then she admits that she herself "when I began to gain some experience of supernatural prayer—I mean the prayer of quiet—I tried to put aside everything corporeal. . . . I thought I was experiencing the presence of God, as proved to be true, and I contrived to remain with him in a state of recollection." She found this so profitable that "no one could have made me return to meditation on the humanity," but afterwards she reproached herself for this as "an act of high treason." She addresses Christ, saying: "Is it possible, my Lord, that for so much as an hour I should have entertained the thought that you could hinder my greatest good?" And she surmised, quite rightly, that there is a kind of pride and human self-conceit in wanting by deliberate effort and technique to attain to an "experience" of the "divine essence" while by-passing the Person of the Man-God as though he were an obstacle.

The problem arises when the *Person* of the God-Man is conceived as being an obstacle to "contemplation of the divine essence." Saint Theresa saw that for a Christian there could be no contemplative experience of the divine essence except through the Person of Christ, the God-Man. However, she distinguished between the state in which Christ lived before his resurrection, and the glorified life in which he lives now:

"I cannot bear the idea that we might withdraw ourselves entirely from Christ and treat that divine Body of his as though it were on a level with our miseries. . . . It may be that our temperament or some indisposition will not allow us always to think of his passion. . . . But what can prevent us from being with him and his resurrection body since we have him so near us in the sacrament, where he is already glorified."

CONTINUES . . .

──────── *W e e k   T w e n t y - n i n e* ────────

Sunday

Never before have men talked so much about peace, and never has there been so little peace in the world. What was said by the prophet Jeremiah of the men of his time applies even more truly to the men of our own: They have said, "Peace, Peace," and there is no peace.

We prescribe for one another remedies that will bring us peace of mind, and we are still devoured by anxiety. We evolve plans for disarmament and for the peace of nations, and our plans only change the manner and the method of aggression. The rich have everything they want except happiness, and the poor are sacrificed to the unhappiness of the rich. Dictatorships use their secret police to crush millions of men under an intolerable burden of lies, injustice and tyranny, and those who still live in democracies have forgotten how to make good use of their liberty. For liberty is a thing of the spirit, and we are no longer able to live for anything but our bodies. How can we find peace, true peace, if we forget that we are not machines for making and spending money, but spiritual beings and sons of the most high God?

Yet there *is* peace in the world. Where is it to be found? In the hearts of men and women who are wise because they are humble, humble enough to be at peace in the midst of anguish, to accept conflict and insecurity and overcome it with love, because they realize who they are, and therefore possess the freedom that is their true heritage. These are the children of God. We all know them. We do not have to go to monasteries to find them. They are everywhere. They may not spend their time talking about peace, or about God, or about Christ our Lord: But they know peace and they know God, and they have found Christ in the midst of battle. They have surrendered their minds and their wills to the call of Christ, and in him they have found reality.

THOMAS MERTON, *THE MONASTIC JOURNEY*

Monday

Imago Dei

God is not a "problem" and we who live the contemplative life have learned by experience that one cannot know God as long as one seeks to solve "the problem of God." To seek to solve the problem of God is to seek to see one's own eyes. One cannot see one's own eyes because they are that with which one sees and God is the light by which we see—by which we see not a clearly defined "object" called God, but everything else in the invisible One. God is then the Seer and the Seeing and the Seen. God seeks himself in us, and the aridity and sorrow of our heart is the sorrow of God who is not known to us, who cannot yet find himself in us because we do not dare to believe or trust the incredible truth that he could live in us, and live there out of choice, out of preference. But indeed we exist solely for this, to be the place he has chosen for his presence. His manifestation in the world, his epiphany. But we make all this dark and inglorious because we fail to believe it, we refuse to believe it. It is not that we hate God, rather that we hate ourselves, despair of ourselves. If we once began to recognize, humbly but truly, the real value of our own self, we would see that this value was the sign of God in our being, the signature of God upon our being.

THOMAS MERTON,

LETTER TO MY BROTHER IN THE WORLD

Tuesday

Coming of age

The change in my own inner climate: The coming of autumn. I am still too young to be thinking about "old age." Really, these years when you approach fifty and get ready to turn the corner are supposed to be the best in your life. And I think that is true. I do not say that for me they have been the *easiest*. The change that is working itself out in me comes to the surface of my psyche in the form of deep upheavals of impatience, resentment, disgust. And yet I am a joyful person, I like life, and I have really nothing to complain of. Then suddenly a tide of this unexpected chill comes up out of the depths: And I breathe the cold air of darkness, the sense of void! I recognize it all right, it does not bother me. And I say to my body: "Oh, all right, then *die*, you idiot." But that is not what it is trying to do. It is my impatience of degrees, and of gradualness, and of time. My body is not sending up signals of emergency and of death, it is only saying: "Let's go a little slower for a change."

Nor is it just "the body" that is talking. Where does this naked and cold darkness come from? Is it *from* myself, or is it a momentary unmasking of my self? Who is it that experiences this sudden chill? What does it mean? When I turn to it, I sense that this chill fear has a friendly and perhaps important message.

THOMAS MERTON, *CONJECTURES OF A GUILTY BYSTANDER*

Wednesday

If I stand back from it and say, "It is nothing," then it returns more forcefully the next time. But if I do not evade it, if I accept it for what it is, I find it is, after all, nothing. What is this nothing which, when you run away from it, becomes a giant? And when you accept it nothing?

I think one must say it is a positive nothing, an unfulfilled possibility—almost an infinite possibility. A frightening one, in the sense that it is a possibility which includes the postulate that I myself cease to exist.

Thus, putting it in the form of a question, it comes out like "Who are you when you do not exist?"

Is this question an absurd one? On the contrary, it is I think a most attractive and fascinating one because of the obscure promises that it contains and because the answer to it can never be grasped by the mind. It is a question into which one must plunge himself entirely before it can make any sense—and that means, in a way, plunging entirely into nothingness, not just struggling with the *idea* of nothingness.

When the question presents itself as an alien chill, it is saying something important: it is an accusation. It is telling me that I am too concerned with trivialities. That life is losing itself in trifles which cannot bear inspection in the face of death. That I am evading my chief responsibility. That I must begin to face the deepest of all decisions—the "answer of death"—*the acceptance of the death sentence*—and with joy, because of the victory of Christ.

THOMAS MERTON, CONJECTURES OF A GUILTY BYSTANDER

Thursday

Monasticism today and the death of faith

The monastic life is a life of renunciation and total, direct worship of God for his own sake. Is this still to be regarded as something a reasonable man will undertake in the twentieth century? Is it simply an escape from life? Is it a refusal of fellowship with other men, misanthropy, evasion, delusion?

A monk must understand the motives which have brought him to the monastery, and he must re-examine them from time to time as he grows in his vocation. But a defensive, apologetic attitude is not in accordance with the monastic life. A monk would be out of character if he tried to argue everybody into admitting that his life is justified. He expects merely to be taken as he is, judged for what he is, because he does not waste time trying to convince others or even himself that he amounts to anything very special.

The monk is not concerned with himself so much as with God, and with all who are loved by God. He does not seek to justify himself by comparing himself favorably with other people: Rather, he sees himself and all men together in the light of great and solemn facts which no one can evade. The fact of inevitable death which puts an end to the struggles and joys of life. The fact that the meaning of life is usually obscure and sometimes impenetrable. The fact that happiness seems to elude more and more people as the world itself becomes more prosperous, more comfortable, more confident of its own powers. The fact of sin, that cancer of the spirit, which destroys not only the individual and his chances of happiness, but whole communities and even nations. The fact of human conflict, hate, aggression, destruction, subversion, deceit, the unscrupulous use of power. The fact that men who refuse to believe in God, because they think that belief is "unreasonable," do in fact surrender without reason to baser forms of faith: They believe blindly in every secular myth, whether it be racism, communism, nationalism, or one of a thousand others which men accept today without question.

THOMAS MERTON, *THE MONASTIC JOURNEY*

Friday

Surrender to the Gospel of Christ

The monk confronts these perplexing facts. And he confronts the religious void in the modern world. He is well aware that for many men, as the philosopher Nietzsche declared, "God is dead." He knows that this apparent "death" of God is in fact an expression of a disturbing modern phenomenon, the apparent inability of man to believe, the death of supernatural faith. He knows that the seeds of this death are in himself, for though he is a believer, he too sometimes must confront, in himself, the possibility of infidelity and failure. More than anyone else he realizes that faith is a pure gift of God, and that no virtue can give man room for boasting in the sight of God.

What is this so-called "death of God"? It is in fact the death of certain vital possibilities in man himself. It is the death of spiritual courage which, in spite of all the denials and protestations of commonplace thinking, dares to commit itself irrevocably to belief in a divine principle of life. It is the seeming death of all capacity to conceive this as a valid possibility, to reach out to it, grasp it, to obey the promptings of the Spirit of divine life, and surrender our heart and mind to the Gospel of Jesus Christ.

A monk has made this surrender, knowing what it costs, knowing that it does not absolve him from the doubts and struggles of modern man. But he believes that he possesses the key to these struggles, and that he can give his life a meaning that is valid not only for himself but for everyone else. That meaning is discovered in faith, though not in arguments about faith. Certainly faith is not opposed to reason. It can be shown to be rational, though it cannot be rationally "proved." But once one believes, one can become able to understand the inner meaning of one's belief, and to see its validity for others. Both this belief and this eventual understanding are special gifts of God.

THOMAS MERTON, THE MONASTIC JOURNEY

Saturday

Infinity we know and feel by our Souls:
And feel it so naturally, as if it were the very Essence and
    Being of the Soul.
The truth of it is, It is individually in the Soul:
for GOD is there,
and more near to us than we are to our selves.
So that we cannot feel our Souls,
but we must feel Him,
in that first of Properties Infinite Space.

THOMAS TRAHERNE (1637–1674)

εaster Sunday

This is the day of the Resurrection,
Let us be illumined, O Christian people,
For this is the day of the sacred Passover of the Lord.
Come, and let us drink of the new river,
Not brought forth from a barren stone,
But from the fount of life
That springs forth from the sepulchre of Christ the Lord.

SAINT JOHN DAMASCENE, EASTER CANON

For the monk in the monastery or hermitage, as for other Christians at home, the joyful festival of the Resurrection of the Lord follows the Lenten period of prayer, fasting, and quiet introspection. But just as we are about to arrive at the celebration of this glorious festival, we spend the last days of Holy Week at the foot of the Cross with Our Lady, in mournful remembrance of the pain and the suffering that her son Jesus underwent for our sake. These are very quiet days in the monastery, for we carry the heavy burden of grief in our hearts. Good Friday is a black fast, when not even dairy products are allowed, the monk makes do with bread and water, tea or coffee. After the stark afternoon liturgy of Christ's Passion, we retire to our cells for more prayer, reading, and meditation. At night, before going to rest, we recite compline and sing the Stabat Mater in a mournful Gregorian chant melody that recalls Mary's solitude in suffering as she wept for her son at the foot of the cross.

Holy Saturday follows, called "the most blessed Sabbath on which Christ sleeps," by the liturgy. I am particularly fond of Holy

Saturday. In a way, it is even quieter than Good Friday, since no liturgy is celebrated, but we share both in the sorrow of the Passion and burial of Jesus and in the anticipated joy of the Resurrection.

BROTHER VICTOR-ANTOINE, *A MONASTIC YEAR*

Monday

O happy tomb! You received within yourself
the Creator and Author of life.
O strange wonder! He who dwells on high
is sealed beneath the earth with his own consent.

BYZANTINE LITURGY

The stillness, the deep silence, and the peace we experience on Holy Saturday, keeping watch by the tomb of Christ, is perhaps the best preparation for the explosive, all-powerful joy of the Resurrection. Very often in life, we are likewise led through loss and sorrow to a new phase of peace and understanding that ultimately culminates in deep joy.

At the end of Holy Saturday, very late and in the darkness of the night, the Paschal Vigil quietly begins with the blessing of the new fire from which the Paschal Candle is lit. A procession forms, and the monks and the faithful, with lighted candles in their hands, solemnly follow the Paschal Candle into the dark church. There the Exultet, the glorious proclamation of the Resurrection of Christ, is announced in song to the whole world. It is a particularly moving moment in the Easter liturgy to hear the haunting Gregorian melody, in perfect unison with the text, proclaim the wonders of God in the Resurrection. After the Exultet, the night vigil proceeds with psalms, and antiphons sung in between. Following the readings we reach the climax of our Easter Vigil, the solemn celebration of the Eucharistic banquet. At the beginning of the Eucharist, the celebrant intones the Gloria. As the monks sing the beautiful Gregorian chant from the Mass 1, *Lux et origo,* of paschaltime, the bells of the monastery peal out in joy, announcing throughout the hills and valleys the glad tidings of the Resurrection.

CONTINUES . . .

Tuesday

At the end of Mass, our Easter lamb, the youngest of our flock and symbol of Christ, the immolated Lamb of God, is blessed with the new Easter water, then taken back to the sheepfold. Easter is a feast when all creation rejoices in the Resurrection of the Creator of all life, so the animals, the plants, and the flowers of the monastery all partake in this rejoicing.

In the early evening of Easter Sunday, the solemn Vespers of the Resurrection are sung in the monastery chapel. They start with the hymn "*Ad Coenam Agni Providi* [The Lamb has been made ready for our feast]," which I consider one of the most beautiful in the entire Gregorian repertory. After the hymn the exquisite antiphons of the feast with their respective psalms are sung, relating to us once more the biblical details of the Resurrection. Our solemn Vespers reaches its climactic point with the proclamation of the Gospel account of Jesus' appearance to the disciples on that first Easter evening. First the book of the Gospels and the Paschal Candle, symbols of Christ, are incensed; then the beautiful account is read. A long silence follows the reading. One can feel the immediacy of the Lord's risen presence.

Vespers concludes, as it always does, with the solemn singing of the Magnificat, Mary's song of praise to God for his great wonders.

The bells ring with alleluias; the chapel is filled with fresh flowers and bright lights; the chant echoes the joy of Christ's Resurrection, as both monks and nuns greet one another with the traditional "Christ is risen" and its reply, "Indeed, he is risen." Spring and Easter are almost synonymous. The season of spring and the mystery of Easter, celebrated together, bring us from sorrow and death to the affirmation of hope and the experience of the renewal of life in our daily existence.

God send us the springtime lamb
minted and tied in thyme
and call us home, and bid us eat
and praise your name.

ANNIE DILLARD, FROM *FEAST DAYS*

CONTINUES . . .

Wednesday

Spring gardening

Behind the abbey, and within the wall of the cloister, there is a wide level of ground; here there is an orchard, with a great many different fruit trees, quite like a small wood. It is close to the infirmary, and is very comforting to the monks, providing a wide promenade or else a pleasant resting place. Where the orchard leaves off, the garden begins, divided into several beds, or still better cut up by little canals. . . . The water fulfills the double purpose of nourishing the fish and watering the vegetables.

ANONYMOUS FRENCH MANUSCRIPT, TWELFTH CENTURY

The Lord God then "took the man and settled him in the garden of Eden to cultivate and take care of it" (Gen. 2:15). At the beginning of time, gardening was recognized as part of God's mandate to man to care for the earth. The early monks in the Egyptian desert took to heart this biblical command, becoming avid gardeners as well as watchful stewards of the land entrusted to them.

An early life of Saint Antony, written by his friend Saint Hilarion, describes Antony's little garden: "These vines and these little trees did he plant; the pool did he contrive with much labor for the watering of his garden; with his rake did he till the earth for many years." Saint Antony cultivated his garden to provide food for himself and to share the rest with his neighbors, especially the poor.

An early medieval manuscript that has survived into our own day shows a plan, drawn up for the Benedictine abbey of Saint Gall in the ninth century, of an ideal monastery, with its dependencies and gardens. There we discover the cloister, with its traditional garden, the physician's herb garden near the infirmary, and the large garden to feed the monastic community. The monks grew fruits and vegetables, flowers and vines, flavoring and healing herbs, and plants that provided dyes, inks, and incense for the monastery.

CONTINUES . . .

Thursday

Gardening within a monastery is both a task and an art, and it's something we only gradually begin to fathom in the early years of our monastic life. The more experienced gardener monks teach us to start slowly. They instruct us on how to improve our soil with compost and other amendments, knowing well that this will have a profound effect on the variety of plants we grow. I learned early, as well, to let Mother Nature be our guide. Her signals often indicate the propitious time for many garden chores. For instance, when the crocus is in bloom, we begin cleaning up the winter's debris. When the forsythia begins to flower, we prune the roses, evergreens, and the plants that have been damaged by the winter. When the soil warms up, we begin to divide and transplant the perennials.

Spring gardening nurtures hope in the monk, then fulfills the promise of new life when all creation is renewed by the power of Christ's Resurrection.

> Though a life of retreat offers various joys,
> none, I think, will compare with the time one employs
> in the study of herbs, or in striving to gain
> some practical knowledge of nature's domain.
> Get a garden! What kind you may get matters not.
>
> WALAFRID-STRABO, *HORTULUS*,
> LATIN MANUSCRIPT, NINTH CENTURY

CONTINUES . . .

A s c e n s i o n   D a y

Friday

The Thursday which follows the fifth Sunday after Easter is the day when monasteries celebrate the feast of the Ascension of the Lord into heaven. Jesus, having fulfilled his earthly mission, went to the Mount of Olives, took leave of his mother and the disciples, and ascended from there to his Father in heaven. It was his final act on this

earth, but it was an act that opens to us, his followers, endless possibilities, for Jesus did not return to the Father alone. Through the
mystery of the Incarnation, Jesus assumed all of humanity into himself, and now all of us are part of him. As the doors of the kingdom
of heaven opened wide to receive the triumphant Lord, the whole
of redeemed humanity was also being received and accepted by the
Father. The feast of the Ascension celebrates not only Jesus' glorifi-
cation by the Father, but also the Father's acceptance of each one of
us. Jesus opens heaven to us, makes it our destination and perma-
nent home, where one day we will also be received into the warm
embrace of a loving Father.

While we are celebrating the Ascension, the liturgical chants
and readings are already making subtle allusions to the Holy Spirit,
the Comforter, whom Jesus will send. The Ascension in a sense is a
necessary prelude to Pentecost.

CONTINUES . . .

P e n t e c o s t

Saturday

O Heavenly King, the Comforter, the spirit of Truth,
Who are everywhere and fill all things,
Treasury of blessings, and Giver of life!
Come and abide in us,
Cleanse us from all our sins,
And save our souls, O Good One!

BYZANTINE PRAYER TO THE HOLY SPIRIT

Pentecost is a time of fruitfulness, of fullness, of completion. The Holy Spirit is being given to us to continue on earth the work Jesus started. At Pentecost the Holy Spirit appears in the forms of wind and fire, two powerful elements of life on our planet. Pentecost takes place at the time of transition from spring to summer. Summer, with its intense mixture of wind and fire, is a symbolic season of the Holy Spirit, who is the life-giver and the maker of all things new. The heat of summer clothes with exuberant colors the flowers in our gardens and gives magnificent texture and taste to our fruits and vegetables. The fire of the Holy Spirit similarly clothes our souls with colors of grace and makes us taste the sweetness of divine life with God.

Monks throughout the ages have had a special affinity and place in their lives for the Holy Spirit. Saint Seraphim of Sarov affirms that "the whole purpose of the Christian life consists in the acquisition of the Holy Spirit." Monks remind themselves daily of the truth of this teaching and try to attune themselves to the whispers of this mysterious presence who dwells within them, whom they know to be the Spirit of God. Without him, monks can do nothing, and he alone can bring a personal monastic life out of chaos into a perfectly unified and harmonious whole. The Holy Spirit upholds the life of God deep within each of us, and his power is the force that mysteriously transforms our lives.

BROTHER VICTOR-ANTOINE, *A MONASTIC YEAR*

Sunday

Our Father

Great, good Father of heaven,
your name is holy for us.
We have entered your kingdom.
We seek to do your will
here on earth as in heaven.

Mother feed us today with our bread of your life:
and free us from our debts,
as we free all who owe to us.
Do not put us to the test.

And may your Spirit free us from the evil one.

AMEN.

A CONTEMPORARY PATER NOSTER

Monday

HENRI J. M. NOUWEN (1932–1996)

The monastery is center of the world

The meeting of John Eudes with Don, Claude and me was very meaningful. We started by asking the abbot about the political influence of monasticism, referring especially to Saint Bernard's great political impact, and moved from there to a discussion of the meaning of monasticism.

John Eudes made it very clear that monasticism may have political, sociological, psychological, and economic implications, but that anyone who enters a monastery with these in mind would leave it soon. He described his own vocation as a response to his world, but a response in which God and God alone became his goal.

He described how the monastic life has three aspects: The *praktikos*, the ascetic practice; the *theoria physica*, a deeper understanding of the inner relationship of things; and the *theologia*, the mystical experience of God. By self-denial, such as fasting, obedience and stability, the monk learns to understand the forces of the world better and to look beyond them to God. John Eudes also explained the full sense of the classic saying that the Christian life consists of "fasting, almsgiving, and prayer." When fasting means self-denial, almsgiving means charity, and prayer the search for union with God, then indeed this short expression summarizes the life of the Christian.

HENRI J. M. NOUWEN, *THE GENESEE DIARY*

Tuesday

"The monastery is the center of the world." This drastic statement by John Eudes in Chapter this morning reminded me of exactly that same statement made by Thomas Merton when he came to the Abbey of Gethsemani for the first time. The monastery is not just a place to keep the world out but a place where God can dwell. The liturgy, the silence, the rhythm of the day, the week, and the year, and the whole monastic life-style with the harmony of prayer, spiritual reading, and manual labor, are meant to create space for God.

The ideal of the monk is to live in the presence of God, to pray, read, work, eat, and sleep in the company of his divine Lord. Monastic life is the continuing contemplation of the mysteries of God, not just during the periods of silent meditation but during all parts of the day.

In so far as the monastery is the place where the presence of God in the world is most explicitly manifest and brought to consciousness, it is indeed the center of the world. This can be said in humility and with purity of heart because the monk, more than anyone else, realizes that God dwells only where man steps back to give him room.

CONCLUDED

Wednesday

The Glory of Christ

Resurrection is not just life after death. First of all, it is the life that burst forth in Jesus' passion, in his waiting. The story of Jesus' suffering reveals that the resurrection is breaking through even in the midst of the passion. A crowd led by Judas came to Gethsemane, "Then Jesus . . . came forward and said to them, 'Whom do you seek?' They answered him, 'Jesus of Nazareth.' Jesus answered, 'I told you that I am he; so, if you seek me, let these men go' " (John 18:4–8).

Precisely when Jesus is being handed over into his passion, he manifests his glory. "Whom do you seek? . . . I am he" are words which echo all the way back to Moses and the burning bush: "I am the one. I am who I am" (see Ex. 3:14). In Gethsemane, the glory of God manifested itself, and they fell flat on the ground. Then Jesus was handed over. But already in the handing over we see the glory of God who hands himself over to us. God's glory revealed in Jesus embraces passion as well as resurrection.

HENRI NOUWEN, *WEAVINGS*. JANUARY 1987

SEEDS OF HOPE, A HENRI NOUWEN READER

Thursday

"The Son of Man," Jesus says, "must be lifted up as Moses lifted up the serpent in the desert, so that everyone who believes may have eternal life in him" (John 3:14–15). He is lifted up as a passive victim, so the Cross is a sign of desolation. And he is lifted up in glory, so the Cross becomes at the same time a sign of hope. Suddenly, we realize that the glory of God, the divinity of God, bursts through in Jesus' passion precisely when he is most victimized. So new life becomes visible not only in the resurrection on the third day, but already in the passion that the fullness of God's love shines through. It is supremely a waiting love, a love that does not seek control.

When we allow ourselves to feel fully how we are being acted upon, we come in touch with a new life that we were not even aware was there. This was the question my sick friend and I talked about constantly. Could he taste the new life in the midst of his passion? Could he see that in his being acted upon by the hospital staff he was already being prepared for a deeper love? It was a love that had been underneath all the action, but he had not tasted it fully. So together we began to see that in the midst of our suffering and passion, in the midst of our waiting, we can already experience resurrection.

CONTINUES . . .

Friday

The face of Christ

For a week now, I have been trying to write a meditation about the icon of Christ the Savior painted by Andrew Rublev. I have not yet been able to write a word, but in fact have experienced increasing anxiety. I looked at some books on iconography, studied some articles on Rublev's particular style, read through Ian Wilson's book on the Turin shroud, and let my mind make all sorts of connections—but could not find words for writing. I feel tired, even exhausted, because I have spent much mental energy but have found no way to channel it creatively.

I am gradually realizing that what restrains me is the direct confrontation with the face of Jesus. I have written about Rublev's icon of the Trinity and about the icon of Our Lady of Vladimir. Yet writing about the icon of Christ's sacred face is such an awesome undertaking that I wonder if I can really do it.

This afternoon I just looked at this seemingly indescribable icon. I looked at the eyes of Jesus and saw his eyes looking at me. I choked, closed my eyes, and started to pray. I said, "O my God, how can I write about your face? Please give me the words to say what can be said." I read in the Gospels and realized how much is written there about seeing and being seen, about being blind and receiving new sight, and about eyes—human eyes and the eyes of God.

I know I must write about Rublev's icon of Christ because it touches me more than any icon I have ever seen. I must come to know what happens to me when I look at and pray with it. One thing is certain: I have read enough about it. I must simply be present to it, and pray and look and pray and wait and pray and trust. I hope that the right words will come, because if they do, perhaps many will begin to see with me and be touched by those eyes.

CONTINUES . . .

Saturday

The eyes of Christ

What makes seeing Rublev's icon such a profound spiritual experience are the eyes of the Savior. Their gaze is so mysterious and deep that any word which tries to describe them is inadequate . . . The Christ of Rublev looks directly at us and confronts us with his penetrating eyes. They are large, open eyes accentuated by big brows and deep, round shadows. They are not severe or judgmental but they see all that is. They form the true center of the icon. One could say "Jesus is all eyes." His penetrating look brings to mind the words of the psalmist:

> O Lord, you search me and you know me
> you know my resting and my rising
> you discern my purpose from afar.
> You mark when I walk or lie down,
> all my ways lie open to you. . . .
> O where can I go from your spirit,
> or where can I flee from your face? (Ps. 139:1–3, 7)

These words do not speak of a fear-inspiring omnipresence, but of the loving care of someone who looks after us at all times and in all places. The eyes of Rublev's Jesus are neither sentimental nor judgmental, neither pious nor harsh, neither sweet nor severe. They are the eyes of God, who sees us in our most hidden places and loves us with a divine mercy. . . .

Alpatov [writes]: "Before the icon of the Savior we feel face to face with him, we look directly into his eyes and feel a closeness to him."

CONTINUES . . .

───────── *W e e k   T h i r t y - t w o* ─────────

Sunday

Light from Light

This face-to-face experience leads us to the heart of the great mystery of the Incarnation. We can see God and live! As we try to fix our eyes on the eyes of Jesus we know that we are seeing the eyes of God. What greater desire is there in the human heart than to see God? With the apostle Philip our hearts cry out: "Lord, let us see the Father and then we shall be satisfied." And the Lord answers: "To have seen me is to have seen the Father. . . . Do you not believe that I am in the Father and the Father is in me?" (John 14:8–10)

Jesus is the full revelation of God, "the image of the unseen God" (Col. 1:15). Looking into the eyes of Jesus is the fulfillment of our deepest aspiration.

It is hard to grasp this mystery, but we must try to sense how the eyes of the Word incarnate truly embrace in their gaze all there is to be seen. The eyes of Rublev's Christ are the eyes of the Son of Man and the son of God described in the book of Revelation. They are like flames of fire which penetrate the mystery of the divine.

They are the eyes of one whose face is like the sun shining with all its force, and who is known by the name: Word of God. They are the eyes of the one who is "Light from Light, true God from true God, begotten, not made, one in being with the Father . . . through whom all things were made" (Nicene Creed).

CONTINUES . . .

Monday

Christ is indeed the light in whom all is created. He is the light of the first day when God spoke the light, divided it from the darkness, and saw that it was good (Gen. 1:3). Christ is also the light of the new day shining in the dark, a light that darkness could not overpower (John 1:5). He is the true light that enlightens all people (John 1:9). It is awesome to look into the eyes of the only one who truly sees the light, and whose seeing is not different from his being.

But the eyes of Christ which see the splendor of God's light are the same eyes which have seen the lowliness of God's people. . . .

The one who sees unceasingly the limitless goodness of God came to the world, saw it broken to pieces by human sin, and was moved to compassion. The same eyes which see into the heart of God saw the suffering hearts of God's people and wept (see John 11:36). These eyes, which burn like flames of fire penetrating God's own interiority, also hold oceans of tears for the human sorrow of all times and all places. That is the secret of the eyes of Andrew Rublev's Christ. . . .

Through the ruins of our world we see the luminous face of Jesus, a face that no violence, destruction, or war can finally destroy.

CONTINUES . . .

Tuesday

The Body of Christ

Being in California is exciting as well as disturbing to me. It is very hard for me to describe the emotions this world calls forth in me. The pleasant climate, the lush gardens, the splendid trees and flowerbeds, the beautiful views over the bay, the city, the island, and the bridges call forth in me words of praise, gratitude, and joy. But the countless car lots, the intense traffic, the huge advertisements, the new buildings going up all over the place, the smog, the noises, the fastness of living—all of this makes me feel unconnected, lonely, and a little lost.

Maybe the word that summarizes it all is "sensual." All my senses are being stimulated, but with very little grounding, very little history, very little spirit. I keep wondering how my heart can be fed in this world. It seems as if everyone is moving quickly to meet some person or to go to some place or some event. But nobody has much of a home. The houses look very temporary. They will probably last a few decades, maybe a century, but then something else will take their place.

The people we meet are very friendly, easygoing, casual, and entertaining; but I keep wondering how to be with them, how to speak with them, how to pray with them. Everything is very open, expressive, and new; but I find myself looking for a space that is hidden, silent, and old.

CONTINUES . . .

Wednesday

This is a land to which people go in order to be free from tradition, constraints, and an oppressive history. But the price for this freedom is high: individualism, competition, rootlessness, and frequently loneliness and a sense of being lost. When anything goes, everything is allowed, everything is worth a try, then nothing is sacred, nothing venerable, nothing worth much respect. Being young, daring, original, and mobile seems to be the ideal. Old things need to be replaced by new things, and old people are to be pitied.

The body is central. The sun, the beaches, the water, and the lushness of nature open up all the senses. But it is hard to experience the body as the temple of the spirit. That requires a very special discipline. To reach that inner sanctum where God's voice can be heard and obeyed is not easy if you are called outward. It is not surprising that California has become a place where many spiritual disciplines are being discovered, studied, and practiced. More and more people feel a need to discover an inner anchor to keep themselves whole in the midst of the sensual world.

So here am I, somewhat overwhelmed by it all and somewhat confused. How am I to be faithful to Jesus in a world in which having a body is celebrated in so many ways? Jesus is the God who became flesh with us so that we could be one with his Spirit. How do I live out this truth in this sun-covered, sensual, nontraditional place?

CONTINUES . . .

Thursday

Berkeley, California, June 1, 1986

Today is the feast of Corpus Christi, the Body of Christ. While Edward Malloy, a visiting Holy Cross priest, Don and I celebrated the Eucharist in the little Chapel of the Holy Cross house in Berkeley, the importance of this feast touched me more than ever. The illness that has severely impaired Don's movements made him, and also me, very conscious of the beauty, intricacy, and fragility of the human body. My visit yesterday to the Castro district, where physical pleasure is so visibly sought and bodily pain so dramatically suffered, reminded me powerfully that I not only *have* a body but also *am* a body. The way one lives in the body, the way one relates to, cares for, exercises, and uses one's own and other people's bodies, is of crucial importance for one's spiritual life.

The greatest mystery of the Christian faith is that God came to us in the body, suffered with us in the body, rose in the body, and gave us his body as food. No religion takes the body as seriously as the Christian religion. The body is not seen as the enemy or as a prison of the Spirit, but celebrated as the Spirit's temple. Through Jesus' birth, life, death, and resurrection, the human body has become part of the life of God. By eating the body of Christ, our own fragile bodies are becoming intimately connected with the risen Christ and thus prepared to be lifted up with him into the divine life. Jesus says, "I am the living bread which has come down from heaven. Anyone who eats this bread will live forever; and the bread that I shall give is my flesh, for the life of the world" (John 6:51).

CONTINUES . . .

Friday

L'Arche, France, Good Friday 1986

Good Friday: day of the Cross, day of suffering, day of hope, day of abandonment, day of victory, day of mourning, day of joy, day of endings, day of beginnings.

During the liturgy . . . Père Thomas and Père Gilbert took the huge cross that hangs behind the altar from the wall and held it so that the whole community could come and kiss the dead body of Christ.

They all came, more than four hundred people—handicapped men and women and their helpers and friends. Everybody seemed to know very well what they were doing: expressing their love and gratitude for him who gave his life for them. As they were crowding around the cross and kissing the feet and head of Jesus, I closed my eyes and could see his sacred body stretched out and crucified upon our planet earth. I saw the immense suffering of humanity during the centuries: people killing each other; people dying from starvation and epidemics; people driven from their homes; people sleeping on the streets of large cities; people clinging to each other in desperation; people flagellated, tortured, burned, and mutilated; people alone in locked flats, in prison dungeons, in labor camps; people craving a gentle word, a friendly letter, a consoling embrace, people—children, teenagers, adults, middle-aged, and elderly—all crying out with an anguished voice: "My God, my God, why have you foresaken us?"

CONTINUES . . .

Saturday

Imagining the naked, lacerated body of Christ stretched out over our globe, I was filled with horror. But as I opened my eyes I saw Jacques, who bears the marks of suffering in his face, kiss the body with passion and tears in his eyes. I saw Ivan carried on Michael's back. I saw Edith coming in her wheelchair. As they came—walking or limping, seeing or blind, hearing or deaf—I saw the endless procession of humanity gathering around the sacred body of Jesus, covering it with their tear-filled eyes; there were hands in hands and arms in arms. With my mind's eye I saw the huge crowds of isolated, agonizing individuals walking away from the cross together, bound by the love they had seen with their own eyes and touched with their own lips. The cross of horror became the cross of hope, the tortured body became the body that gives new life; the gaping wounds became the source of forgiveness, healing, and reconciliation. Père Thomas and Père Gilbert were still holding the cross. The last people came, knelt, and kissed the body, and left. It was very, very quiet.

Père Gilbert then gave me a large chalice with the consecrated bread and pointed to the waiting crowd standing around the altar.

I took the chalice and started to move among those whom I had seen coming to the cross, looked at their hungry eyes, and said, "The body of Christ . . . the body of Christ . . . the body of Christ" countless times. The small community became all of humanity, and I knew that all I needed to say my whole life long was "Take and eat. This is the body of Christ."

CONTINUES . . .

Sunday

The peace that is not of this World

During the past two years I moved from Harvard to Daybreak, that is from an institution for the best and the brightest to a community with severe learning disability. Daybreak, close to Toronto, is part of an international federation of communities called L'Arche—the Ark—where mentally handicapped men and women and their assistants try to live together in the spirit of the Beatitudes. I live in a house with six handicapped people and four assistants. None of the assistants is specially trained to work with people with a mental handicap, but we receive all the help we need from doctors, psychiatrists, behavioral management people, social workers, and physiotherapists in town. When there are no special crises, we live together in a family, gradually forgetting who is handicapped and who is not. We are simply, John, Bill, Trevor, Raymond, Adam, Rose, Steve, Jane, Naomi, and Henri. We all have our gifts, our struggles, our strengths and weaknesses. We eat together, play together, pray together, and go out together. We all have our own preferences in terms of work, food, and movies, and we all have our problems in getting along with someone in the house, whether handicapped or not. We laugh a lot. We cry a lot too. Sometimes both at the same time. Every morning I say, "Good morning, Raymond," he says, "I am not yet awake. Saying good morning to everyone each day is unreal." Christmas Eve Trevor wrapped marshmallows in silver paper as peace gifts for everyone and at the Christmas dinner he climbed on a chair, lifted his glass, and said, "Ladies and gentlemen, this is not a celebration, this is Christmas." When one of the men speaking on the phone with someone was bothered by the cigarette smoke of an assistant, he yelled angrily, "Stop smoking; I can't hear." And every guest who comes for dinner is received by Bill with the question, "Hey, tell me, what is a turkey in suspense?" When the newcomer confesses ignorance, Bill, with a big grin on his face, says, "I will tell you tomorrow."

CONTINUES . . .

Monday

That is L'Arche; that is Daybreak; that is the family of ten I am living with day in and day out. What can life in this family of a few poor people reveal about the peace of Christ for which people are searching? Let me tell you the story of Adam, one of the ten people in our home, and let him become the silent spokesman of the peace that is not of this world.

Never having worked with handicapped people, I was not only apprehensive, but even afraid to enter this unfamiliar world. This fear did not lessen when I was invited to work directly with Adam. Adam is the weakest person of our family. He is a twenty-five-year-old man who cannot speak, cannot dress or undress himself. cannot walk alone or eat without much help. He does not cry, or laugh, and only occasionally makes eye contact. His back is distorted and his arm and leg movements are very twisted. He suffers from severe epilepsy and, notwithstanding heavy medication, there are few days without grand mal seizures. Sometimes, as he grows suddenly rigid, he utters a howling groan, and on a few occasions I have seen a big tear coming down his cheek. It takes me about an hour and a half to wake Adam up, give him his medication, undress him, carry him into his bath, wash him, shave him, clean his teeth, dress him, walk him to the kitchen, give him his breakfast, put him in his wheelchair, and bring him to the place where he spends most of the day with different therapeutic exercises. When a grand mal seizure occurs during this sequence of activities, much more time is needed, and often he has to return to sleep to regain some of the energy spent during such a seizure.

CONTINUES . . .

Tuesday

I tell you all this not to give you a nursing report but to share with you something quite intimate. After a month of working this way with Adam, something started to happen to me that never had happened to me before. This deeply handicapped young man, who by many outsiders is considered an embarrassment, a distortion of humanity, a useless creature who should not have been allowed to be born, started to become my dearest companion. As my fears gradually decreased, a love started to emerge in me so full of tenderness and affection that most of my other tasks seemed boring and superficial compared with the hours spent with Adam. Out of this broken body and broken mind emerged a most beautiful human being offering me a greater gift than I would ever be able to offer him. It is hard for me to find adequate words for this experience, but somehow Adam revealed to me who he was and who I was and how we can love each other. As I carried his naked body into the bathwater, made big waves to let the water run fast around his chest and neck, rubbed noses with him and told him all sorts of stories about him and me, I knew that two friends were communicating far beyond the realm of thought or emotion. Deep speaks to deep, spirit speaks to spirit, heart speaks to heart. I started to realize that there was a mutuality of love not based on shared knowledge or shared feelings, but on shared humanity. The longer I stayed with Adam the more clearly I started to see him as my gentle teacher, teaching me what no book, school, or professor could have ever taught me.

CONTINUES . . .

Wednesday

Am I romanticizing, making something beautiful out of something ugly, projecting my hidden need to be a father on this deeply re-tarded man, spiritualizing what in essence is a shameful human con-dition that needs to be prevented at all cost? I am enough of a psychologically trained intellectual to raise these questions. Recently—during the writing of this story—Adam's parents came for a visit. I asked them: "Tell me, during all the years you had Adam in your home, what did he give you?" His father smiled and said without a moment of hesitation: "He brought us peace . . . he is our peacemaker . . . our son of peace."

Let me, then, tell you about Adam's peace, a peace which the world cannot give. I am moved by the simple fact that probably the most important task I have is to give words to the peace of one who has no words. The gift of peace hidden in Adam's utter weakness is a gift not *of* the world, but certainly *for* the world. For this gift to become known, someone has to lift it up and hand it on. That, maybe, is the deepest meaning of being an assistant to handicapped people. It is helping them to share their gifts.

CONTINUES . . .

Thursday

A Dwelling Place for God

Marriage is not a lifelong attraction of two individuals to each other, but a call for two people to witness together to God's love. The basis of marriage is not mutual affection, or feelings, or emotions and passions that we associate with love, but a vocation, a being elected to build together a house for God in the world, to be like two cherubs whose outstretched winds sheltered the Ark of the Covenant and created a space where Yahweh could be present (Ex. 25:10-12; I Kings 8:6-7). Marriage is a relationship in which a man and a woman protect and nurture the inner sanctum within and between them and witness to that by the way in which they love each other. . . . Celibacy is part of marriage not simply because married couples may have to live separated from each other for long periods of time, or because they may need to abstain from sexual relations for physical, mental, or spiritual reasons, but also because the intimacy of marriage itself is an intimacy that is based on the common participation in a love greater than the love two people can offer each other.

The real mystery of marriage is not that husband and wife love each other so much that they can find God in each other's lives, but that God loves them so much that they can discover each other more and more as living reminders of God's presence. They are brought together, indeed, as two prayerful hands extended toward God and forming in this way a home for God in this world.

HENRI NOUWEN, *SEEDS OF HOPE*

Friday

EVELYN UNDERHILL (1875–1941)

The way we enter a retreat is very important. Often, we waste the first day getting our bearings. I want to speak especially to those at their first retreat. I remember my own first retreat and all the apprehension and vagueness with which I entered it. But what a wonderful revelation it was! I remember my alarm at the idea of silence, the mysterious peace and light distilled from it, and my absolute distress when it ended and the clatter began.

Silence is the very heart of a retreat. We get away from the distractions of talking, interchange, and action. We sink into our souls where God's voice is heard. It is an *elected silence*. We cannot find it in the world. We must come together in a special place, protected by our own rule from distractions, interests, surface demands.

Remember that this is your personal retreat. It is not a joint undertaking in which we all do the same thing. Each of us is at a different stage in defining our needs and problems. . . . I will not press you in special paths. There are one thousand ways to God.

I am no more the authority over your real journey than the conductor of a bus. Disregard what doesn't suit you. Let yourselves be led by God. A retreat is your time *with Him*, for facing realities in his light, for thinking in his presence.

EVELYN UNDERHILL,

THE WAYS OF THE SPIRIT

Saturday

The first recommendation tonight is: don't let us waste much time gazing at ourselves. A deepened and enriched sense of God is far more important than increased and detailed knowledge of the self. *God,* our redeemer and sustainer, is all and does all, and is the one Reality. Life comes with such thoughts. Plunging more deeply in him with faith and love will do more than self-concerned efforts. We can do nothing of ourselves but depress ourselves and get fussy.

Don't behave like the inexperienced motorist who goes for a drive and spends all day lying in the road under the machine examining the works. The soul is a delicate and intricate machine. When it needs pulling to pieces, it is best to leave it to God. Our prayer should be that of Saint Augustine: "The house of my soul is narrow. Enlarge it, so that you may enter in. It stands in ruins: do you repair it and make it fair."

First to last, put all emphasis on God. Attend to him. Forget yourselves if you can. Bathe in his light. Respond to the unmatched attraction. Be energized by his power. Try to realize a little of the perpetual molding action of his Spirit on your souls.

Have you ever seen the popular experiment of iron filings in the field of a magnet? Those little specks of matter are nothing in themselves, but when they are placed in the field of a magnet, each becomes a centre of energy, instantly influenced by an invisible power. They align themselves parallel to the lines of the magnet's force.

EVELYN UNDERHILL,

THE WAYS OF THE SPIRIT

Sunday

Offertory

With expectation have I awaited the Body and Blood of Christ the Lord upon his holy altar. Let us all offer it with fear and praise, crying with the angels "Holy, holy, holy is the Lord our God."

The poor shall eat, and be satisfied with the Body and Blood of Christ set forth upon this altar. Let us all offer it with fear and praise, crying with the angels "Holy, holy, holy is the Lord our God."

May all glory be given to the ever-glorious Trinity, world without end; and may Christ who was sacrificed as an oblation for our salvation and has commanded that we should offer sacrifice in memory of his Passion, Death and Resurrection, receive this sacrifice from our hands through his grace and love.

LITURGY OF MALABAR,

TRANS. EVELYN UNDERHILL

Monday

For those in Trouble

Remember, O Lord, Christians travelling by land or sea, those in foreign lands, those in bonds and in prison, those in captivity, in exile, in mines, and in torture and bitter slavery, our fathers and brethren.

Remember, Lord, the sick, the feeble, those beset by unclean spirits, and grant them speedy healing and salvation which is from God.

Remember, Lord, every Christian soul in tribulation and distress, in need of thy help and pity, O God, and of turning from the way of error.

Remember, Lord, all men for good; Master, have pity on all; be reconciled to us all; make thy many peoples live in peace. Scatter hindrances; bring wars to an end; make the divisions of the churches and the uprising of heresy to cease. Undo the wanton insolence of the nations. Give us the hope of all the ends of the earth.

LITURGY OF SAINT JAMES, TRANS. EVELYN UNDERHILL

Tuesday

What is the spiritual life?

This is a task in which all may do their part. The spiritual life is not a special career, involving abstraction from the world of things. It is a part of every man's life; and until he has realized it he is not a complete human being, has not entered into possession of all his powers. It is therefore the function of practical mysticism to increase, not diminish, the total efficiency, the wisdom and steadfastness, of those who try to practise it. It will help them to enter, more completely than ever before, into the life of the group to which they belong. It will teach them to see the world in a truer proportion, discerning eternal beauty beyond and beneath apparent ruthlessness. It will educate them in a charity free from all taint of sentimentalism; it will confer on them an unconquerable hope; and assure them that still, in the hour of greatest desolation, "There lives the dearest freshness of deep down things."

EVELYN UNDERHILL,

PRACTICAL MYSTICISM, INTRODUCTION

Wednesday

The World of Reality

The practical man may justly observe that the world of single vision is the only world he knows: that it appears to him to be real, solid, and self-consistent: and that until the existence—at least, the probability—of other planes of reality is made clear to him, all talk of uniting with them is mere moonshire, which confirms his opinion of mysticism as a game fit only for idle women and inferior poets. Plainly, then, it is the first business of the missionary to create, if he can, some feeling of dissatisfaction with the world within which the practical man has always lived and acted; to suggest something of its fragmentary and subjective character. We turn back therefore to a further examination of the truism—so obvious to those who are philosophers, so exasperating to those who are not—that man dwells, under normal conditions, in a world of imagination rather than a world of fact; that the universe in which he lives and at which he looks is but a construction which the mind has made from some few amongst the wealth of materials at its disposal.

The relation of this universe to the world of fact is not unlike the relation between a tapestry picture and the scene it imitates. You, practical man, are obliged to weave your image of the outer world upon the hard warp of your own mentality; which perpetually imposes its own convention, and checks the free representation of life. As a tapestry picture, however various and full of meaning, is ultimately reducible to little squares; so the world of common sense is ultimately reducible to a series of static elements conditioned by the machinery of the brain. Subtle curves, swift movement, delicate gradation, that machinery cannot represent.

CONTINUES . . .

Thursday

. . . It leaves them out. From the countless suggestions, the tangle of many-coloured wools which the real world presents to you, you snatch one here and there. Of these you weave together those which are the most useful, the most obvious, the most often repeated: which make a tidy and coherent pattern when seen on the right side. Shut up with this symbolic picture, you soon drop into the habit of behaving to it as though it were not a representation but a thing. On it you fix your attention; with it you "unite." Yet, did you look at the wrong side, at the many short ends, the clumsy joints and patches, this simple philosophy might be disturbed. You would be forced to acknowledge the conventional character of the picture you have made so cleverly, the wholesale waste of material involved in the weaving of it: for only a few amongst the wealth of impressions we received are seized and incorporated into our picture of the world. Further, it might occur to you that a slight alternation in the rhythm of the senses would place at your disposal a complete new range of material; opening your eyes and ears to sounds, colors, and movements now inaudible and invisible, removing from your universe those which you now regard as part of the established order of things. Even the strands which you have made use of might have been combined in some other way; with disastrous results to the "world of common sense," yet without any diminution of their own reality.

CONTINUES . . .

Friday

Preparation

Richard of Saint Victor has said that the essence of all purification is self-simplification; the doing away of the unnecessary and unreal, the tangles and complications of consciousness: we must remember that when these masters of the spiritual life speak of purity, they have in their minds no thing, abstract notion of a rule of conduct stripped of all color and compounded chiefly of refusals, such as a more modern, more arid asceticism set up. Their purity is an affirmative state; something strong, clean, and crystalline, capable of a wholeness of adjustment to the wholeness of a God-inhabited world. The pure soul is like a lens from which all irrelevancies and excrescenses, all the beams and motes of egotism and prejudice, have been removed; so that it may reflect a clear image of the one Transcendent Fact within which all other facts are held.

> All which I took from thee I did but take,
> Not for thy harms,
> But just that thou might'st seek it in My arms.

CONTINUES . . .

Saturday

Recollection itself, so long as it remains merely a matter of attention and does not involve the heart, is no better than a psychic trick. You are committed, therefore, as the fruit of your first attempts at self-knowledge, to a deliberate—probably difficult—rearrangement of your character; to the stern course of self-discipline, the voluntary acts of choice on the one hand and of rejection on the other, which ascetic writers describe under the formidable names of Detachment and Mortification. By detachment they mean the eviction of the limpet from its crevice; the refusal to anchor yourself to material things, to regard existence from the personal standpoint, or confuse custom with necessity. By mortification, they mean the resolving of the turbulent whirlpools and currents from your own conflicting passions, interests, desires; the killing out of all those tendencies which the peaceful vision of recollection would condemn, and which create the fundamental opposition between your interior and exterior life.

What then, in the last resort, is the source of this opposition; the true reason of your uneasiness, your unrest? The reason lies, not in any real incompatibility between the interests of the temporal and the eternal orders; which are but two aspects of one Fact, two expressions of one Love. It lies solely in yourself; in your attitude towards the world of things. You are enslaved by the verb "to have"; all your reactions to life consist in corporate or individual demands, appetites, wants. That "love of life" of which we sometimes speak is mostly cupboard-love. We are quick to snap at her ankles when she locks the larder door: a proceeding which we dignify by the name pessimism. The mystic knows not this attitude of demand. He tells us again and again, that "he is rid of all his asking; that henceforth the heat of having shall never scorch him more."

CONTINUES . . .

Sunday

You must begin this great adventure humbly; and take, as Julian of Norwich did, the first stage of your new outward-going journey along the road that lies nearest at hand. When Julian looked with the eye of contemplation upon "something small, about the size of a hazelnut that seemed to lie in my hand as round as a tiny ball" it revealed to her the oneness of the created universe. Her deep and loving insight perceived successively three properties, which she expressed as well as she might under the symbols of her own theology: "First, God had made it; second, God loves it; and third, that God keeps it." Here are three phases in the ever-widening contemplative apprehension of Reality. Not three opinions, but three facts, for which she struggles to find words. The first is that each separate living thing, budding "like a hazelnut" upon the tree of life, and these destined to mature, age, and die, is the outbirth of another power, of a creative push; that the World of Becoming in all its richness and variety is not ultimate, but formed by Something other than, and utterly transcendent to, itself. . . .

From this Julian passes to that deeper knowledge of the heart which comes from a humble and disinterested acceptance of life; that this Creation, this whole changeful natural order, with all its apparent collisions, cruelties, and waste, yet springs from an ardor, an immeasurable love, a perpetual donation. Blake's anguished question here receives its answer: the Mind that conceived the lamb conceived the tiger too. Everything, says Julian in effect, whether gracious, terrible, or malignant, is enwrapped in love. . . .

Lastly, this love-driven world of duration—this work within

which the Divine Artist passionately and patiently expresses his infinite dream under the finite forms—is held in another, mightier embrace. It is "kept," says Julian.

EVELYN UNDERHILL,

EXTRACTS FROM *PRACTICAL MYSTICISM*

Monday

A TOUCH OF GOD

Three Monastics Tell Their Tale

At this time came the Second Vatican Council and I was repeatedly impressed by the discovery that the outside and the inside, the life of the Church and my own life, were astonishingly in tune. . . . I knew that the same Spirit was stirring the longings at these different levels and I had an enormous sense of identification with the searching Church, the Church of joy and hope and tension, the Church called by the Spirit to trust and openness.

This experience suggests something to me about the place of monastic life in the whole life of God's people. I cannot understand my vocation in purely individual terms, highly personal though it is. I have already mentioned that the Easter perspective is primordial for me: in many ways and at many levels I experience my life as sharing with Christ in his suffering, death, resurrection and communication of the Spirit; if this were not so, the monastic life would make no sense to me. Yet to say this is to make no claim to any special monastic prerogative, for it is in every Christian that Christ lives out his mysteries, in every Christian that the Church is present and alive. At most one could say that certain features of monastic observance—particularly listening to the word of Scripture, the daily celebration of the liturgy and the experience of a close-knit community—foster such an awareness and make it explicit. It seems to me that the meaning of the monastic vocation is to be sought not on the periphery but in the centre of the Christian life, indeed of human life and experience.

DAME MARIA BOULDING,

A TOUCH OF GOD

Tuesday

Monks are really no different from the rest of mankind and one thing I discovered at this time was that I was going through the motions of prayer, but not really praying. As a result I seemed to draw no closer to God. I think many people have this experience. It is what Fr Simon Tugwell calls the two dangers: "In our relationship with God, one of the main problems is that half the time we just forget about it. . . . Habits must begin somewhere. And just where we need to build up good habits is often precisely the occasion where we simply forget all about it." Yes, this was me. My life as a monk was habit-forming: the routine of the day is divided into periods in which one is brought to God's house so that one does not forget God. And yet even here there were dangers. Unless one turns oneself consciously to be aware of prayer, the praise and the worship one is offering and unless one forms good habits rather than just habits, so much of one's time is spent in merely going through the motions of prayer and, in my case, through the motions of monastic life as well. What happened to me and brought about an understanding of the difference between "just habit-forming" and "good habit-forming" was that in the early 1970s there seemed to grow up within the Church as a whole, and also in the monastery, a response to the call for renewal. We were asked to take a good hard look at ourselves, at the way we were living our lives and at the fullness of that life. I soon discovered that in order to get more out of my life, I have to put more in, that the whole relationship with God was a two-way relationship.

DOM LEONARD VICKERS

Wednesday

Apart from the whole business and techniques and forms of prayer it was Dom Leander [my confessor as a novice] who taught me how to cope with "the abyss" and recognize it for what it was. After a period of almost delirious joy in my praying I had an early experience of annihilation: I felt that I was being sucked into a "black hole." It was a *positive* experience of nothingness. It was the most horrific experience I have ever had: I seemed to be teetering on the edge of becoming nothing. This was not physical, it was not precisely in the mind, it was in the spirit, in the very roots of my being. I went to Dom Leander in a real terror, feeling that at any moment I was going not only out of my mind, but out of existence. And when I told him of it in words of panic and desperation, he replied, "This is marvellous! This is the best thing that could happen to you; I wish I were there with you in this." And I said, "If you can say that, then you have no comprehension of what I am talking about." He assured me that he did, and that I was experiencing the infinity and total otherness of God.

In prayer we keep making concepts or ideas of God, and then making these into God, but as we remain faithful to God, and God to us, he has to break out of everything that appears to contain him. The bottom has to drop out of the world and the effect *appears* to be one of annihilation. It is the best possible foretaste of death. It is the experience of the Passion.

DOM PHILIP JEBB

Thursday

A Carthusian Master Guides His Novices

It might have been more satisfactory to be able to present you with a complete formation program, the principles on which it is based, my own personal preferences, etc.

But I will spare you all of that; firstly, because that would have been very difficult to effect, even for one who had exercized the charge of Master of Novices for many years; almost impossible for someone like myself who takes it up for the first time. Secondly, because it might have given a false impression of monastic formation.

Monastic formation is not a question of a body of doctrine which the novice is to learn. It is the transmission of a life—incarnate life, because we have a share in humanity; incarnate life, therefore, body and soul. The body manifests the practical expression of the way members of a group live together and the rules and customs that govern their common life. The soul carries them onward; the love that gives life to their outward observance, that quality that lies beyond definition: The spirit that gives them life; the spirit which has its source in the self-outpouring of God, because it is their response to a particular call of God that is continually kindled at this divine flame—otherwise there would be a corpse, not a body.

A CARTHUSIAN, THE WAY OF SILENT LOVE

Friday

The outward body of our life makes no sense without regard to a reality that surpasses the human sphere and all created reality: The self-communication of divine life that the Father gives us through Christ by the working of the Holy Spirit.

At its heart, the wellspring of our Carthusian life is divine love, and the goal of our lives is divine love; and the way into which formation seeks to move us can be nothing other than divine love, that is to say, the love of God poured out in our hearts by the Holy Spirit who dwells in us (Rom. 5:5). The Spirit alone can search the depth of God, the Spirit alone communicates the life and love of God, the Spirit alone, the anointing that teaches us from within, is able to guide us in the ways of God, unto the Father.

CONTINUES . . .

Saturday

For the solitary whose gaze seeks God alone beyond all that is created, the ultimate guide can only be the divine Master who dwells in the heart. So then, what use is a Father Master? Not very much if one sees in him only a man with certain qualities, a particular experience, prudence, and a specific monastic polish. Of course he can transmit an abundance of useful information at a certain level; he can ground the outward person in a certain discipline that allows insertion into the monastic milieu without too many hard knocks; he can mould a certain moral and ascetic perfection—but he cannot bestow God, he cannot enable entry into the intimacy of divine life.

He is not able to do this for himself by means of his own resources and his own wisdom.

But as an instrument of God, if God wishes to use him, he can support, affirm, give a certain visible and concrete reality to the teaching and action of the Master within. He can remove in ourselves the more or less hidden obstacles to that action. We are so clumsy, so deaf, so blind because of our passions and egotism that we easily deceive ourselves in regard to what the Spirit wishes to say to us. We need to have it confirmed by a voice other than our own. And in the end, God, who knows our weakness, has adapted the economy of his salvation to our condition. This is the principle of the incarnation.

> For it is the God who said, "Let light shine out of darkness," who has shone in our hearts to give the light of the knowledge of the glory of God in the face of Christ (II Cor. 4:6).

> And we all, with unveiled face, beholding and reflecting the glory of the Lord, are being changed into his likeness from one degree of glory to another; for this comes from the Lord who is the Spirit (II Cor. 3:18).

A CARTHUSIAN, *THE WAY OF SILENT LOVE*

Sunday

Spring and New Birth

Jesus is thrice born. Christian tradition honors his human birth at Bethlehem as a visible event between two invisible births: His eternal birth as a Son of the Father in the splendors of the Trinity, and his birth by grace in the life of every human being who accepts him. All three of these births are real, but not all are historical. His Trinitarian birth as the Father's Word is outside history, in the eternal Now of God's life. His human birth of Mary, from the stock of Israel, is an event in historical time, more or less datable. His hidden birth in people's lives takes place again and again, and will continue through all the time of human history.

Advent and Christmas celebrate all three births, but it is not possible to separate them and deal with each in turn. They are intertwined in mystery beyond mystery, depth beyond depth. The eternal, divine birth of the Son is the foundation of all else. The coming to be of the whole created universe is an echo of that primordial utterance, as John declares:

> In the beginning was the Word, and the Word was with God, and the Word was God. He was in the beginning with God; all things were made through him, and without him was not anything made (John 1:1–3).

MARIA BOULDING, *THE COMING OF GOD*

Monday

The Father's being, identity and joy are to pour himself out unreservedly in his self-gift to his Son. The Son's being and delight are to have nothing as of himself but all as received in the gift of love, and to breathe his answering love to the Father. The New Testament speaks of the Son as the radiant splendor of the Father's glory; the Creed calls him "God from God, Light from Light, true God from true God." Early Christian writers speak of the Source and the Spring. These are images; as long as we remember that the reality behind them is infinitely personal they may help, but language breaks under the strain. The eternal begetting of the Son who is the Father's glory is beyond our understanding and imagination, because it is the innermost mystery of God.

Yet we can hear and speak, even of God, even of that primal birth, because God has made us in his image, as creatures who communicate, and our clumsy efforts to understand and to love are an echo of his Word. Every movement of self-surrendering love in human relationships, every response of beloved to love, every real personal communication and meeting of minds, is a shadow of that glory. Every utterance of passionate beauty proclaims it. All that we know of the dignity and joy of parenthood on earth points towards it. Life and love in our experience are flow and reflow, giving and receiving; the more we give, the more we receive and the more there is to give, and this is because we are a little like God. His life is not solitude, self-sufficiency or a frozen, static perfection. He is eternal exchange, infinite unselfishness. Love is never cornered, pinned down, halted in its flow, because it never finds a self to trap

it and appropriate it. The three Persons are a dance of utter delight:
They exist for one another.

MARIA BOULDING, *THE COMING OF GOD*

Tuesday

Preface Weekdays VI

*The ordinary working-day preface to the canon of the mass reminds all
Christians of the everyday recurrence of God working our salvation.*

Father, it is our duty and our salvation,
always and everywhere
to give you thanks
through your beloved Son, Jesus Christ.

He is the Word through whom you made the universe,
the Savior you sent to redeem us.
By the power of the Holy Spirit
he took flesh and was born of the Virgin Mary.

For our sake he opened his arms on the cross;
He put an end to death
and revealed the resurrection.
In this he fulfilled your will
and won for you a holy people.

And so we join the angels and saints
in proclaiming your glory:

Holy, holy, holy . . .
Lord God . . .

Wednesday

THE CARTHUSIAN EXPERIENCE

Joining the Family

Once admitted within the confines of a Charterhouse, we find ourselves right in the midst of Carthusian life itself. Now begin the surprises, even if we knew in advance what we would find at the heart of a community life. We came with the idea of isolating ourselves completely, and casting ourselves upon God alone. Now we find ourselves caught in the complicated network of obligations involved in family life. We thought to find ourselves surrounded by saints and, to our horror, discover a prevailing mediocrity. Even worse, we end up realizing that the Absolute has vanished within us: Nothing remains of that for which we came. Does this mean that we have been side-tracked, or is it some new "trick" of God, who is revealing himself in a way we did not expect?

When there are so few dwelling in the heart of the same desert, drawn by the same ideal, there is no question of living side by side with strangers. He who has no wish to join in the life of the family will be rejected by it and soon discover that his life in the cell is radically undermined. If he truly wishes to persist in his search for the Absolute, there is no alternative but to accept this family life and to join it wholeheartedly, in loyalty and honesty.

This social dimension is quickly revealed as being at the very heart of Carthusian life. No one can find God while forsaking the road laid down in the Gospels, that is the path of charity. It would be fruitless to seek the Absolute and, at the same time, seek to dispense ourselves in any way from the love of our brothers. For the teaching of Jesus and of the beloved disciple is clear: The love which binds together the children of God is the very same love that unites the Father and the Son. To join the Carthusian family is to enter fully into the life of the divine family and, with the risen Jesus, to penetrate the veil and come into the presence of God. Yet, in a Charterhouse, this human image of the divine family seems limited and constrained and only makes sense when placed within the context of that great family of the children of God—the mystical body of Christ, his church.

A CARTHUSIAN, *THE WOUND OF LOVE*

Thursday

The Kingdom of Mediocrity

It is impossible to overestimate the mental adjustment often required of the young monk in this apparent reversal of values. Having come to lose himself in an Absolute which had totally overwhelmed him, he suddenly discovers this Absolute to be completely different from what he had imagined. The "Absolute" is a way we have of imagining God: The reality of God is the Son who is in the bosom of the Father, and who revealed this reality to us when he said that the Father loved the Son, and that they both loved us and would come to us. In the end, it is a crucifying choice that we have to make; either the Absolute which contents us by enclosing us within ourselves, or the relationship that will open us to the infinite, but at the cost of wrenching us asunder and exposing us to all those around us, whatever affinity we may or may not have for them.

One does not need to spend very long in a Charterhouse to become aware that it is rampant with many petty problems and the presence of ordinary human weaknesses, even if everyone is doing his honest best to strive towards that perfection of which the Father is the supreme model. There is nothing new about this. Historical accounts of life in the Charterhouse, as well as the annals of the Order, show that individuals of great sanctity or distinction are very rare in our communities. The life of most Charterhouses is a dull sort of gray. One encounters disputes with neighbors and little incidents within the communities.

CONTINUES . . .

Friday

A deeper insight into souls gradually allows us to discover that behind these disappointing exteriors often lie real treasures of interior life, of generosity, and of an authentic search for God. Nevertheless, it cannot be denied that these precious gems are often buried in unattractive dress. How could it be otherwise, face to face with the Absolute? Is this not the price of such dangerous proximity to fire? For it highlights all our faults, all our roughness of character and all the petty misery which in other circumstances would be swallowed up in the surrounding sea of trivialities. To wish to come face to face with the light of God is deliberately to consent to expose all our faults and pettiness to the hard light of day. These first become apparent to others, and then, as we become enlightened, to ourselves. We first discover mediocrity in others and afterwards, in ourselves.

CONTINUES . . .

Saturday

Risks are always involved when our aim is high. Seeing ourselves apparently ever more distant and removed from our goal is a painful suffering. On a more prosaic level, this mediocrity is the consequence of our separation from the world. To the extent that solitude is effective, it deprives us of a great many advantages which might introduce into the community an *élan* or a renewal which would mask the mediocrity or remedy it in some way. The critical choice must be made: Either choose God and accept that perfection must come first and foremost from within, or leave open certain gates to the world so that certain means, other than those proper to the desert, play a part in one's life. The usual choice in the Charterhouse is the former. To make such a decision quite deliberately represents a very real sacrifice—an entry into solitude at a very exacting price. In effect, it is a conscious decision to leave untapped a part of our human potential so that God may well up from within. Such conditions are only suitable for those who have already attained a certain level of human maturity and self-motivation in their spiritual and intellectual life.

CONTINUES . . .

Sunday

The discovery of mediocrity first in others and then in oneself is a step towards an even more disconcerting discovery. Holiness, perfection and virtue—all these qualities which, without realizing it, we believed to be reflections of the Absolute within ourselves—begin to vanish. Everything which tends to make the ego a point of reference or an autonomous centre must disappear in order to conform with the resurrected Christ who is but pure relation to the Father. Even his humanity is now endowed with divine names. All created riches have been stripped away in order to be nothing but pure relation.

Such is the direction which the monk must take little by little: First, in his interior life and then in all his activities, whether in cell or in community. He must learn never to focus on himself but to be taken up in the movement of a divine love which has neither beginning nor end, neither goal nor source, neither limit nor shape. He must surrender to the breath of the Spirit, without knowing whence he comes nor whither he goes.

A CARTHUSIAN, *THE WOUND OF LOVE*

Monday

In the Presence of the Word

This feeling of being in the presence of a Person should permeate all intellectual endeavor. We should always be aware that through the concepts and words a Person is revealing himself, leaving traces of his presence. This is the theological principle of Saint Thomas.

> Now, whoever believes, assents to someone's words (someone who sees what we cannot); so that, in every form of belief, the person to whose words assent is given seems to hold the chief place and to be the end as it were; while the things one holds on that person's authority hold a secondary place *(Summa Theologica 2/2, XI, 1, c)*.

It is this personal end we must keep in mind when we study, when we read the Word of God, when we celebrate the liturgy, when we encounter our neighbors. "When you have done this, you have done it to me" (Matt. 25).

A CARTHUSIAN, *THE WAY OF SILENT LOVE*

Tuesday

This is the personal encounter that fills with presence the soul that is empty of concepts. Facing someone we love, by whom we know we are loved, the mystery of personality does not trouble us. On the contrary, love discovers delight in it, because it has a presentiment of inexhaustible riches, and it rejoices even more in the measure that these riches surpass its powers of comprehension. "Glory to God in the heavens." In one sense, the mystery is necessarily involved in personal love. The attraction of a woman is all the greater because she remains mysterious always, even in the gift of her whole self. There remains a more intimate communion to desire.

In heaven, the mystery of God, precisely as mystery, will be our eternal blessedness. From the point of view of the intellect, too, this

will be forever, the blessedness of poverty. Here once more purity
and poverty signify the same thing, because together they speak the
language of love. Purity of heart in its aspect of purity of the intellect is the striving of love towards the hidden Person behind the veil
of words and signs. It is the desire for personal communion that always goes further to enter the purity of light without form in the
solitude of a silence that surpasses all speech. It is poverty of spirit,
pure receptivity before pure truth, that knows God is all in all, and
that the two are one.

> Deep calls to deep (Ps. 42:7).
> The Spirit and the Bride say, "Come."
> Amen. Come, Lord Jesus! (Rev. 22:17 and 20).

A CARTHUSIAN, THE WAY OF SILENT LOVE

Wednesday

Macrina of Cappadocia and the First Nuns

It goes without saying that men as well as women were influenced
by contact with Jesus Messiah, and were led to dedicate their lives
to God in prayer, poverty and perpetual chastity, as the Acts of the
Apostles prove. But the first to seize upon the exact implications of
the gospel with its new and revolutionary evaluation of woman was
precisely woman herself. At a single stroke, the prohibition of di-
vorce translated the moral equality of the sexes into deeds; but that
did not go far enough. It was left to the virgins, "God's chosen ones,
brides of Christ," to proclaim their right to the full prerogatives of
human personality: A fulfilment of their womanhood, no longer dependent on physical qualities but attained through spiritual and intellectual values. To be childless would cease to be a synonym for

withered barrenness, to be unmarried neither misfortune nor curse.

Whereas Christian monasticism dates roughly from A.D. 300, consecrated virgins are of apostolic origin. Acts (21:9) refers to Philip of Gaza's four virgin daughters who prophesied; Tertullian (160–225), the African church Father, speaks of the *virgines sacrae* devoted to psalmody and prayer; Origen of Alexandria (185–254) observes that their number was unbelievably great; in 280, before going into solitude, the Egyptian Antony, Father of Monks as he is called, placed his young sister in a well-established parthenon of "known and trusted virgins." When later on the monastic ideal spread, men and women tended to join forces and work in close collaboration. Elder sisters of a family played an important part in moulding the character and outlook of brothers who were to assume leadership.

DAME FELICITAS CORRIGAN, O.S.B., *BENEDICTINE TAPESTRY*

Thursday

Thus in Cappadocia, Macrina (d. 379), eldest of ten, took in hand her brilliant brother Basil when he returned home, laurel-crowned and insufferably conceited after completing his studies in Constantinople and Athens, and transformed him under her tutelage into the humble monk whom Benedict, Patriarch of the West, was to salute in his Rule, as "our holy Father Basil." Two more brothers, Gregory of Nyssa and Peter of Sebaste, find a place in the calendar of saints; Peter, her youngest brother, revered her as "father, teacher, guide and mother." Her task of education complete, Macrina continued to live in the family estate, presiding over a large community of nuns. When she came to die, a few months after her brother Basil, she did so stretched out on two wooden boards, her face turned towards the East. Whispering prayers for forgiveness of her sins, she finally sealed eyes, mouth and heart with a large sign of the cross, drew a deep breath, and closed life and prayer together, just as the lamps were being lit for Vespers.

Her brother Gregory (whose theological influence since the Second Vatican Council equals, if it does not surpass, that of Thomas Aquinas) insisted on laying out her virginal body with his own hands, but such was her poverty that he himself had to supply the linen, since her personal possessions amounted to little more than the coarse veil of her consecration, and a hood.

DAME FELICITAS CORRIGAN, O.S.B., BENEDICTINE TAPESTRY

Friday

Our Father

All holy Father
who makes your home in the heavens,
adored in the gladness of glory.
Because of your works, be your name hallowed
by the sons of men; for you are men's savior.
Your kingdom come far and wide,
and your will be exalted below heaven's high roof,
as also on this ample earth.
Lend us today a lawful blessing,
our loaf of bread, Benefactor of men,
the eternal One, true-sworn Lord.
Let not temptation assault us too strongly,

but give us deliverance, Leader of nations,
from every evil until endless ages.

EXETER BOOK, ANGLO-SAXON C. TENTH CENTURY

Saturday

Blessed the Pure of Heart
Set me as a seal upon your heart
as a seal upon your arm;
for love is as strong as death,
jealousy as cruel as the grave.

SONG OF SOLOMON 8:6

The primary seat of God's action in the human person is the heart in the sense that the Bible and the Fathers of the Church have given to this word. It does not denote perceptible and superficial activity, but rather the intimate center from which arise our deepest urges, the wellspring that pours out intentional and intellectual activity, the living centre of the person.

"Blessed are the pure in heart, for they shall see God" (Matt. 5:8). All of the ascetical striving of the monk, striving that is simply the visible side of the hidden action of the Spirit in us, aims at the purification of the heart. This is above all true for the solitary whose striving in large measure is purely interior. When we speak of purity of heart, we mean the quality of the deepest essence of a human life, the life of knowledge and love. God has commanded us to love him with "all your heart, all your soul, and all your mind" (Matt. 22:37), and we desire to love utterly in this way. It is this that motivates our choice of the monastic life. But the drama is that of ourselves we are incompetent. We want to love purely, but we also don't want to entirely, not yet. We are so weak, so easily diverted from our true Good, from true Beauty, like children who are easily distracted by all sorts of trifles.

A CARTHUSIAN, *THE WAY OF SILENT LOVE*

_____ *W e e k   T h i r t y - e i g h t* _____

Sunday

Our heart is corrupt. This is our human inheritance; it is also the fruit of our personal choices. It demands ascesis: A hard, long struggle. But we are not alone. Christ has taken upon himself our nature and our sad heritage; he has redeemed us and he communicates his energy to us, the power of his Spirit, that enables us to enter the divine life that makes us children of God, and gives us the power to live, in the light, as children of God, after the pattern of Christ. But not without us, not without our free co-operation, our personal response to his love.

The monastic quest for purity of heart and co-operation with the Holy Spirit in us, docility to the interior Master, are therefore two aspects of the same reality, Christ in us, the way to the Father. The divine action precedes, gives birth to and sustains our activity. All is grace. But the activity of the Spirit grows increasingly predominant as the work continues and the image of Christ becomes apparent. As the work continues and one approaches God, the process proves more delicate, beyond human ways of working. To facilitate the activity of the Spirit, God endows us with a sensitivity to this activity of the Spirit, receptivity, a readiness to follow these impulses (what we usually call gifts of the Spirit), that enable us to work in a way beyond our limited potential according to a divine potential, because this is the wisdom of God who is the guide. This implies a certain passivity on our part, a passivity that is able to be consciously felt (as occasionally happens in divine contemplation); we cannot link it to a specific feeling (and feeling has no relation to the intensity of divine activity). Alone, the action of the Spirit can bestow purity of heart, "the eye, by whose serene gaze the Spouse is wounded with love; that eye, pure and clean, by which God is seen" (Carthusian Statutes).

A CARTHUSIAN, *THE WAY OF SILENT LOVE*

Monday

A Saturday prayer at 6:50 A.M. on BBC radio
"Blessed be God who was and is and is to come. I have slept and have arisen and I am still with thee."

Benedictine nun that I am, in speaking of prayer I naturally turn to the psalms for they are the bread-and-butter so to say of my daily spiritual diet. For at least three to four hours every day, the psalms are on our lips, praising and thanking God, and invoking his blessing upon the world we live in. To that must be added two periods of private prayer, and I should like to share with you a very homely, personal experience. Feeling very tired one afternoon, I decided to make my prayer out of doors in what we call "the dingle," a deeply-wooded place full of mystery and delight, interlaced branches of trees overhead, carpeted with all kinds of wild flowers underfoot and resounding with birdsong. As I put on a shawl, I noticed a senior nun changing her shoes. "I'm going out to pray, but haven't a decent thought in my head," I said to her. "Please give me one."

"Yes," she promptly replied. "Try this!" Slowly she ticked each phrase off on the fingers of her left hand.

"God loves me as nobody else loves me, and as He loves nobody else." No artist—and God is the supreme artist—discards the work of his own hands. God made me. There is no mass production with the Almighty.

CONTINUES . . .

Tuesday

The psalmist tells us that God has made hearts one by one. There may be hundreds of millions of other human beings on this tiny planet spinning amid a spiral of millions of other stars, yet the fact remains that there is only one me and one you. All of us have eyes, a nose, a mouth—but no two faces, no blood count, no finger-print, nothing whatever in all those millions is identical. This surely is the true meaning of human rights. However deep within every one of us is a secret space which none save God himself can enter. We all know that there are things we could not tell others, even if we would, and things we would not tell even if we could. This is the secret place of prayer where we meet the all-seeing eye, the compassionate heart, and the all-forgiving love of the God who made us and knows us through and through. That is why I ask you now to join with me in repeating with worship and thanksgiving those two lines first given to me, that I gave you at the beginning of this exchange:

> "God loves me as nobody else loves me, and as He loves nobody else. I love God as nobody else loves Him, and as I love nobody else."

DAME FELICITAS CORRIGAN, A NUN OF STANBROOK ABBEY

Wednesday

Prayer: A Mystery of Silence

To "make" prayer. The expression is strange since it suggests the idea of doing something, of obtaining a result, of producing or creating. There, one finds again the old temptation of Western contemplative thinking symbolized in the juggler of Notre Dame. The story is touching in so far as it shows us that God hardly pays attention to what one does for him, since he sees the heart and not the deeds. Therefore it is sad to see that the poor juggler little realized that it was enough to let his heart rest in the presence of the Lord in order to give him the very best. He had to do his juggling. It was not our Lady who needed him to dance, it was the juggler himself who needed to do something. It was for him a matter of "making" prayer.

It is not a question of "making" prayer or even of making silence. Silence is not contrived. When one comes before the Lord with the mind full of images, with strong emotions and one's thoughts still in movement, one realizes the need for silence; the temptation then is to make silence. As if it were a question of clothing oneself in silence, or throwing over all the inner murmurings a cape which would hide or smother it. This is not to be silent; it is rather to cover up the noise or shut it up within ourselves, so that it is always ready to emerge at the slightest opportunity. There is no need to create silence or to inject it from without. It is already there and it is simply a matter of letting it rise from within us so that it eliminates by its very presence the noise that distracts or invades us. Silence of the mind can be mere nothingness: The silence of the

stone, the silence of the mind numbed and deadened by its involve-
ment with the material and exterior. This is not true silence. The
only silence that counts is the presence of him who is no-thing.

A CARTHUSIAN, THE WOUND OF LOVE

Thursday

Does not prayer often mean returning gradually and simply to true
silence? Certainly, not by doing anything or imposing some kind of
yoke or burden on ourselves but, on the contrary, by letting all our
activity subside, little by little, into that true interior silence that
will begin to assert itself and resume its rightful place. Once we
have heard this silence we thirst to find it again. We must, however,
free ourselves from the idea that we can of ourselves reproduce
it. It is there: It is always there even if we no longer hear it. Indeed,
there are days when it is impossible to recapture it, for the mill of
the mind is grinding and it is hard then to stop the workings of the
imagination and the senses. Yet, silence does abide in the depths of
our will as a peaceful and tranquil acceptance of the noise and dis-
turbances that hinder our coming to serenity of mind. Normally,
though, it should be possible by means of a certain physical and intellectual asceticism (breathing, posture, etc.) to calm the undisci-
plined impulses of the mind in order to achieve at least a little
stillness. All the same, silence is more profound than all accepted
forms of meditation: *Lectio divina,* lights from the Lord that help us
penetrate his mysteries, reflections on themes that merit our attention, etc. All this is good and helps us to approach the truth. It is all
very necessary in its own time.

CONTINUES . . .

Friday

Silence, however, is deeper still and nothing can replace it. There are days when we must forgo silence in order to give our spirit the nourishment it needs. Yet we must not become light-headed with the wine of a partial truth which becomes clear to us; our thirst is deeper still and aims at a truth as near as possible to the absolute Truth. Only silence, even if it is darkness, draws us to total light. Indeed, even the work of God only reveals to us its riches if it is the bearer of silence. The Divine Office only achieves its balance when it breathes forth in the depth of the soul the silence contained in the eternal Word.

We cannot, therefore, do anything. There is nothing to give. God does not wait for us to give him little gifts. He has no use for bulls or wild rams; what he wants is the spiritual sacrifice of our hearts. Must we say, therefore, that if we have nothing to give that is outside of us, we must give our very selves? Not even that. He does not ask us to become agitated, to invent formulas or methods of offering ourselves. Besides, if we really thought about it, what could that possibly mean? To go out of ourselves? But that would mean to lose ourselves, to renounce being ourselves, taking our soul in our hands and offering it to God. If it is then not a question of our making a formal offering, should we, therefore, be receiving a gift from the hands of God? Not that either. We do not receive a gift from God, whether little or great; it is God himself that we receive. Yet what does this mean? Does he come to us in regal splendor, arrayed in majesty? In reality, we know that when we are silent God does not speak to us, nor does he reveal himself in any way, and yet he gives himself.

CONTINUES . . .

Saturday

God gives himself to me. Yet, we must be careful not to act like frogs and puff ourselves up in an attempt to become as God. The gift of God is not something foreign to us; in a way, it is not different from us at all. For God, to give himself to us is to give us to ourselves. He gives me my being as child of God, ever springing forth anew. Experience shows that silence brings us back to ourselves. The danger would be to turn in on ourselves, and find contentment in a sort of self-complacency. To be truly oneself is to drink deeply at the wellsprings of our being, or more exactly, to be the spring nourished and sustained at the heart of God himself. God creates us in love and it is our being that we receive from him in love. At one and the same time, we become ourselves and we receive God himself. In fact, we are God, not through pantheism or monism, obviously, but by shared sonship. God begets me even before I know or desire it; but he also gives me his Spirit who allows me to receive this gift, of which I cannot clearly say whether it is he or I myself. It is simply a question of being oneself, or better, of becoming oneself at every moment, together with the Son who, from all eternity, in one unchanging moment receives his being from the Father.

A CARTHUSIAN, *THE WOUND OF LOVE*

Sunday

Friends and Foes

From our perspective, it is hard to realise the explosive nature of the Church's first experience of Christianity; from early days, monks and nuns were at the epicentre of this convulsive force.

It staggers the mind to realize that Saint Athanasius to whom Saint Antony left his sheepskin cloak was but thirty-three and recently ordained as Bishop of Alexandria when Basil of Caesarea was born in 329, his bosom-friend Gregory Nazianzen followed one year later and his younger brother Gregory of Nyssa two years after. These three were boys when John Chrysostom was born about 347. In 360, Saint Benedict's hero, Martin of Tours, was forty-four, Ambrose twenty-one, Jerome nineteen, Paulinus of Nola seven, Augustine six. Almost all these [Church Fathers] came into contact with one another, sometimes as friends, occasionally as foes. Many of the Eastern Fathers were monks; in the West, Jerome alone had embraced the monastic life, and it was he, the Latin educated in Rome, Antioch and Constantinople, who resolved the tension, built the bridge linking East and West, and set the pattern of monastic life that was to permeate the Middle Ages.

The pages of the Rule prove that Saint Benedict had studied Jerome assiduously; he quotes directly from him six times and, like Jerome, has little time for monks who lived alone or in twos or threes as self-will dictated. "Live in a monastery under the control of one father and with many companions," Jerome wrote to Rusticus (Eph. 29). "Things at first compulsory will become habitual" (cp. Prologue to Benedict's Rule).

No art is ever learned without a master and these will teach you, one humility, another patience, another silence, a fourth meekness. You will eat what you are told to eat, wear what clothes are given you, obey one you do not like, go to bed tired out, be forced to rise before you have had sufficient rest.

DAME FELICITAS CORRIGAN, O.S.B.,

BENEDICTINE TAPESTRY

Monday

ψ

So long as you seek Buddhahood,
specifically exercizing yourself for it,
you shall never find success.
Yung-chia Ta-shih

How does any man set himself in harmony with Tao?
I am always out of harmony.
Shih-t'ou

How can I take hold?
Never make hold.
What I am left with is my Self.
Panchadasi

I can tell you: Simply stay—
whether in God or close to God;
and ask nothing more,
unless he prompts you.
Francis de Sales

⌐

Tuesday

Novices at Play

20 March 1959

. . . Dame Hildelith wonders whether you received copies of *The Monotype Recorder* devoted to the work of Eric Gill? Also, can you give me any idea how much Joan Hassall would charge for illustrating a book? And in my last letter, I said I should try to get hold of a copy of the novices' Ophelia parody. It is too long to send, so I only send you these snippets. Polonius warns Ophelia:

> How now, Ophelia, does dream of Hamlet still?
> But thou must be obedient to my will.
> That Fellow's good for naught, dishonest, too,
> I fear that to his vows he'll prove untrue.

To which Ophelia replies:

> . . . But if I spurn him, maybe he'll be bowed
> With sorrow, and perhaps he may go mad,
> Or be a Jesuit, which is just as bad.

(Song: When a wooer goes a-wooing.)
Hamlet enters unobserved.

OPHELIA *(aside)*

> He little knows I want to be a nun
> And all my love for Hamlet's only done
> To hide the truth because full well I know
> If he suspected, he'd not let me go.

HAMLET *(aside)*

> They little dream I want to be a monk
> And yet I really am in a dreadful funk,
> I know Ophelia really loves me so,
> If she heard this, she'd drown herself for woe.

EXEUNT OPHELIA AND POLONIUS

Wednesday

HAMLET:

> To go or not to go, that is the question
> I've worried o'er it till I've got indigestion.
> Whether it is nobler in the mind to bear
> The heartaches and the dreadful wear and tear
> Of worldly life, or leave it all behind
> And live in cloister with a quiet mind.
> To pray and spend one's time in quiet oration
> Indeed methinks this a consummation
> Devoutly to be wished. I must not shirk
> The issue of to pray perchance to work.
> To work; aye, there's the rub that gives me pause.
> For who knows what may lie beyond those doors?
> And once they've got me in, I dread to think
> What I may have to do at kitchen sink,
> Sorting potatoes, picking apple trees,

Or cleaning dirty floors on hands and knees.
For who would fardels bear, a novice be
When he might smoke and drink and watch TV?
Thus fancy doth make cowards of us all.
Some leer within and some without the wall.

DAME FELICITAS CORRIGAN, O.S.B.,

A LETTER TO SIR SYDNEY COCKERELL,

A BENEDICTINE TAPESTRY

Thursday

Go to the Jesuits

Saint Theresa of Avila writes to her brother [1576]
I should not like you to forget this, so I am putting it down here.
Unless you begin now and take great trouble with those boys, I am
very much afraid they may get friendly with some stuck-up set in
Avila. So you must send them to the Company (of Jesus) at once—
I am writing to the Rector, as you will see when you go there—and
if good Francisco de Salcedo and Master Daza agree, let them wear
college caps. One of Rodrigo's daughter's six children is a boy,
which is fortunate for him: they have always kept him at his studies
and he is now at Salamanca. A son of Don Diego de Aguila did what
I am recommending to you. In any case you will hear there what is
usual. Pray God my brother's boys may not grow up to think too
much of themselves.

Friday

You will not be able to see much of Francisco de Salcedo, or of the Master, unless you go to their houses, for they live a long way from Peralvarez; but you ought to be alone with them for talks like these. Do not forget that you should not fix on any particular confessor just now, and you should have as few servants in your house as you can manage with. It is better to engage more than to have to get rid of some. I am writing to Valladolid to get the page to come; but, even if the boys have to go without one, for a few days, there are two of them, and they can go together, so it does not much matter. But I am writing to have him sent to you.

You are inclined to think a great deal of your prestige—you have already demonstrated that. You must mortify yourself in this respect and not listen to everybody, but follow the advice of these two in everything, and also of Father Muñoz, of the Company, if you think well, though the other two are sufficient in serious matters, and you can abide by what they say. Remember you may begin things without realizing at first that you are doing harm and that you will gain more in the eyes of God, and indeed in the eyes of the world, by keeping back your money for almsgiving, and your children will gain too.

I should not favour you buying a mule just yet. Get a little pony which will be useful for journeys and also for use at home. There is no reason at present why those boys of yours should not go on foot: let them keep to their studies.

SAINT THERESA OF AVILA, A LETTER TO HER BROTHER

Saturday

THOMAS KEATING

Contemplative Prayer

The modern contemplative prayer movement is spreading rapidly. In response to a perceived thirst for prayer that can be described as universal, a number of charismatic leaders and teachers have offered their own path to prayer. First the Benedictine John Main and now the Trappist Thomas Keating have sought to spread the peace and prayerful practice of the cloister into the modern world. The response has been heartening: both movements are now worldwide.

Letting Go

The root of prayer is interior silence. We may think of prayer as thoughts or feelings expressed in words, but this is only one of its forms. "Prayer," according to Evagrius, "is the laying aside of thoughts." This definition presupposes there *are* thoughts. Contemplative prayer is not so much the absence of thoughts as detachment from them. It is the opening of mind and heart, body and emotions—our whole being—to God, the ultimate mystery, beyond word, thoughts and emotions—beyond, in other words, the psychological content of the present moment. We do not deny or repress what is in our consciousness. We simply accept the fact of whatever is there and go beyond it, not by effort, but by letting go of whatever is there.

THOMAS KEATING, *OPEN MIND, OPEN HEART*

Sunday

Lessons of the Transfiguration

Jesus took with him the three disciples, who were best prepared to receive the grace of contemplation, who had made the most headway in changing their hearts. God approached them through their senses by means of the vision on the mountain. At first, they were overawed and delighted. Peter wanted to remain there forever. Suddenly, a cloud covered them, hiding the vision and leaving their senses empty and quiet, yet attentive and alert. They fell upon their faces, a posture of adoration, gratitude and love all rolled into one. The voice from heaven awakened the consciousness to the presence of the Spirit, who had always been speaking within them, but whom until then they had never been able to hear. Their interior emptiness was filled with the luminous presence of the divine. At Jesus' touch they returned to their ordinary perceptions and saw him as he was before but with the transformed consciousness of faith. They no longer saw him as a mere human being. Their receptive and active faculties had been unified by the Spirit; the interior and exterior word of God had become one. For those who have attained this consciousness, daily life is a continual and increasing revelation of God. The words they hear in scripture and in the liturgy confirm what they have learned through the prayer of contemplation.

CONTINUES . . .

Monday

Infused Love

In a remarkable passage in *The Living Flame of Love* in which John of the Cross describes in detail the transition from sensible devotion to spiritual intimacy with God, he says that when one cannot reason discursively or make acts of the will with any satisfaction during prayer, one should give the situation a quiet welcome. One will then begin to feel peace, tranquillity, and strength because God is now feeding the soul directly, giving his grace to the will alone and attracting it mysteriously to himself. People in this state have great anxiety about whether they are going backward. They think that all the good things they experienced in the first years of their conversion are coming to an end, and if they are asked how their prayer life is, they will throw up their hands in despair. Actually, if questioned further, they reveal that they have a great desire to find some way to pray and they like to be alone with God even though they can't enjoy him. Thus, it is evident that there is a secret attraction present at a deep level of their psyche. This is the infused element of contemplative prayer. Divine love is the infused element. If it is given a quiet rest, it will grow from a spark to a living flame.

CONTINUES . . .

Tuesday

At the Heart Is Contemplative Prayer

Inquirer: The Cloud of Unknowing *has a lot to say about being ready for this movement into contemplative prayer. It presupposes that not everyone is called to this. It gives signs for telling whether you are called or not. Yet today it seems to be offered to everyone, not only by teachers of centering prayer, but also by teachers of Eastern meditation. It is as if it is open to all.*

With regard to the Christian tradition, Origen, a fourth-century exponent of the theological school of Alexandria, considered the Christian community in the world to be the proper place of ascesis. It was only through Antony's example and Athanasius's report of it that the practice of leaving the world became the standard way to pursue the Christian path to divine union. Antony had no intention of making this the only way to achieve it, but when mass movements occur, popularizations also take place, and these may fossilize or even caricature a movement. A new wave of spiritual renewal has to arise before the necessary distinctions can again be made. This may take a long time when movements have become institutionalized. The essence of monastic life is not its structure but its interior practice, and the heart of interior practice is contemplative prayer.

THOMAS KEATING, *OPEN MIND, OPEN HEART*

Wednesday

Centering Prayer in Folsom State Prison

In the suburbs of Sacramento, California, there's a small town aptly named Repressa. It has its own post office and a small housing community. In the back yard of several homes stands a thirty-foot granite wall. Behind this wall are housed approximately 4,000 people. The place is Folsom State Prison.

Three years ago, something very unusual started to happen. With the help of an outside sponsor, the inmates of Folsom started their own contemplative prayer group. We were small to begin with, about fifteen inmates, mostly lifers and long-termers. This small core of inmates, that once met on Friday nights, now meets in one form or another every day of the week.

Our group has chosen Centering Prayer as taught by Fr Thomas Keating. It is a remarkable situation in that we are convicted felons from different ethnic backgrounds and have different religious beliefs, yet we set all that aside and meditate together as a family. There have never been any problems with violence or discipline within the group.

We now have representatives in every building in the prison: Inmates who used Centering Prayer to improve their lives. It has become a real tool of rehabilitation. In the three years that the group has been meeting, inmates who have been active members have not returned to Folsom after being released. This fact is extraordinary since the normal return rate to prison is over 80 percent.

It is now time for us to combine contemplation with action. Our group is looking to expand its efforts into other prisons. There are over thirty prisons in the State of California alone. This program should be in every one of them and in every prison across the country because it is changing lives.

ARTICLE IN CONTEMPORARY OUTREACH NEWS

Thursday

Faith is opening and surrendering to God. The spiritual journey does not require us to go anywhere because God is already with us and in us. It is a question of allowing our ordinary thoughts to recede into the background and to float along the river of consciousness without our noticing them, while we direct our attention toward the river on which they are floating. We are like someone sitting on the bank of a river and watching the boats go by. If we stay on the bank, with our attention on the river rather than on the boats, the capacity to disregard thoughts as they go by will develop, and a deeper kind of attention will emerge.

THOMAS KEATING, OPEN MIND, OPEN HEART

Friday

Abraham Encounters God

It is certain that Abraham did not yet know the name of Yahweh. His God is *El, El Shaddai ("God of the Mountain")*. He is in a real sense the "God of Abraham, Isaac and Jacob," the God who lives and acts, who intervenes decisively in the story of Abraham in order through him to inaugurate both the revelation and the realization of his economy of grace, whose history we shall attempt to trace from the standpoint of God's presence dwelling among men. At the point we have now reached, God does not yet dwell among men. He does not even announce his intention of doing so. He has not yet established his dwelling place on earth. He is in heaven, he is the "Most High God" invoked by Melchisedech (14:18–20). He only reveals himself on earth, he only "appears." In the life of Abraham, Yahweh intervenes in a vision and makes his double promise of an inheritance and an heir, and this promise is accompanied by a convenant sealed during a sacrifice by Yahweh's appearance under the form of fire. At the oak of Mamre, Yahweh shows himself in human form. He is one[15] of three men to whom Abraham offers hospitality. God is a passing

---

[15] In the Iconic tradition of the Eastern Church, the three "men" are represented as angels and prefigure the revelation of the Trinity.

"guest." But he remains for two days at least while the two other men go on to Sodom, and Abraham speaks to him with that familiarity full of both assurance and respect, which is revealed to us in the admirable scene of his intercession on behalf of Sodom.

YVES M.-J. CONGAR O.P., THE MYSTERY OF THE TEMPLE

Saturday

As Jacob's story unfolds, we see a similar pattern of relations with God. For the most part, the Patriarchs love to "consult Yahweh" in the same place (Gen. 25:22). When the aged Jacob goes down into Egypt to be reunited with his son Joseph, he stops at Bersabee to offer sacrifices to the God of his father Isaac (Gen. 46:1). It was at Bersabee that Yahweh had appeared to Isaac in order to renew the promise. Isaac had built an altar there and had called upon the name of Yahweh (Gen. 26:23–25).

Jacob does likewise at Sichem. . . . He buys the piece of land where he pitched his tent and erects on it an altar which he calls "El, the God of Israel" (Gen 33:18–20). But it is above all at Bethel that Jacob meets God. There he sees in a dream a ladder linking heaven and earth and angels going up and down it as a token of the familiar lasting relations between the Most High God and mankind. Hence Jesus, in order to show Nathaniel that with his (Jesus') coming, we pass from prophecy to the reality of God's presence, refers to Jacob's vision (John 1:51). Jacob set up the stone that had been his pillow at the place of the vision and consecrated it with oil. It was to be the dwelling-place or house of God—El. . . . It is obvious that Jacob had there a very vivid experience of God's Presence. . . . "What a fearsome place is this! This can be nothing other than the house of God; this is the gate of heaven." Jacob's experience at Bethel stands as a type of the real Presence of God among men.

CONTINUES . . .

W e e k   F o r t y - o n e

Sunday

Moreover it is marked by two characteristics whose union is typical of the Judeo-Christian religious economy, namely transcendence and proximity, or better, transcendence and communication. The God of Abraham and of Jacob is the Most High God but he is at the same time the God who comes to meet us and enters into our history. The Most High God is "my God," "the God of my salvation," who casts his eyes on me and looks after me as if I were infinitely precious to him. The psalms are full of this twofold feeling. Better than all else they educate us in that sense of the two values of infinite respect and of tender confidence which determine the impulse of the religious soul and "our consciousness of God." From as far back as the age of the Patriarchs, God, at the very moment when he intervenes in their story and follows their only too human activities, reveals himself to them as the Most High God and inspires in them a religious awe and at the same time a feeling of his nearness to them.

The Gospel, when its time comes, will reveal all the depth and truth of these two inseparable values which Jesus will bring together in his prayer with sublime simplicity. He will teach us to say "Our Father" but only by making us add at once "who are in Heaven." At one and the same time, he will reveal to us that God who is Father in the mystery of his transcendent life and that by virtue of this very fatherhood of his, he communicates himself to men in a way we should never have dared imagine. Distances are abolished, communication between heaven and earth is established in Jesus, the Word made flesh. But Jesus in whom the two are joined becomes the inner principle of our own life and at the same time is for us an object of faith and adoration—*Tu solus Altissimus, Jesu Christe.*

YVES M.-J. CONGAR O.P.,

THE MYSTERY OF THE TEMPLE

Monday

Dies Irae
Rex tremendae majestatis,
qui salvandos salvas gratis,
Salve me, fons pietatis.
Recordare Jesu pie,
Quod sum causa tuae viae;
Ne me perdas illa die.

My most majestic king,
who freely gives salvation,
save me, from the goodness of your heart.
Be mindful, good Jesus,
why you lived your life;
let me not perish on that day.

SEQUENCE FROM MASS FOR THE DEAD

Tuesday

Lord, never trust me for one moment: I am sure to fail you—unless you stand by me.

SAINT PHILIP NERI

We consist in the humility of the ancients; we are Christians, Jesus is merely a Savior, a name of mystery, Christ is Anointed, a name of communication, of accommodation, of imitation; and so this name, the name of Christ, is *Oleum effusum* (as the Spouse says); an ointment, a perfume poured out upon us and we are Christians. In the name of Jesus Saint Paul abounded, but in the name of Christ more. . . . If we will call ourselves or endanger or give occasion to others to call us from the names of men, Papists or Lutherans or Calvinists, we depart from the true glory and serenity, from the lustre and splendor of the Sun; this is *Tabernaculum Solis*: Here in the Christian church God has set a tabernacle for the sun; and as in nature man has light enough to discern the principles of reason; so in the Christian church (considered without subdivisions or name and sects) a Christian has light enough of all things necessary to salvation.

JOHN DONNE

Wednesday

CARTHUSIAN REFLECTIONS

A finger pointing

The figure of John the Baptist is a powerful symbol of the eremetical life. He stands before us stark and clear-cut, his whole being a finger pointing towards an invisible reality. Solitude is his milieu of life, silence the mantle he wears. What is silence, what is solitude for the contemplative?

Solitude is not isolation, the cutting off of oneself from others. It is rather a mystery of communion, a being-with in a deeper way; a being with God, with Christ and, potentially, with all people. It is a being grafted into the vine of Christ so as to become one with his body which is the Church. It is being enabled to intercede from within a real solidarity with all people in Christ. It is a being caught up into the paschal mystery of his redemptive love.

Likewise silence is not the mere absence of speech. It is listening to God, receiving the word he communicates to us in his creation and in the history of salvation. It is entering into communion with his superabundant life, a life of mutual knowledge and love. It is speaking with God as one would speak with a friend, with words and without words at that point where all the partial words come together in the reality of pure communion. It is this silence that animates and gives substance to the song of our adoration and praise, for it is, as it were, the hidden presence of the unique Word in whom the Father, through the Spirit of his Love, says eternally all that was, that is and that will be.

Our life, like that of John the Baptist, should be a living witness to the reality of God through such a silence and such a solitude. May it be so a little more each day, and especially this day, for all of you, in Christ our Lord.

Thursday

A hidden name

Receiving the monastic habit signifies the entry into the monastic life. You are crossing a threshold that will radically change you. The habit signifies Christ. In putting it on, you are being clothed in Christ, not just the body but the heart and soul as well. Your task is to realise this, to make it real by the grace of God, in your whole being and life.

The fact that this should happen on the feast of the Assumption of Our Lady is symbolic. In Our Lady we see the fulfilment of our spiritual journey. Just as she entered, body and soul, into the definitive life won for us by Christ, so, hopefully, will each one of us. During our life, we will try to cultivate the seed of life that is given to us, letting all our being, our attitudes, our acts be informed by the Spirit, opening ourselves in joyful trust and thanksgiving to the outpouring love and light that is the life of God. This is our goal.

The way is Christ, being conformed to his death and to his life. In choosing the Carthusian life, you have chosen to follow Christ completely in response to the special and personal call he has addressed to you. He has called you by your name. We each have a hidden name that designates the inmost part of our being which is turned towards and, as it were, in immediate contact with God. This name will be revealed only in the beatific vision. The name we bear in this world can, to some extent, signify it, at least pointing towards the way we are to follow.

RECEIVING THE HABIT
OF A CONVERSE BROTHER,
THE SPIRIT OF THE PLACE

Friday

Your name, Joseph, is particularly apt for the life you have chosen, that of a Converse Brother. We know little of Joseph. There were dramatic moments in his life, of course: Bethlehem, the flight into Egypt, the temple episode, but my feeling at least is that for the essential Joseph, the body and substance of his life was in the ordinary, simple, working, family life in Nazareth. The child and his mother depended on him for food, a home, love, basic education, a place in the social fabric of their village. He seems to have been a simple man, hidden in his ordinariness, "only" Joseph the carpenter. He did not have any part in Christ's public life of preaching. It would seem he was dead by then. More profoundly, his contribution to Christ's work was situated at another level, at the level of his personal relationship with Christ, what he gave of himself to the human person of Jesus. We know how important this is in the development of the personality. Judging by the fruits, he loved much and wisely.

As a Brother, your contribution to the body of Christ which is the Church will have some of the same characteristics. It will be simple yet essential. It will be very much incarnated, yet the fruit of the Spirit. It will be concerned with the material well-being of a small group of Christ's disciples, yet it will be Jesus whom you will serve in them. Its truth will be plain to see, verifiable in a very concrete obedience, effort, humility and charity, yet it will receive all its energy from within, from a deep, personal love of Christ and a willingness to carry the burdens of his cross as they present themselves in the vicissitudes of real life. Prayer and work will be inextricably interwoven in the silent world of the monastery, not the silence of absence of life, but the harmonious silence of well-ordered activity. Like Mary and Joseph you will follow the way, not of riches or power, but the humble hidden path of Nazareth and so enter, day by day, more deeply into the kingdom of God.

Relying on the intercession of Our Lady and of Saint Joseph will you thus follow Christ to the Father?

RECEIVING THE HABIT

OF A CONVERSE BROTHER,

THE SPIRIT OF THE PLACE

Saturday

Called to be saints

The trouble is that we are called to be saints, not just good people, virtuous, wise, well-balanced, not doing harm to others. We are called to be holy as God is holy, to be perfect as our heavenly Father is perfect, merciful as he is merciful, loving as Christ loves us, that is totally, to the point of giving our life for our brothers and sisters.

This is surely a tall order. If we look at our own experience in life, if we look at ourselves and the people we know and have known, do we see many saints, do we see any? Would I be able to recognise a saint if I saw one? This is not at all certain. It would imply that I know exactly what makes a saint a saint. In an abstract way I could perhaps say something on that subject. I could say that a saint is someone who has responded fully to the gift of God communicating himself to a human person in the reality of his historical existence, this person thus becoming godly, begotten as a child of God, living and to live for all eternity from God's life. I could say that a saint is someone wholly animated and transformed by the Spirit of Christ, becoming like Christ in his or her heart and actions. I could say that a saint is someone utterly empty of self, given wholly in service of God and his or her neighbor. I could say that a saint is a person of profound faith, hope, love, goodness, humility, generosity, prayer, truthfulness. I would be right, of course, although I am then rather describing the effects of sanctity than touching on its core.

FEAST OF ALL SAINTS, *THE SPIRIT OF THE PLACE*

W e e k   F o r t y - t w o

Sunday

The essential of the saint, it seems to me, is the divine spark of grace in a saint's soul, that something of God's Spirit that is freely given and as freely received. This is what lifts a human life to a plane other than the realisation of a human project or ideal to something more sublime but also disconcerting. God ultimately is mystery, transcending all our categories and reasonable previsions and the saint, who lets God shine through, is equally mysterious and unpredictable. Touched by God, the saint is creative of what is new. How often in the history of the Church have saints been the initiators of original ways of being Christ in the world. What an enormous variety there is in the styles of life and personal being they have manifested. The vitality of the Gospel of Christ is nowhere more clear as it responds to the needs of each epoch. In that respect the canonisation of some saints (there were many more uncanonised saints, perhaps the majority) can be falsely understood if it is regarded as imitative, that is, we must imitate them in exactly their way of living. We cannot all be like Saint Thérèse of Lisieux! Christ alone is to be imitated in the strict sense, and then, as it were, from within, under the guidance of his Spirit. The example of the saints encourages us to something of the same quality of commitment but embodied according to the particular grace of each one. Let us not be afraid to be original in this sense, as long as it is the expression of the originality of the Holy Spirit.

CONTINUES . . .

Monday

This, of course, is why we might not recognise a saint. He or she might not fit any one of our familiar models. We tend to see only the exterior discrepancies from what we expect in a saintly person and the inevitable limitations, that may have nothing to do with his or her liberty and hence sanctity. Perhaps we are surrounded by saints that we fail to recognise, just as Christ was not recognised in the poor and hungry and naked (Matt. 25:31–46). It is not for us to judge. Let us receive and cherish Christ in each one of our brothers and sisters and, for our part, be faithful to the grace we have received. Then our voice will blend perfectly, without losing its original tone, with the voices of all the saints throughout all time, in all places, as we sing the praises of our God and Father in the melody of his Son and the breath of his Spirit, We will start to do that hopefully in the office we are about to celebrate. Happy feast!

FEAST OF ALL SAINTS,

THE SPIRIT OF THE PLACE

Tuesday

Indwelling love

Today, we celebrate, not some aspect of revelation, not some saint, but God himself in his innermost being. Hence the importance of the feast. Even though it dates only from the mid-fourteenth century, the Sundays following it used to be named with relation to it: 1st, 2nd, etc. Sunday after Trinity.

The explicit celebration of the Holy Trinity is fundamental to the knowledge we have of God and of ourselves. It is easy to slip into an idea of God derived from the abstract reasoning of Platonism, combined with monarchical imperialism. The inscrutable God of predestinarian Calvinism, the implacable God of Jansenism, and the distant God of the eighteenth-century Deism, have alike imprinted a pattern on the Western understanding of God, which had little place for God as Trinity. It is this God that not only Marx, Freud and Nietzsche rejected, but also a sincere modern humanism. This negative image of God is often at the root of conflict with or revolts towards God to be found in the hearts of many believers.

As if by reaction from such a remote and arbitrary God, in modern times the immanence of God has been stressed to the point that God seems often to be so telescoped into the world as to be identified with it. There is nothing more. As Coleridge put it, "Pantheism is but a painted atheism—and the doctrine of the Trinity the only sure and certain bulwark against it." Why? Because God as Trinity is a God of grace, the Lord and Giver of life, a God who saves.

FEAST OF THE MOST HOLY TRINITY,

THE SPIRIT OF THE PLACE

Wednesday

And as our God is, so is our understanding of ourselves. There is here a circular influence. Human projections inevitably shape our image of God, but conversely our image of God shapes our understanding of what it means to be human. All too often the person is identified with the individual with adverse consequence. Persons are related by definition, individuals are not. Persons experience solitude, individuals isolation. Atomised individualism—me, me—and an equally destructive collectivism—we, we—have characterised much Western thought and political life in recent centuries. Both can be seen as flowing from a distorted doctrine of God, what has been called the pathology of Western Christianity, a failure to take Trinitarian theology seriously.

The heart of the doctrine of God is the conviction that God is a communion of persons. The Greek Fathers, in particular the fourteenth-century Cappadocians, spoke of that communion as *perichoresis*, a divine circulation of mutually indwelling love. This is God as he revealed himself in the person of Jesus Christ, this is how we must conceive of him as he is known through his self-giving and transforming love.

The Trinity is what we mean when we say that God is Love. That communion of Love is the key to our human identity as those made in the image of God. We come from each other in order to live for each other. And that is true socially as well as personally.

The feast of the Holy Trinity invites us to discover our true identity as persons in relationship, made in the image of the God of love, distinct from one another yet receiving and giving all of ourselves one to the other. We need to listen to what Gerard Manley Hopkins called "the crying of those three, the Immortals of the Eternal Ring, utterer, uttered, uttering." God, who is the source and goal of our being, is grace and communion. "It is the glory of his high estate. He is an act that doth communicate" (Traherne). And he that dwells in love, dwells in God, and God in him (cf. I John 4:16). Let us, today, celebrate with joy and simplicity the fountain of love and life that God is.

FEAST OF THE MOST HOLY TRINITY, *THE SPIRIT OF THE PLACE*

Thursday

The invisible man

Patrick wakes up to find he has become invisible. He looks at his watch. He sees the watch, he reads the hour, but his wrist he does not see. Frightened, he jumps out of bed. His pyjamas stand upright but there is no one in them. All at once, he understands that he has become really invisible: he has separated himself from all that rendered him visible to himself and to others. If he does not find another form of presence to himself, he will disappear altogether. He sets off in quest of himself.

At first, it is amusing. He sees people who cannot see him. He sees much good but also much evil. He sees people true to life. Then he hears what they say of him—even his friends (and that is not pleasant). Eventually, he begins to feel very isolated, alone, misunderstood. Then he discovers that by using make-up and clothes he can be seen by others. He clothes himself, with satisfaction.

Thereupon, he makes a terrible discovery. The others also are invisible, but they do not know it! It is not real persons who speak to each other but persons constituted by make-up and clothes. Basically, there are only four or five styles of clothes—like four or five uniforms. Those wearing blue range themselves against those wearing red. Not only are individuals reduced to being ciphers of a common type, but they are divided into cliques, each clique divided from and fighting the others. Finally, their true identity, they are invisible, unknown and terribly alone.

FEAST OF THE BODY AND BLOOD OF THE LORD,

THE SPIRIT OF THE PLACE

Friday

Nudus, nudum Christum sequere
Naked, to follow the naked Christ

What is to be done? Patrick has a blinding intuition—like a child seeing the sun rising in the morning for the first time. Naked, he will follow the naked Christ. Throwing off his uniform, washing all the make-up from his face, he stands naked. He accepts the solitude of the mystery of his being and his total poverty.

He enters a church where Mass is being said. For the first time he understands and lets himself be taken up into the movement of Christ's sacrifice, this total gift to the Father for the love of humankind, where he receives everything. The priest, a truly spiritual man, with the eyes of faith and hope, sees him in his invisibility. When Patrick eats the Body of Christ, his own body takes on again its true substantiality. He is there, visible, but different. He "sees," in his turn, the others around him in their Christic bodies, and for the very first time, he can communicate with them—person to person. And in this communion—in loving his brothers—he discovers who he is. He is saved. He is no longer alone.

FEAST OF THE BODY AND BLOOD OF THE LORD,

THE SPIRIT OF THE PLACE

Saturday

If God exists

If God exists, the taking of the Carthusian habit today has sense, is even rigorously coherent. If God does not exist, then you are a fool, the victim of a self-destroying illusion. Everything hangs on this one question, and will go on depending on it every day and night of the years that will be given to you to live. The contemplative life is not primarily a business of heroism. It is rather the common-sense ordering of our attitudes and acts according to the vision of things given to us by faith. Faith is the key, animated by the love of him who is the source and end of all that is, and sustained by the hope that awaits the fulfilment of his promise. If God exists, we must surely adore him in his majesty, obey him in his commands, receive his gift of life with gratitude and trust, love him in his goodness and his beauty, live in communion with him in so far as we are able, see and love all creatures, particularly our brothers and sisters, as he sees and loves them, up to the giving of our life for them in Christ, if this is asked of us. All this follows necessarily, if God exists.

The problem is that the act of faith reaches out beyond the limits of our rational mind and points towards a mystery it cannot circumscribe or control. Love of the Good seen in shadow and enigma alone can bear our mind on the wings of trust into direct contact with the reality of God as he is in himself. The ultimate guarantee of our faith must paradoxically be God alone. Our act of faith is his own light gifted to us and is its own truth. Light is light. It is a fact that faith becomes, not visions, but vision, the simplest and clearest of all. But it is also this leap in trust in God, and this aspect may be foremost at certain key moments.

RECEIVING THE HABIT AS A CLOISTER MONK,

FEAST OF THE PRESENTATION OF THE LORD, *THE SPIRIT OF THE PLACE*

W e e k   F o r t y - t h r e e

Sunday

You yourself have used the expression *"le saut de l'ange."* This refers to a dive from the high board into a swimming pool with arms outstretched until the very last second. Only, in this case, the diver cannot see for himself whether he is diving into water or on to a cement surface. People gathered around the pool tell him to jump, the pool is full of water—let us say they represent the Church—while others, the non-believers, cry that the pool is empty and you will crash on to a cement floor. This illustrates well the place of the testimony of the Church in our faith, but the saints who have jumped do not come back to tell us how it was. Again, ultimately, with the whole Church, we must put our trust in the Word of God himself who invites us to take him at his word and enter into his kingdom and life, by adhering to Christ and following in his footsteps, through death to life eternal. Perhaps we of all people will experience the anguish of this act at certain moments, for we are suspended from an unique cord. Perhaps the essence of the contemplative life is to believe in God because he is God, to love him for his own sake, and to hope for nothing less than God himself, giving himself to each one of us in a total communion of life and love.

CONTINUES . . .

Monday

For you, of course, there is the added complication that the pool in question is situated in an English garden! The Carthusian ideal has always been seen by you clothed in the form of a certain natural setting: the glory of the mountains, the purity of snow, the silence of high spaces [La Grande Chartreuse nestles in the mountains above Grenoble]. The Lord in his providence has led you to pitch your tent in another setting, with a less obvious poetry. As in so many areas of your life, you are invited to relinquish an exterior reality in order to accede to a deeper spiritual reality. England, behind the more bland appearance, is indeed a spiritual desert in many ways and has desperate need of the witness of men of prayer to the reality of God. You show that you have the intuition of the value of witness of a life given totally and publicly consecrated to God by your devotion to a great English martyr, Saint Thomas More. His initial attraction to the Charterhouse took the final form of suffering physical death for his faith. Perhaps your initial and enduring call to the priesthood may find its concrete realisation in the offering of your whole life, day after day, body and soul, as what Saint Paul calls "a living sacrifice, holy and acceptable to God, which is your spiritual worship" (Rom. 12:1).

In today's feast, Simeon and Anna receive and acknowledge the Savior in a little child. Each one of us must learn to discern the image of Christ engraved in the Child within us—the Child who, in his spontaneity and vulnerability yet dares to dream great dreams and to go forward towards their realisation in the joy of hope. That Child will not be crushed by a life dedicated to Christ for he is, in truth, "Christ within you, the hope of glory" (Col. 1:27). Believing in him who is, who was, and who will be, and putting on Christ Jesus, your lord and Savior, will you now, this day, set forth on this way?

RECEIVING THE HABIT AS A CLOISTER MONK,

FEAST OF THE PRESENTATION OF THE LORD, *THE SPIRIT OF THE PLACE*

Tuesday

In praise of beginnings
But I, being poor, have only my dreams. . . .
Tread softly because you tread upon my dreams.

W. B. YEATS

Life, as we know it, is a constant succession of beginnings. The mark of God's work is to make all things new, even that which was deformed and distorted.

Let us look at some images of beginnings so as to put ourselves, as it were, in tune with God's Spirit. There is the hypothetical Big Bang: the immense variety of cosmic matter issuing out from a single point of intense density, giving birth to time and space.

There is spring: nature stretching forth its new green shoots to the sun. There is the break of dawn, a fresh day setting out with dewy locks on its ordained course.

Then there are human beginnings. The apparently random lottery of conception. Birth itself. The first smile. The first words spoken, the first steps taken, entering into school, starting to work, perhaps falling in love, waking up each morning to the glory of another day.

And there are spiritual beginnings. The awesome gift of baptism, the beginning of a new life in God. The eternal newness of the

Eucharist: always the same, Christ's unique sacrifice, always new, making of each successive moment the sacrament of his Spirit; assuming, transforming time. The sacrament of reconciliation, renewing by the grace of pardon what has been damaged by our falls, setting us free to live and love in him again. Beyond the celebration of the sacrament, our attitude towards ourselves and others should be inspired by that of God towards us, for we are inconstant and weak.

FEAST OF THE BIRTHDAY OF THE BLESSED VIRGIN MARY,

THE SPIRIT OF THE PLACE

Wednesday

The sacraments of marriage, of healing, and of order are all entries into new modes of life. Every time Christ touches us there is new life, a new beginning. He is indeed the Lord of the resurrection. For our part, we must be poor enough to receive the newness of his gifts, for the Spirit is infinitely creative. We must not cling to the past, good or bad. It is but to cling to an image of ourselves and shut ourselves off from the abounding vitality of the Father. Rather we must have the courage, in faith, to let go of all that encumbers us and to dare to trust and hope in God alone. Then will the beginnings of Christ be realised in our lives. In him every day, every moment can be a new beginning, traversed by a spark of his creative energy. "Your joy no one will take from you" (John 16:22).

I wish you that joy that showed itself so gracefully in the Virgin Mary whose birthday we celebrate today.

FEAST OF THE BIRTHDAY OF THE BLESSED VIRGIN MARY,

THE SPIRIT OF THE PLACE

Thursday

God's life in our mortal veins

For some reason my mind keeps coming back to the Eucharist these days. It is, after all, the sacrament of the Paschal Mystery, its symbolic representation. Through this simple rite, Jesus tried to make his disciples grasp the meaning of what was to happen.

It is so simple and so profound. Jesus knows he is about to die. He gathers his disciples about him and eats with them, Judas included, remember; his presence is essential: Jesus will give his life for him perhaps in a special way. Christ's lonely journey into the ultimate stripping of death concerns them all, even to their weakness and their sin. He will not leave them, he will be with them as a leaven of healing and spirit-life. Let us listen to the terse narrative in the second Eucharistic Prayer:

> Before he was given up to death, a death he freely accepted,
> he took bread and gave you (Father) thanks.
> He broke the bread, gave it to his disciples and said:
> Take this, all of you and eat it:
> this is my body which will be given up for you.
> When supper was ended, he took the cup.
> Again he gave you thanks and praise,
> gave the cup to his disciples and said:
> Take this all of you and drink from it:
> this is the cup of my blood,
> the blood of the new and everlasting covenant.
> It will be shed for you and for all,

so that sins may be forgiven.

Do this in memory of me.

Friday

This is the meaning of my sacrifice, Jesus is saying, and this is the way you must follow if you are to love as I have loved, if you wish to enter into the life of the resurrection. Let us look at things very simply from this angle today, enumerating some of the qualities of life and love of which Christ gives us here the example. What are they?

- Liberty: with conscious freedom to give our life, the heart's choice beyond all exterior or interior constraint.
- Total gift: not this or that, but our life itself, all we have, be it but a widow's mite.
- Grateful acceptance: of our humanity and of all creation in a spirit of thanksgiving and of praise. We take the bread and wine that symbolise them and we give thanks.
- Sharing: we break the bread and we give it: the bread of our human lives, our hearts, our thoughts, our time, our dreams, our disappointments, our pain, our faults, our hopes. Take, eat, this is my body.
- Solidarity: this is my body given up for you. Christ took his place among us, as it were, beside us. He did not look down upon us from a position of invulnerable superiority, He accepted us, each and all as we are in

truth, and tied his lot to ours. So doing he could apply the healing gift of his Spirit to our very real wounds from within and restore us to God's friendship. "This is the cup of my blood, the blood of the new and everlasting covenant. It will be shed for you and for all, so that sins may be forgiven."

CONTINUES . . .

----------- *Week   Forty - four* -----------

Sunday

In this pardon, from this covenant, the Church and our community are born. Only in shared pardon and in communion with Christ can it continue to exist. In practice, this is a hard saying: it is not easy to accept a real solidarity with each and every one of my brothers, not only with the amenable, the gifted and the well-disposed towards me, but also with the less agreeable, the less gifted, the less well-disposed, even hostile. Or I accept only those parts of their personalities that I approve of, as if a person could be divided. It is hard not to exclude from our hearts through arrogance or defensiveness or judgement. We religious are far too prone to sit in judgement on others, even though we know in our hearts that we are no better ourselves. Let us learn of Christ to judge no one, to exclude no one, to accept as a precious gift each of our brothers and sisters. This is not "charity," it is their right in Christ. We must learn to suffer, not only from them, as may sometimes happen, but with them; to sustain them by our pardon, to carry them in our heart's prayer: to help them carry their cross, from which they are the first to suffer, rather than pharisaically to condemn their weaknesses. Community implies sacrifice, it is found in the cup of Christ's blood. Remember this when you drink the chalice. . . . Beyond any exterior thing, it lies, or so it seems to me, in this real solidarity in Christ's love. All the rest will follow.

And it is thus that we will know that we are risen in Christ, by the Spirit that has been poured out in our hearts, God's Life in our mortal veins. Already we are risen in Christ: in a hidden way, the eternal realities are present. Sacramentally we see them and in faith we try to live them. As in Christ's humanity the divinity was truly present but unseen to human eyes, so now is the life of the resurrection present in us, here and now to be lived, but under the veil of our humanity, shining obscurely through, often, in a strange way, through the wounds of our hearts.

We come back in full circle to the image of Christ crucified, but now transfigured, bearing the crown of his triumph, as the Eastern Fathers loved to portray him.

I wish you the fullness of his joy this day.

EASTER DAY, *THE SPIRIT OF THE PLACE*

Monday

East and West

Humanity is divided because man is divided in himself. The two great traditions of East and West stand as the two sides of understanding of man. So far these two traditions have grown independently with little relation beyond occasional rivalry. The time has come to integrate them.

In the West today the masculine aspect, the rational, the aggressive power of mind is dominant, while in the East the feminine aspect, the intuitive aspect of the mind prevails.

The future of the world depends on the "marriage" of these two minds, the conscious and the unconscious, the rational and the intuitive, the active and the passive. This "marriage" must take place first within the individual. Then only can external union take place.

BEDE GRIFFITHS,
THE UNIVERSAL CHRIST

Tuesday

Finding space

For anyone who is on a spiritual path, that is the path to God, there must be an element of renunciation in this life.

In India renunciation is seen as an essential part of spiritual growth and awakening. A man may leave his family at a certain stage of his life and go into the forest, there to find God within his soul. He gives up the comforts of life for a greater good. We do not need to follow this practice literally in order to find our "true selves," but we must be prepared to sacrifice legitimate things in order that we may find the space in which the spiritual life can blossom.

This is the way of the cross which leads to a kind of death and resurrection.

CONTINUES . . .

Wednesday

The universe within

There is a space within the heart in which all space is contained. Both heaven and earth are contained within. Fire, air, sun and moon, lightning and stars—everything exists within.

When we pass beyond the mind with its measuring faculties, with its categories of time and space, we find the very ground of the universe. There all things are not dead matter as Western science has told us for so long. They are life and intelligence.

Western man has been turning outwards to the world of senses for centuries and losing himself in outer space. The time has now come to turn inwards, to learn to explore the inner space within the heart, and to make that long and exciting journey to the Centre. Compared with this the exploration of the moon and planets is the play of children.

CONTINUES . . .

Thursday

Be still

Inner stillness is necessary if we are to be in perfect control of our faculties and if we are to hear the voice of the Spirit speaking to us.

There can be no stillness without discipline, and the discipline of external silence can help us towards that inner tranquillity which is at the heart of authentic religious experience.

In meditation we take steps to achieve this stillness. We quieten

our bodies and our emotions, then gradually allow the mind to become single-pointed.

Stillness within one individual can affect society beyond measure.

CONTINUES . . .

Friday

Making all things new

Jesus was a man in whom body and soul were pure instruments of
the indwelling spirit. In him human destiny has been fulfilled.

Whereas in the universe as we know it there is conflict at every
level, and body and soul are in conflict with one another, in Jesus
this conflict has been overcome. Body and soul have been restored
in unity with the spirit, and a power of unification has been released
into the world.

So we are able to see the death of Jesus and the free surrender
of his life on the cross to the Father as a cosmic event.

> Jesus said to his disciples:
> "I still have many things to say to you
> but they would be too much for you now.
> But when the Spirit of truth comes,
> he will lead you to the complete truth,
> since he will not be speaking from himself
> but will say only what he has learnt;
> and he will tell you of the things to come.
> He will glorify me,
> since all he tells you
> will be taken from what is mine.

Everything the Father has is mine;
that is why I said:
All he tells you
will be taken from what is mine."

JOHN 16:12–15

CONTINUES . . .

Saturday

The love of total surrender

Certain events, that is, the emergence of life on this planet, the awakening of consciousness in man, mark critical changes in the evolution of the world. The death of Jesus was an event of this kind.

It marked the point of transition of the human consciousness to the Divine, the point where the human being was totally surrendered, body and soul, to the divine Being. In this sense the death of Jesus can be called "a redemptive sacrifice"; it is an offering of human nature to the divine which "redeems," that is, restores human nature to its unity with the divine nature.

CONTINUES . . .

Week Forty-five

Sunday

True ecumenism

Christianity came out of the Semitic world of Jewish culture. Its teaching, definitions and thought were largely formed by Greek culture and philosophy. For nearly two thousand years the movement of the Church has been westwards.

The twentieth century has witnessed a powerful convergence of Western and Eastern cultures and this is profoundly affecting today's Church. Meditation, once thought to be the prerogative of the Eastern and non-Christian religions, has thus opened the door into a Christ-centred spirituality for thousands of Westerners.

The immanence of indwelling God always central to Eastern spirituality is now by many seen to be at one with the Pauline doctrine of "Christ in you, the hope of glory" (Eph. 3).

God is one. Knowledge of the one God comes to all human beings through the opening of the heart. This is the true ecumenism. It is the true interior religion of Christ for which today there is a great yearning.

BEDE GRIFFITHS, *THE UNIVERSAL CHRIST*

Monday

FRANCIS KLINE, O.C.S.O.

Opening the Monastery Gates

In the beginning, grace often acts upon a person in the way of an avalanche which at once overwhelms and forever qualifies the individual. Only time and reflection upon the event can clarify the experience and translate it into concepts about God and actions for God. At first the person is lifted up by undifferentiated feelings of grandeur which affect the senses and also inspire the mind. But almost immediately, the person feels an unworthiness as a sort of reality check upon the experience. When, after a bit, one's eyes become accustomed to the place and one is able to begin to see clearly the assembly and the hall, reflection is possible and time must be given to it. This explains the alteration between hearing the Word of God in the assembly and the dark pauses for reflection when all the groups of beings digest the Word of God in prayer. The constant return to and fro between time together and time apart becomes the norm for Christian liturgy. Only within this rhythm can the full impact of what has happened in the sacraments be absorbed.

FRANCIS KLINE, O.C.S.O., *LOVERS OF THE PLACE*

Tuesday

Somewhere during this event of the heavenly liturgy, our subject ceases to be just an individual and becomes part of one of the groups. Now he is a member of Christ's body, a member in such a way as to continue to make progress into the unknown realm of faith. This process of belonging is based on the dialectic of the inner world of spiritual growth and the outer world of Christian liturgy. It is accomplished by means of the Three Degrees of Truth, first formulated by Saint Bernard in the twelfth century. An ever-increasing self-knowledge of my issues, that is, my shadows and my sinful patterns, gradually gives way to a concomitant knowledge and appreciation of my neighbor's situation, which I presume must be similar to my own. Thus, knowledge and an inchoate compassion on myself naturally leads to an understanding and compassion toward my neighbor. The move to compassion takes sovereign place here, lancing the boils of my own jealousy and envy, calming my own fears and worries about the aggression of my neighbor. Suddenly, I can be at peace with myself because my fears about my neighbor have been dissolved.

CONTINUES . . .

Wednesday

I can now afford to go out of the castle without fretting over who will defend it while I am away. I can leave in order to meet the other person without fear of any advantage the other may take of me. Ironically, my own castle grows and prospers even while I am away. At this point in the process, I begin to notice the Lamb in the center, the Truth in itself. Knowing my own truth and that of my neighbor, I can now view for the first time the ultimate Truth as it is in itself. Worship takes on new dimensions. Anything I thought I was given of myself in compassion towards my neighbor I now receive back many times over as I worship the Lamb and as the light and warmth of his divinity play over me. I become aware of the person of the Word, his incarnation and the human instruments by which he came to us. Their flesh which beheld him first is still the best filter for our eyes to see him, as the theology of the East constantly proclaims in their churches. Yet, in the sacrament, he is revealed to the heart without mediation. Still, the heart must grow in its capacity to receive him. Only the constant application of the Spirit's gifts in the hearing and doing of the word can open the heart to move from graces momentarily received to true and lasting growth in God's own life. This is the true content of faith.

CONTINUES . . .

Thursday

The colors of their garments

The groupings of beings [within this great building that is the Church] show how they have received the theological virtue of faith by the colors of their garments. These not only identify their place in the Church, but also their reception of that designation. As the sacraments feed them with the life of God, their activity in the Church increases. Their song grows fuller and their garments grow richer in color because of the gifts of the Spirit which exercise their hearts. So the interchange between the promptings of the Spirit and the growth in the content of their faith result in the holiness of their lives. The various colors exhibited in the assembly demonstrate the complexity of God's life among his people, with all their diverse roles and occupations. His revelation spreads throughout the human spectrum to include the married, unmarried, the vowed and the non-vowed, the professional and the laborer, the professional religious and the lay person. All are called to holiness, because all are taught by God. None was rejected by Jesus in his public ministry. We can delve further into this mystery by considering the apparent washout on color in the assembly where the monastics are found.

CONTINUES . . .

Friday

The monastics seem pale in comparison with the others. They are positioned in the places under the windows with clear glass. If the sun should ever move past these windows, the monastics would have to take it full in the face. And, in fact, this happens at one point during the heavenly liturgy. All had to shield their eyes when the uncircumscribed light pierced the hall. What does the paleness and neglect of light signify? And will it indicate what the explosion of light might mean?

The paleness of their robes indicates the quieting of apostolic activity among the monastics. It is to be assumed that, while their gifts were being developed and the spiritual life was growing in content, their robes had enjoyed a deeper hue. But now, a deeper action of God's has begun to empty out their former richness. We may call it the movement into hope, where a purification must occur on the way to love.

The richness of the monastic tradition took centuries to mature. All the possible applications of the virtues of faith, hope and love to every possible variation of culture, human ability and variety have resulted in charisms of incredible versatility. The monastic tradition has seen and done almost everything in its long history. Its most lasting achievement, however, has been to chart the royal way of holiness for the entire Church. When others were busy preaching the gospel to foreign lands and building up the fabric of social concern in the West, the monastics remained hidden in their cloisters, living the gospel among themselves in controlled conditions, as they had been called to do. . . . This intentional atmosphere allowed them the freedom to develop the full use of the gifts of the Spirit for the sake of growth in the life of God, that is, in faith, hope and love.

CONTINUES . . .

Saturday

The classic three stages

The living of the gospel can be put on gradually like a garment. But it has its own internal order and structure. This structure has been best described in three stages which the tradition has identified and never wavered from, although there are differences in the accidentals of it. These are faith, hope and love, or the stages of striving, proceeding and possession, or the stages of purgation, progress and union. They are not mere descriptions of the life of God acting in the person, but are guideposts on the way to a complete identification with God. For these three virtues or stages have as their goal the transformation of the human person into Christ. While they are always active in whatever order in the life of grace by the reception of the sacraments and virtuous living, they are only transformational, that is fully effective, in their proper order. A person may live for long years in the realm of faith before moving slowly on to hope and love. While it is possible to slip out of one of these stages back below to the introductory stages, it is more than likely that God will preserve on in full faith and move that person on to hope and to love, according to his good pleasure.

CONTINUES . . .

Week Forty-six

Sunday

Faith put to the test

First is faith, when, after a certain discipline and observance of rules, the person begins to accept the first participation in the life of God. This faith is never achieved without living through the *dura et aspera* [when the going gets tough] of the spiritual journey. Here all the waywardness of the human heart must be confronted and expelled, at least to the point where a certain constancy can be lived. God, who is never compelled to act upon us, waits until the soil of the human heart is plowed enough for him to plant his seed, and for the subsequent grain to spring up and grow into food for others.

The terrain of faith is wide and broad, with many varied features in the landscape. Here, the outward apostolic life flourishes, gifts of preaching and teaching are perfected, the moral life is deepened as all the disparate elements of the heart gradually coalesce into a single focus of commitment. When the seed of faith has been sufficiently matured, and when the human person has lived all its effects for the time that God judges to be fitting, then God begins to act further on the person by testing one's resolve by the withdrawal of consolation or by the emptying out of gifts, or if not the emptying, then the removal of the reward from them that one formerly enjoyed. Jesus described this journey from faith to hope very frequently in his teaching. The Lukan Beatitudes (Luke 6:20–26) can serve as an example.

FRANCIS KLINE, O.C.S.O., *LOVERS OF THE PLACE*

Monday

DAVID STEINDL-RAST

The surprise of life

A close brush with death can trigger that surprise. For me, that came early in life. Growing up in Nazi-occupied Austria, I knew air raids from daily experience. And an air raid can be an eye-opener. One time, I remember, the bombs started falling as soon as the warning sirens went off. I was on the street [a boy of twelve]. Unable to find an air raid shelter quickly, I rushed into a church only a few steps away. To shield myself from shattered glass and falling debris, I crawled under a pew and hid my face in my hands. But as bombs exploded outside and the ground shook under me, I felt sure that the vaulted ceiling would cave in any moment and bury me alive. Well, my time had not yet come. A steady tone of the siren announced that the danger was over. And there I was, stretching my back, dusting off my clothes, and stepping out into a glorious May morning. I was alive. Surprise! The buildings I had seen less than an hour ago were now smoking rubble. But that there was anything at all struck me as an overwhelming surprise. My eyes fell on a few square feet of lawn in the midst of all this destruction. It was as if a friend had offered me an emerald in the hollow of his hand. Never before or after have I seen grass so surprisingly green.

BROTHER DAVID STEINDL-RAST, *GRATEFULNESS, THE HEART OF PRAYER*

Tuesday

Alive

The fact that you are not yet dead is not sufficient proof that you are alive. It takes more than that. It takes courage—above all, the courage to face death. Only one who is alive can die. Aliveness is measured by the ability to die. One who is fully alive is fully able to die. In the peak moments of aliveness we are reconciled with death. Deep down within us something tells us that we would die the moment our life reached fulfillment. It is fear of death that prevents us from coming fully alive.

CONTINUES . . .

Wednesday

Peak experience

Abraham Maslow, who put the Peak Experience on the map of psychology, insisted that it could in no way be distinguished from mystic experience as described by the mystics. And yet, most (if not all) of us have Peak Experiences, moments in which we are overwhelmed by a sense of belonging, of universal wholeness and holiness, moments in which everything makes sense. Acceptance is a word often used in describing Peak Experiences. For a moment that seems outside time, we feel fully accepted and can fully accept all that is. Gratefulness pervades every aspect of these peaks. The religiousness at the core of a person's religion is fueled by those moments of overwhelming gratefulness. One's religion is seen as valid in the light of those experiences of heightened awareness. It is measured by standards glimpsed from those peaks of grateful acceptance. That is why we can call gratefulness the root of religion.

BROTHER DAVID STEINDL-RAST, *GRATEFULNESS, THE HEART OF PRAYER*

Thursday

I did not find him

On my bed, at night, I sought him
whom my heart loves.
I sought but did not find him.
So I will rise and go through the City;
in the streets and the squares
I will seek him whom my heart loves.
. . . I sought but did not find him.

SONG OF SONGS 3

Friday

Prayers and prayerfulness

Sooner or later we discover that prayers are not always prayer. That is a pity. But the other half of that insight is that prayer often happens without any prayers. And that should cheer us up. In fact, it is absolutely necessary to distinguish between prayer and prayers. At least if we want to do what Scripture tells us to do and "pray continually" (Luke 18:1), we must distinguish praying from saying prayers. Otherwise, to pray continually would mean saying prayers uninterruptedly day and night. We need hardly think to realize that this would not get us very far. If, on the other hand, prayer is simply communication with God, it can go on continually. In peak moments of awareness this communication will be more intense, of course. At other times it will be low key. But there is no reason why we should not be able to communicate with God in and through everything we do or suffer and so "pray without ceasing" (I Thes. 5:17).

Maybe I shouldn't have mentioned uninterrupted prayer at all. The very thought may seem overawing and scare someone off. Many of us might, in fact, say: "Praying at all times? Goodness! From where I find myself it would be a long way even to praying at those times when I am saying my prayers!" All right, then, let us start once again where we are. What is it that makes our prayers truly prayer? If only we could somehow catch on to the secret of that spontaneous prayerfulness. That would be the clue to praying when we are saying prayers. Eventually it may even lead to praying at all times.

BROTHER DAVID STEINDL-RAST,

GRATEFULNESS, THE HEART OF PRAYER

Saturday

The eye wherein I see God is the same eye wherein God sees me.

MEISTER ECKHART

It is no mere coincidence that the personal pronoun "I" in the English language cannot be distinguished by its sound from the word "eye" for the organ of sight. This adds an additional layer of meaning to Eckhart's famous saying "The eye by which I see God is the very eye by which God sees me."

When we understand our I in this sense, we give it its deepest meaning and escape from the prison of the individualistic little self.

BROTHER DAVID STEINDL-RAST,

GRATEFULNESS, THE HEART OF PRAYER

Week Forty-seven

Sunday

The guardian of Israel
I lift my eyes to the mountains:
Where is help to come from?
Help comes to me from Yahweh,
who made heaven and earth.

PSALM 121

Monday

God

Since this book is based on experience and appeals to experience, God comes in as basic to everyone's experience, and only under this aspect. "Restless is our heart." This is a basic fact of human experience. Saint Augustine continues the sentence: "Restless is our heart until it rests in God." But this does not mean that we first know God, so that our thirst for God is one among various things worth mentioning. Rather, all we know at first is the restlessness of our heart. And to the direction of our restless yearning, we give the name God. By pooling insights gained by the heart, we can come to know a little bit about God, especially when we listen to great explorers into God. Yet, what matters is never knowledge *about* God, but knowledge of God—as the magnetic North of the human heart.

BROTHER DAVID STEINDL-RAST,

GRATEFULNESS, THE HEART OF PRAYER

Tuesday

Heart

Whenever we speak of the heart, we mean the whole person. Only at heart are we whole. The heart stands for that center of our being where we are one with ourselves, one with all others, one with God. The heart is ever restless in its quest for God, and yet, deep down, it is ever at home in God. To live from the heart means to live out of the fulness of this longing and belonging. And that means to live fully.

BROTHER DAVID STEINDL-RAST,

GRATEFULNESS, THE HEART OF PRAYER

Wednesday

A prayer in trouble
In you, Yahweh, I take shelter;
never let me be disgraced.

In your righteousness rescue me, deliver me,
turn your ear to me and save me!
Be a sheltering rock for me,
a walled fortress to save me!
For you are my rock, my fortress.
My God, rescue me from the hands of the wicked,
from the clutches of the tyrant!

PSALM 71

Thursday

Authority

For a long time now, our society seems to have had a blind spot regarding authority. We blindly assume that human beings are by nature resistant against external authority. The opposite is true. The average person is excessively prone to yield to the pressure of external authority, even when it conflicts with the inner authority of one's conscience. Examples are the atrocity committed by ordinary citizens in Nazi Germany and other dictatorships, or the widespread submission to peer pressure in every society. Given this human weakness, the task of external authority is not to entrench and enforce itself, but rather to build up the inner authority responsibly by constantly encouraging those subject to it to stand on their own two feet. Putting words in print gives them an appearance of authority. This book appeals to one authority only: the reader's own experiences of the heart. This appeal is a twofold one. It is a question and a challenge. The question is: Does this ring true to your heart's experience? The challenge is: wake up and allow your heart to experience the full range of reality.

DAVID STEINDL-RAST *GRATEFULNESS, THE HEART OF PRAYER*

Friday

Becoming

All we know of being is becoming. Being alive, being grateful, means becoming alive, becoming grateful. Being human means becoming what we are. If you stopped becoming, you would cease to be. Yet, in the process of becoming you cease to be what you were. T. S. Eliot says:

> In order to arrive at what you are not
> You must go through the way in which you are not.

The movement of life is the process of becoming. Yet, in this process being and non-being, fullness and emptiness are inextricably one. Remembering this may save us from speaking too glibly about the fullness of life.

CONTINUES . . .

Saturday

Death

In death, two events happen at once: being killed and dying. Nothing is more passive than being killed, even if it's merely old age that kills one. But nothing is more active than dying. The verb "dying" does not even have a passive voice. I can say "I'm being killed," but I can't say "I'm being died." Being dyed would make me colorful, not dead. Dying is something I must do. It can't happen unless I give myself willingly to change. I die to what I was and come alive to what I will be. Every moment is, in this sense, a dying into life. Being afraid of death would mean being afraid of life. Learning to die means learning to live.

CONTINUES . . .

─────── *Week Forty-eight* ───────

Sunday

Divine life

To speak of divine life as something we know from experience may seem presumptuous. But it would be even more presumptuous to speak about it without knowing it. We either know something by experience, or we do not really know it. There are moments when, altogether gratuitously, we get an inkling of the ground of our being. We realize that we are both at home there and on the way there. Some are bold enough to call this starting point and goal of our heart's journey "God." Nothing else deserves this name. We can call the two poles of this experience God's immanence (closer to me than I am to myself) and God's transcendence (beyond the beyond). If God were merely transcendent, it would indeed be presumptuous to claim any knowledge of God. But a transcendence worthy of God must be so transcendent that it transcends our logical limits of transcendence and is, therefore, perfectly compatible with God's immanence. Would it not be presumptuous to deny this? The fact that I am not simply God needs little proof. And yet, according to Piet Hein,

> Who am I
> To deny

That, maybe,
God is me?

CONTINUES . . .

Monday

Mystic experience

If we think of it as an experience of communion with Ultimate
Reality, we have a fair working definition of mystic experience. We
will do well not to introduce the term "God" into our definition.
Not all people feel comfortable calling "Ultimate Reality" God. But
all of us, regardless of terminology, can experience moments of universal communion. Those are our own mystic moments. The men
and women we call mystics differ from the rest of us merely by giving these experiences the place they deserve in everyone's life.
What counts is not the frequency or intensity of mystic experiences,
but the influence we allow them to have on our life. By accepting
our mystic moments with all they offer and demand, we become the
mystics we are meant to be. After all, a mystic is not a special kind
of human being, but every human being is a special kind of mystic.

CONTINUES . . .

Tuesday

Jesus Christ

In speaking not merely of Jesus, or merely of Christ, but of Jesus
Christ, we stress the tension between two points of reference. One
is in time: the historic Jesus. The other is timeless: the Christ-reality
in him and in all of us. We must maintain the creative tension be-

tween these two aspects, for if we allow it to snap, our relationship to Jesus Christ will be polarized. We will either be unable to look beyond the historic frame of reference, or else run the risk of losing our historic anchorage altogether. The historic Jesus provides an objective standard for the life of Christians. This prevents their awareness of the Christ within them from drifting off into mere subjectivity. Yet the historic Jesus is merely one point of reference in a genuine encounter with Jesus Christ. The other is expressed in the words, "Christ lives in me" (Gal. 2:20).

CONTINUES . . .

~

Wednesday

Communication

Although communication is basic to our world, most people have a crippled notion of how it works. They realize that communication aims at communion (mutual understanding, a sense of community, common action). But they fail to see that communion is not only the fruit, but the root of communication. Unless we have already something in common before we start to communicate, communication is impossible. Of course, our common ground expands as we build on it and is enriched in the process. We know that communication broadens and deepens communion. What we tend to forget is that communication also presupposes communion. We need at least the basics of a common language before we can begin to communicate. There could be no communication across the gap of an absolute vacuum. Fortunately, there is no such gap anywhere. At heart, everything hangs together with everything. All communication is rooted in this most basic communion. This insight becomes relevant when we conceive of prayer as communication with God. If there is a gap, God is on our side before we ever start to bridge it. Or, as Thomas Merton put it, prayer does not consist in an effort to get across to God, but in opening our eyes to see that we are already there.

CONTINUES . . .

Thursday

Sin

In our day and age, the word "sin" is so prone to be misunderstood that it has become quite useless. The reality once called sin is still with us, however, so that our times had to find its own term for it. What other ages called sin, we call alienation. Living language hit upon an apt word here. Alienation suggests an uprootedness from one's true self, from others, from God (or whatever else ultimately matters), and all this with one word. The word "sin," too, suggests uprooting and separation. It is related to the word "asunder." Sin tears asunder the wholeness in which all belongs together. Sin alienates. An action is sinful to the degree to which it causes alienation. Without alienation there is no sin. Drawing the consequences could prove liberating for many, indicting for others. It could mean a significant shift of emphasis in ethics from a preoccupation with private perfection to social responsibility. It could help us see that in our time "working out our salvation" means overcoming alienation in all its forms. The path from alienation to belonging is the path from sin to salvation.

CONTINUES . . .

Friday

Silence

There is a negative meaning to silence and a positive one. Negatively, silence means the absence of sound or word. In these pages we focus on its positive meaning. Silence is a matrix from which the word is born, the home to which word returns through understanding. Word (in contrast to chatter) does not break the silence. In a genuine word, silence comes to word. In genuine understanding, word comes home into silence. For those who know only the world of words, silence is mere emptiness. But our silent heart knows the paradox: the emptiness of silence is inexhaustibly rich; all the words in the world are merely a trickle of its fullness.

BROTHER DAVID STEINDLE-RAST,

GRATEFULNESS, THE HEART OF PRAYER

Saturday

Making links
Having become familiar with this book over the weeks and months, readers will begin to make links between different readings across the centuries. Not merely will they see connections for themselves between this reading and that, they will also link these with other material of their own. This final section offers examples of such links and how they come about. But, necessarily, all such connections remain highly personal.

Gazing at the Light that never changes
And then I was brought up short so that I returned to my true self.

With you as my guide I entered the depths of my soul;
I could only do so because you were my helper (Ps. 30:10).

And as I entered so I saw, with the eye of my soul, such as it was, and far beyond the eye of my soul, even above my whole mind, and I was gazing at the Light that never changes.
No ordinary light which we may see day by day; nor was it the same only far brighter, capable somehow to fill the whole universe with its light.
No, this was no such a light, but another far removed from all earthly light.

And it shone above my mind, not as oil will float upon water, nor even as the heavens arch themselves above the earth.
Simply, it was above my soul because it made me;
I was below, since I was made by it.

All who know truth, know this Light at once for what it is; and all who see this Light know eternity. And love alone may see this Light.

FROM AUGUSTINE'S CONFESSIONS (CF. WEEK THIRTEEN, SATURDAY)

--------- *Week Forty-nine* ---------

☞

Sunday

JULIAN OF NORWICH

And so it is that in our making God almighty is Father of our substance; and God all wisdom is Mother of our substance; with the love and the goodness of the Holy Spirit; which is all one God, one Lord. In the knitting and the oneing he is our very own spouse, as we are his beloved wife and fair maiden; with his own wife he may never be displeased. For he says as much: "I am loving you, and you are loving me: and our loving shall never be parted in two."

JULIAN OF NORWICH, *REVELATION OF LOVE*, TRANS. JOHN SKINNER

Monday

I beheld the working of all the blessed Trinity, and in this beholding I saw and understood these three properties: the property of fatherhood, the property of motherhood, and the property of the lordship in one God. In our Father all mighty we have our keeping and our bliss as regards our human substance, which is ours by our making without beginning. And in the Second Person, in wit and wisdom, we have our keeping as regards our sensuality, our restoring and our saving: for he is our mother, brother and saviour. And in our good lord the Holy Spirit we have our rewarding and our recompense for our living and our labours which will far exceed anything we can desire, due to his marvellous courtesy and his high plenteous grace.

For our whole life is in three.[17] In the first we have our being, and in the second we have our increasing, and in the third we have our fulfilling. The first is kind, the second is mercy and the third is grace. In the first, I saw and understood that the high might of the Trinity is our Father; and the deep wisdom of Trinity is our Mother; and the great love of the Trinity is our Lord: and all this we have and own in our natural kind and in the making of our substance.

CONTINUES . . .

---

[17] In one of her finest chapters Julian is boldly wrestling with the unsayable: how the economy of the Trinity impinges upon our reality and our experience of that reality.

Tuesday

And more than this, I saw that the Second Person, who is mother of our substance, the same most dear Person is become our mother sensual. For we are doubly of God's making: that is to say, substantial and sensual. It is our substance that is the higher part, this we have in our Father, God all mighty; and the second person of the Trinity is mother in nature, in our substantial making, in whom we are grounded and rooted; and he is also our mother in mercy in taking our sensuality. And so our mother works in diverse ways for us, so that our parts are held together. For in our mother Christ we profit and increase as in mercy he reforms and restores us, while, by the power of his passion and his death and rising, he ones us to our substance. And so our mother works in such a merciful way with all his children making them buxom and obedient.

And grace works alongside mercy, that is to say in two properties as was shown; as for this working, it belongs to the third person, the Holy Spirit. He works by rewarding and giving: rewarding is a generous gift of truth which the lord gives to those who have laboured; while giving is a courteous working which he freely performs by his grace, overpassing all that a creature deserves.

CONTINUES . . .

Wednesday

Thus in our Father, God all mighty, we have our being; and in our Mother of mercy we have our reforming and restoring, and in whom our parts are oned and we all made perfect Man; and by the recompense and giving in grace of the Holy Spirit we are fulfilled. And our substance is our Father, God all mighty, and our substance is our Mother, God of all wisdom, and our substance is in our lord the Holy Spirit, God of all goodness; yet our substance is whole in each person of the Trinity, which is one God. While our sensuality is only in the second person, Christ Jesus, yet in Him is the Father and the Holy Spirit. And in him and by him we are mightily taken out of hell and out of this wretchedness on earth, and gloriously brought up into heaven and blissfully oned to our substance, with every increase in riches and nobility, all by the power of Christ and by the grace and working of the Holy Spirit.

A REVELATION OF LOVE, CHAP. 58

Thursday

JOHN OF THE CROSS

To keep the [Carmelite] sisters going while he was away, John wrote cards for each of them. One which he spread fairly widely (he made an estimated sixty copies) was a sketch of a mountain, with wide paths leading to dead ends, and one narrow path going direct to the summit. On the central path is the word *"nada"*— "nothing." It is repeated all the way up—*nada, nada, nada, nada, nada, nada,* and on the broad, spacious, sunkissed summit, *nada:* "Here there is no road, because for the just there is no law; she is her own law."

This "nothing" gets developed in the longer writings.

> To come to savor all
>   seek to find savor in nothing;

to come to possess all,

 seek possession in nothing

to come to what you know not

 you must come by a way you know not . . .

to come to what you are not

 you must go by a way where you are not.

Friday

This then is one image for "progress": ascent. The image is demanding, radical, all-embracing. Here we come close to the gospel Jesus who asks for everything and evidently believes he is worth such a price. We come close to the essence of loving, which, unless its dynamic is frustrated, will tend towards totality.

At the same time, it is important to understand the "nothing" correctly. Here are some of the things it is not saying:

"Christian progress means forsaking whatever gives joy." Of course not.

"Christian progress means striving for perfection." Not quite this either, though John can use the word.

Apart from the fact that John intends to open a path to joy, and that his priority is not self-realisation (perfection), but relationship (union), a view of the journey from those perspectives would suggest that Christianity is one more test of excellence, which, in exalting the prima donna, tells the majority not to bother auditioning. If God is so far away, and it is so hard, better to let the demands of the gospel, and its promise, slip off into the shadows.

Trying again, "Christian progress means: searching for the one who is giving joy to my life, who seems to believe in me, who makes me alive. When I am with him, every moment is a discovery; and being without him is like dying."

This is, partly, what John is saying. That is why he writes, first, poetry, and why his poems relish the image of the lover's quest. Beloved—you wounded me—I went out—you were gone . . .

If progress is an ascent, then it is not the lonely labor of the athletic Christian. John steps out with vigor because the Other's love has "wounded" him, and there can now be only one thing to care about.

Ascent; lover's quest, but both belong to one family of images, where the onus is on the person to take the steps towards the encounter.

CONTINUES . . .

☙

Saturday

However, another kind of image is primary. We have seen it already in the symbol, "flame." In this case, it is the flame that does the entering; and the essential activity belongs, not to us, but to the Other, to "the Spirit of her Bridegroom." In the *Living Flame* the entry is unimpeded and incandescent. Previously, as John portrays the journey, the approach felt more aggressive—like fire burning into wood, first making it sputter and steam, blacken and crackle, until the wood itself becomes flame. But whether the flame is purifying or glorifying, it is the same "fire of love" that is approaching, entering.

This thrust keeps recurring: sunlight shining, eyes gazing, a mother feeding, water flowing, images of a God who initiates and invades. In this family of images, the emphasis is not on our forging a way, but on our getting out of the way. Progress will be measured, less by ground covered, more by the amount of room God is given to manoeuvre. "Space," "emptiness," are key words; or, as John puts it, *nada*.

CONTINUES . . .

Sunday

This is what gets a person up the mountain. It has to be so. If John's writing springs from the impact of an invasive God, lavish in bestowing himself "wherever he finds space," the only meaningful kind of asceticism would be the kind that clears the ground to make way for the onrush. All John has to say about our task must be interpreted in this light.

Writing [to his nuns], John speaks of people who "do not stay empty, so that God might fill them with his ineffable delight; so they leave God just as they came—their hands were already full, and they could not take what God was giving. God save us from such unhappy burdens which keep us from such far and wholesome freedom!"

Hands empty and cupped to receive what God is giving: that does evidently depend on John's first word, a self-giving God. Otherwise, space just leaves you with space. *Nada* would be a sad word pronounced on its own. Instead, it is blessed because it always announces the presence of an "everything" being given in exchange.

So it is with John's sketch of the mountain, the summit is a huge space—"and on the mountain nothing"—because it holds a total Presence: "On this mountain dwells only the honor and glory of God."

"For the soul: all things are nothing to her. In her eyes, she herself is nothing. For her, only her God is everything."

This emptiness is gospel, not law; poetry, not prose. It is welcome to a God who is coming in to fill.

IAIN MATTHEW, *THE IMPACT OF GOD*

Monday

The "J" Account of Creation

Although Moses is credited as author of Genesis, scholars now accept that it is an amalgam of four documents. The "J" source, in which God is named Yahweh, is the most ancient, belonging to the ninth century, when it was first committed to writing in Judah.

The Lord God said, "It is not good that the man should be alone. I will make him a helper as his partner." So out of the ground the Lord God formed every animal of the field and every bird of the air, and brought them to the man to see what he would call them; and whatever the man called each living creature, that was its name. The man gave names to all cattle, and to the birds of the air, and to every animal of the field; but for the man there was not found a helper as his partner. So the Lord God caused a deep sleep to fall upon the man, and he slept; then he took one of his ribs and closed up its place with flesh. And the rib that the Lord God had taken from the man he made into a woman and brought her to the man.

Tuesday

EDITH STEIN (1891–1942)

"How I came to the Cologne Carmel"

December 18, 1938

Perhaps I shall leave this house soon after Christmas. The circumstances which have forced us to initiate my transfer to Echt [Holland] are strikingly reminiscent of the situation at the time of my entrance to Carmel. It is likely that there is a subtle connection between the two.

When the Third Reich was established early in the year 1933, I had been an instructor at the German Institute for Scientific Pedagogy in Münster, Westphalia for about a year. I lived in the "Collegium Marianum" amidst a large number of nuns who were students and who belonged to the most divers orders as well as a small group of other women students, lovingly taken care of by the Sisters of Our Lady.

One evening during the vacation I returned late from a meeting of the Society of Catholic Academics. I don't know whether I had forgotten to take my key or whether there was a key stuck in the lock from the inside. At any rate, I could not get in. . . . A passerby asked whether he could help me. When I turned to him, he bowed deeply and said, "Dr. Stein, I didn't recognize you." He was a teacher at the Institute. He excused himself for a moment to tell his wife and then returning said: "My wife would like to invite you to spend the night at our house."

[Returning to their home] the man began to relate what American newspapers had reported concerning cruelties to which Jews had been subjected. They were unconfirmed reports; and so I do not wish to repeat them. I am only interested in the impression I got that evening. True, I had heard of rigorous measures against the Jews before. But now a light dawned in my brain that once again God has put a heavy hand upon his people and that the fate of this people would also be mine.

AUTOBIOGRAPHICAL NOTES
WRITTEN TWO WEEKS
BEFORE FLEEING GERMANY

Wednesday

On Thursday of Passion week, I traveled to [the Benedictine monastery of] Beuron. Since 1928 I had spent that week and the Easter holiday there each year and had quietly held my own private retreat. This time a special reason drew me there. During the past weeks I had constantly given thought to whether I could do something about the plight of the Jews. Finally I had made a plan to travel to Rome and to ask the Holy Father in a private audience for an encyclical. But I did not want to take such a step on my own. Years ago I had taken private vows. Since I had found a kind of monastic home in Beuron, I was permitted to regard Archbishop Raphael [Abbot of Beuron] as "my abbot" and to put before him all important problems for his judgement. It was not certain, however, that I would find him there. In early January he had gone on a trip to Japan. But I knew he would do his utmost to be home during Passion week.

Although it suited my nature to make such an overt move, I sensed that this was not "of the essence." But I did not yet know what this "essence" really was. I interrupted my travels in Cologne from Thursday afternoon until Friday morning. I was instructing a catechumen there, and had to devote some time to her at every possible opportunity. I wrote and asked her to find out where we could attend the Holy Hour in the evening. It was the eve of the first Friday of April, and in this Holy Year, 1933 [celebrated as the nineteen hundredth anniversary of Christ's death], the memory of the Passion of our Lord was being observed with particular solemnity everywhere.

CONTINUES . . .

Thursday

The fate of the Jews

At eight o'clock in the evening, we arrived for the Holy Hour at the Carmel Cologne—Lindental. A priest gave a homily and announced that from then on this worship service would be held there every Thursday. He spoke beautifully and movingly, but something other than his words occupied me more intensely. I talked with the Savior and told him that I knew that it was his cross that was now being placed upon the Jewish people; that most of them did not understand this, but that those who did, would have to take it up willingly in the name of all. I would do that. He should only show me how. At the end of the service, I was certain that I had been heard. But what this carrying of the cross was to consist in, that I did not yet know.

Next morning I continued my trip to Beuron. When I changed trains that evening I met Dom Aloys Mager and learned that Father Archabbot had returned. . . . So that, too, was in order.

Through my inquiries in Rome I ascertained that because of the tremendous crowds I would have no chance for a private audience. At best I might be admitted to a "semi-private audience," i.e., in a small group. That did not suit my purpose. I abandoned my travel plans and instead presented my request in writing. I know that my letter was delivered to the Holy Father [Pius XI] unopened; some time thereafter I received this blessing for myself and my relatives. Nothing else happened. Later on I often wondered whether this letter might have come to his mind once in a while. For in the years that followed, that which I had predicted for the future of the Catholics in Germany came true step by step.

CONTINUES . . .

Friday

My last day at home was October 12, my birthday. It coincided with a Jewish holiday, the end of the Feast of Tabernacles. My mother attended services in the synagogue of the rabbinical seminary. I accompanied her, because we wanted to spend as much of this day together as possible. Erika's favorite teacher, an eminent scholar, gave a beautiful sermon. On the way there on the trolley we had not talked very much. In order to comfort her a little, I had said that at first there would be a probationary period. But that was no help.

"If you take on a probationary period, I know you will pass."

Now my mother asked to walk home, a distance of about forty-five minutes, and this at eighty-four years of age! But I had to consent, for I knew well that she wanted to talk with me undisturbed a little longer.

"Wasn't it a beautiful sermon?"

"Yes, it was."

"It's possible then to be devout as a Jew also?"

"Certainly, if one has not come to know anything else."

Now she replied, sounding desperate: "Why did you have to come to know it? I don't want to say anything against *him*. He may have been a very good man. But why did he make himself into God?"

Many visitors came that afternoon and evening; all the brothers and sisters, their children, my women friends. That was good, because it was distracting. But as one after the other said goodbye and left, it became difficult. Finally, my mother and I were left alone in the room. My sisters were still busy with dishwashing and cleanup. Then she covered her face with her hands and began to weep. I stood behind her chair and held her silvery head to my breast. Thus we remained for a long while, until she let me persuade her to go to bed. I took her upstairs and helped her undress, for the first time in my life. Then I sat on the edge of the bed till she herself sent me to bed. . . . I don't think either of us found any rest that night.

CONTINUES . . .

Saturday

I arrived in Cologne late at night. My godchild [her catechumenate who had now been received into the Church] had asked me to spend one more night at their house. I was not supposed to be received within the enclosure until the next day after Vespers.

In the morning I announced my arrival at the convent and was permitted to come to the grille for a welcome. Soon after lunch we were back again to attend Vespers in the chapel; first Vespers of the Feast of our Holy Mother [Saint Theresa of Ávila]. Earlier, while kneeling in the sanctuary, I heard someone whisper at the sacristy turn: "Is Edith outside?"

Then a bunch of big white chrysanthemums was delivered to

me. Teachers from the Palatinate had sent them in welcome. I was supposed to see the flowers before they were used to decorate the altar. After Vespers we were asked to have coffee. Then a lady arrived, who introduced herself as the sister of our dear Mother Teresa Renata [Prioress at Cologne and later Edith's biographer]. She asked which one of us was the postulant; she wanted to offer some encouragement. But there was no need of that. This sponsor and my godchild accompanied me to the door of the enclosure. At last it opened, and in deep peace I crossed the threshold into the House of the Lord.

"HOW I CAME TO THE COLOGNE CARMEL"

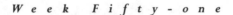

Week   Fifty-one

Sunday

Edith Stein wrote a number of poems, or verse meditations, which also carry a strongly autobiographical story, set as they are against the dark history of Nazi Germany.

Vineyard of Carmel

Come, love, to the vineyard
In the morning dew,
There we'll watch in silence,
If vineyards bloom anew,
If the grapes are growing,
Life with vigor glowing,
Fresh the vine and true.

From the heights of Heaven
Holy Mother descend,
Lead unto your vineyard
Our beloved friend.
Dew and rain let gently
Drop from his kind hand
And the balm of sunshine
Fall on Carmel's land.

Young vines, newly planted,
Tiny though they be,
Grant them life eternal
A gift of grace from thee.
Trusted vintners strengthen
Their frail and feeble powers,
Shield them from the enemy
Who in darkness cowers.

Monday

I shall stay with you . . .
Your throne is at the Lord's right hand,
Within the realm of his eternal glory,
God's word from when the world began.

You reign upon the highest throne of all,
Even in transfigured human form,
Since you fulfilled your task on earth.

So I believe, because your word has taught me,
And, thus believing, know that this delights me,
And blessed hope blooms out of it.

For where you are, there also are your dear ones.
And heaven is my glorious fatherland,
With you I share the Father's throne.

The Eternal One, creator of all being,
Who, holy thrice, encompasses all life,
Retains a quiet realm all to himself.

The inmost chamber of the human soul
Is favorite dwelling to the Trinity,
His heavenly throne right here on earth.

CORPUS CHRISTI, 1935

Tuesday

Aphorisms in the month of June 1940
The Lord is stomping grapes,
And blood-red is his gown.
He sweeps with broom of iron
Through hamlet and through town.
Proclaims in the storm's resounding
That he will come again,
We hear the awesome pounding.
Our Father alone knows when.

Within your heart lives peace eternal.
You want to pour it into our hearts.
And into each of them you want to flow,
But there's no opening where you can go.

When you knock gently, they give no ear.
A hammer's blows they will surely hear.
When the long night is past, morning will dawn,
In the painful labour your kingdom's born.

From night to light who'll be our guide?
How will the horror end?
Where will the sinners be justly tried,
When will our fortunes mend?

From the Mount of Olives his anguished plea
To the Father in heaven he hurled.
His agony gained him the victory,
Determined the fate of the world.
There prostrate yourselves and pray, and then
Ask no more: Who? How? Where? or When?

Judge not lest you be judged in turn,
Appearances cloud our view,
We guess at the truth, but only learn
God alone knows that is true.

Wednesday

He covers you with his feathers,
and you find shelter underneath his wings . . .
his faithfulness is shield and buckler.

PS. 91:4

Thursday

To God, the Father

Bless the mind deeply troubled
Of the sufferers,
The heavy loneliness of profound souls,
The restlessness of human beings,
The sorrow which no soul ever confides
To a sister soul.

And bless the passage of moths at night,
Who do not shun spectres on paths unknown.
Bless the distress of men
Who die within the hour,
Grant them, loving God, a peaceful, blessed end.

Bless all the hearts, the clouded ones, Lord, above all,
Bring healing to the sick.
To those in torture, peace.

Teach those who had to carry their beloved to the grave,
    to forget.
Leave none in agony of guilt on all the earth.

Bless the joyous ones, O Lord, and keep them under
    your wing—
My mourning clothes you never yet removed.
At times my tired shoulders bear a heavy burden.
But give me strength, and I'll bear it
In penitence to the grave.

Then bless my sleep, the sleep of all the dead.
Remember what your Son suffered for me in agony of
    death.
Your great mercy for all human needs
Give rest to all the dead in your eternal peace.

Friday

Pentecost, 1942

Who are you, sweet light that fills me
And illumines the darkness of my heart?
You guide me like another's hand.
And if you let me go, I could not take
Another step.
You are the space
That surrounds and contains my being.
Without you it would sink into the abyss
Of nothingness from which you raised it into being.
You, closer to me than I to myself,

More inward than my innermost being—
And yet unreachable, untouchable,
And bursting the confines of any name:

Holy Spirit—
Eternal love!

Rosa (1883–1942), an older sister of Edith, also became a Catholic after their mother had died; she was portress at Echt, the Carmel in Holland, where the sisters had transferred for greater security. In 1942, the Dutch bishops issued a public condemnation of Nazi treatment of the Jews: the German reaction was immediate and ruthless. All known Catholics of Jewish race were arrested. Rosa and Edith were apprehended on August 2, 1942: "Come, Rosa, we do this for our people," were Edith's final comforting words as they left Carmel. The two sisters perished together in Auschwitz probably one week later.

⌒

Saturday

A Carthusian Eucharist

Mass is always sung, using the ancient Latin plainsong version of the proper, yet the daily celebration remains starkly simple. The altar, a plain table at the head of the choir stalls, yet the focal point of the first part of the mass, the liturgy of the word, is centred on the reading lectern with the monks facing each other outwards in their stalls. As with everything Carthusian, both gesture and ritual are simple. But nothing can conceal that coming together in order to celebrate the Eucharist presents the sum total of their life aim. If the Carthusian seeks to be closer each day to the Father, modelling himself on Christ's life, this bread and wine is the very sustenance of his journey. More, the enactment of Christ's free gift of himself on Calvary is for the monk a source of wonder, of thanks and his consummate goal. There is no hiding the truth that, as the Carthusian is in love with God, this is where he finds him. Mass is unmistakably intimate and private although enacted by the whole community. Its central passage, the canon of the mass from the sanctus to the Pater Noster, is prayed in silence, the community at their stalls in upright prayer. At the moment of the consecration, all kneel. The Host is raised. High above the priest's head, a great brown numinous disc, wafted in real time while an age is held.

Now, as the priest reaches for the great silver goblet to take hold of its two side handles, each monk prostrates to lie upon his side in the Carthusian manner—an almost foetal tuck—while the chalice too is elevated unseen. His prayer to Christ might be the *Anima Christi*: those mediaeval words "In your own wounds hide me; never let me part from you. . . ."

JOHN SKINNER, HEAR OUR SILENCE

W e e k   F i f t y - t w o

Sunday

I was puzzled at the singing. Or lack of it. Gone was the bullish to and fro of the Night Office. Now all was diffidence and hanging back. The deputed cantor was left to carry the day.

Familiar with the first plainsong text, a votive mass of the Holy Name that was identical to the proper for the mass of Saint Ignatius, I joined in confidently on that second morning. The next day, was a mass of the dead with which once more I was familiar. And then it occurred to me that their style was not to "perform" so much as to pray the mass; it was not necessary to attempt a mass with choirs of the Rhondda Valley effect. Here it was different. We were in "real time," the time of birth and of death, when man finds his clock has ceased and he is without time as normally experienced but in this new, stretched moment. As more than one medieval hymn puts it, "thine age at mass shall not increase."

When we listen again to Christ's own words of promise, none of this can come as a surprise.

> "If you only knew what God is offering
> and who it is that is saying to you:
> Give me a drink,
> you would have been the one to ask,
> and he would have given you living water."   John 4:10

> "I tell you most solemnly,
> it was not Moses who gave you bread from heaven,
> it is my Father who gives you the bread from heaven,
> the true bread;
> for the bread of God
> is that which comes down from heaven
> and gives life to the world."   John 6:23

> "I tell you most solemnly,
> if you do not eat the flesh of the Son of Man
> and drink his blood,
> you will not have life in you.
> Anyone who does eat my flesh and drink my blood

has eternal life,
and I shall raise him up on the last day." John 6:52

JOHN SKINNER, *HEAR OUR SILENCE*

Monday

Homage

Holy Trinity,
one God,
receive the homage of our ministry.
We, your unworthy servants,
have offered to you this sacrifice of praise:
receive it, we pray,
and pour out on us
and on all those for whom we have offered it
your peace and joy
of eternal life.
In the name of the Father,
and of the Son, and of the Holy Spirit. Amen.

FROM THE CARTHUSIAN EUCHARIST

Tuesday

Making himself known by silence

Better be silent and be than speak without being. It is good to
teach, if the teacher acts on his own teaching. There is in fact but a
single master, one who spoke and at the same time was. What he accomplished in silence was worthy of his Father. He who truly pos-

sesses the word of Jesus can hear even his very silence; then he will
be perfect, acting by his word and making himself known by his
silence.

IGNATIUS OF ANTIOCH

Wednesday

You have only one physician,
for body and spirit alike,
born and unborn,
he is made flesh and he is God himself;
at the very heart of death, he is true life,
born of Mary, born of God,
at first subject to suffering,
but now beyond every pain:
he is none other than our Lord Jesus Christ.

CONTINUES . . .

Thursday

Do not allow anyone to lead you astray; moreover you must never
give way to betraying yourself, for you belong solely to God. If you
refuse any place for quarrelling among you, which might so easily
tear you apart, then you will truly live according to God.

All those who live according to the flesh cannot perform the
works of the spirit, and those who live according to the spirit cannot do deeds of the flesh (Rom. 8:4). In the same way, faith cannot
work with infidelity, nor can unbelief treat with faith. But even the

deeds you do that are of the body are deemed to be of the spirit: that
is because everything you do is done in the name of Jesus Christ.

IGNATIUS OF ANTIOCH

Friday

Therefore I prayed, and understanding was given me;
I called on God, and the spirit of wisdom came to me.
I preferred her to sceptres and thrones,
and I accounted wealth as nothing in comparison with
    her.
Neither did I liken to her any priceless gem,
because all gold is but a little sand in her sight.

WISDOM 7:7–9

Saturday

I did not find him
On my bed, at night, I sought him
whom my heart loves.
I sought but did not find him.
So I will rise and go through the City;
in the streets and the squares
I will seek him whom my heart loves.
. . . I sought but did not find him.

SONG OF SONGS 3

Who's Who

IGNATIUS OF ANTIOCH (35–107) Ignatius, who was born shortly after Christ's death, became a disciple of Saint John the apostle and later Bishop of Antioch. Arrested and put into chains, he was taken by ship along the coast of Asia Minor to his martyrdom in Rome. He wrote seven letters to the various churches along the route and they tell us a good deal about the customs and organization of the early Christian communities. His raw and passionate accounts of what it means to him to be a Christian are among the most moving documents in the entire archives of the Church. We begin and end our selection with his words.

SAINT IRENAEUS (C. 130–200) Bishop of Lyons and martyr, Irenaeus originated from Smyrna, where as a boy he heard Polycarp (the disciple of John) preach. Thus he was a bare two generations from Christ.

Having studied in Rome, he came to Lyons as a presbyter and was made bishop after the martyrdom of Pothinus.

Irenaeus had to suffer divisions within his church and persecution from without; his chief work, "Against Heretics," as its name implies, was an attempt to still the fierce debates. But it is also a vivid and highly original exposition of the early Christian understanding of the faith which remains as vibrant today as when it was first written.

THE LETTER TO DIOGNETUS This anonymous letter dates back to very early Christian times—probably the second, maybe the third century—when, to the inquiring outsider who receives the letter, the Christian way of life was still a mystery. The letter comes to us by means of a single thirteenth- or fourteenth-century MS which was itself lost when Strasbourg was torched in 1870, during the final stages of the Franco-Prussian War. It could have come from the hand of Quadratus, a bishop of Asia Minor, and may have been addressed to Hadrian when he was Emperor of the East. We shall never know. But to read so early an account of what the Christian way of life meant to believers then provides us with a good ground for heart searching about how we live out our Christian task today. If we listen keenly—with Diognetus—we may be able to find the simple, universal truth that is the shared birthright of all Christians.

SAINT CLEMENT OF ALEXANDRIA (C. 150–215) Probably Athenian by birth, Clement studied Christian theology and philosophy in several places before arriving at Alexandria to head up the catechetical school. Writing to explain early Christianity to non-Christians, he used their own language in a lyrical, poetic Greek style. He was succeeded by his brilliant young pupil, Origen.

ORIGEN (C. 185–C. 254) It would be hard to overemphasize Origen's influence upon the Patristic tradition: he is the source of spiritual themes and intuitions which the whole of Christendom continued to digest, develop, and correct for centuries after his death. One of his main themes was to reconcile the Jewish and Christian faiths by demonstrating that both Old and New Testaments told the same, continuous story: the journey of the People of God toward the fulfillment of his Covenant in Jesus Christ. But Origen was not merely a brilliant scholar, he was also an ardent follower of Christ: an early attempt as a boy to follow his father to martyrdom was only foiled by his mother hiding his clothes. Later he took the Gospel maxim about offending members literally and, tragically, mutilated himself.

He took over the catechetical school of Alexandria from his master Clement at the age of seventeen, continuing to teach for the next twenty-eight years. In 216, while visiting Palestine, Origen was invited to be ordained by the Bishop of Jerusalem. But this only caused trouble since his own bishop had not been consulted. Later he was deprived of his priesthood and forbidden to teach. Settling in Caesarea, he founded a school of letters, philosophy, and theology. Under the Emperor Decius persecutions began once more: Origen, now aged sixty, was imprisoned and tortured. Released after a year, he was now a broken man and died three years later.

SAINT CYPRIAN (D. 258) A pagan rhetorician, Cyprian became a Christian around 246 and within two years became Bishop of Carthage. He had few ambitions other than to study the Scriptures and the writings of his beloved master, Tertullian. Gentle Cyprian went into exile and ruled his see by letter; he finally returned to Carthage where he was martyred in 258. His commentary on the Lord's Prayer has remained a classic spiritual text since first it was written.

ANTONY ABBOT (250–353) Antony was the first of the Desert Fathers to draw other monks to him by reason of his immense courage and tenacity at living the ascetic life of the desert. When he at last came to die, he was over a hundred years of age; such was his fame throughout the Christian world that Athanasius of Alexandria, the great bishop who had tackled the Arian crisis, wrote his *Life of Antony Abbot* to be a model for the monks of the desert. His example was so magnetic that, rather like Thomas Merton in our day, a huge influx of young monks flocked to the desert in order to imitate his way of life.

THE JESUS PRAYER The earliest sources of this prayer go back to the Desert Fathers, where it appears to have provided the bedrock of a monk's daily prayer life. As a living tradition it has flourished far more in the Eastern Church, where it still has a central role today.

THE PHILOKALIA The Philokalia is a collection of spiritual writings of the Fathers from the earliest development of Christianity immediately following the Peace of Constantine in 313. It shows a way, the way toward God, the Way of Christ. And this art of arts and science of sciences—as it was declared to all who would listen—would take a man to the highest levels of perfection. Its simplest and most effective form, it was claimed, lay in the practise of the Jesus Prayer.

SAINT BASIL, "THE GREAT" (330–379) Basil, known as the Great, is the first of the three Cappadocian Fathers of the Church who were so influential in bringing Christianity to Asia Minor and imparting both unity and a deeper understanding of the Christian faith to the Church at large. Together with his brother, Gregory of Nyssa, and the great orator Gregory of Nazianzus, whom he met and befriended while they were both studying as young men in Athens, he established a vigorous network of Christian communities in Cappadocia together with a flourishing monastic movement. This was fully two centuries before Benedict was to follow his example in the West. Basil—who wrote two sets of Rules for his monks—is considered to be father of Eastern monasticism as is Benedict in the West.

Two hallmarks of Basil's teaching are his constant insistence that God is always beyond our understanding and that the Holy Spirit acts in each one of us in a completely different manner.

SEVERUS OF ANTIOCH (C. 465–538) Greek monk-theologian and bishop who lived as monk in Palestine; became a leading exponent of monophysitism (the heresy which taught that Christ had only one nature). He wrote a very great deal and came to the notice of Emperor Anastasius, who made him Patriarch of Antioch in 512. But six years later, on accession of Justin I, he fled to Egypt. From here he spread the monophysite movement both in Egypt and adjacent Syria. In the Coptic Church he is considered a saint and martyr.

GREGORY OF NYSSA (330–395) Gregory was the younger brother of Basil the Great and like him was educated in Athens where he took a wife and became a rhetor. Doubtless under the formidable influence of his eldest sister, Macrina, he became a monk and later Bishop of Nyssa. (We are not told what befell his wife!) Lacking Basil's administrative skills, Gregory became a wise spiritual teacher. In his commentary on the Song of Songs, he gives a vivid and intimate account of the Christian soul's mystical and ascetic journey toward God.

JOHN CASSIAN (C. 360−435) Cassian was responsible for bringing monasticism from East to West and it is from his tradition that Benedict derived his Rule. Originally a monk in Bethlehem, he moved on to Egypt, seeking out wise and holy monks and learning their ways; there he became deacon in the church of Constantinople and was sent by Saint Chrysostom to Pope Innocent I. Afterward, settling near Marseilles, he founded two monasteries which continued to flourish after his death.

His *Conferences*, an account of his many conversations with the monks of Egypt, provide the direct link between Eastern and Western traditions.

SAINT AMBROSE (340−397) Ambrose first studied law before entering the Roman civil service. His outstanding talents were soon recognized; while still only thirty, he was appointed consular magistrate for the whole of northern Italy. Based in Milan, his wisdom and fairness so endeared him to the people that, when the see fell vacant four years later, he was bishop by the people's acclaim.

For almost a quarter of a century he wielded immense influence right across the Christian world. But his chief influence beyond his own immediate lifetime was through his relationship with Saint Augustine. At first, a distant yet tantalizing figure who stood for everything Augustine had rejected, the tormented newcomer to Milan was inevitably drawn toward the bishop, especially by his sermons. But apart from this public contact, Ambrose would have little to do with him.

All he will say, agonizes Augustine in his *Confessions*, is: "Tomorrow, I shall find it. . . ." And he was right. In due time, Augustine sought baptism and became a Christian.

Fourteen years his senior, Ambrose's influence on the future Bishop of Hippo was immeasurable: He had brought him to a new way of life which offered reconciliation to his spirit, mind, and body.

SAINT AUGUSTINE (354–430) When, in 410, Augustine of Hippo, bishop, celebrated theologian and controversialist, preacher, ascetic, spiritual director, published ten books of *Confessions*, he was not indulging in a taste for literary self-congratulation or self-advertisement. As Peter Brown has emphasized in his magnificent study, *Augustine of Hippo* (Chapter 16), this was a new *kind* of book. It was a work in which the writer's struggles were worked out on the written page, in which a meaningful life had to be created in words. Augustine is never merely remembering; he is searching for significant patterns, *making* a biography. Again and again the questions recur. *Why* was this so? Where is the hand of God in this or that experience? And yet the question repeatedly modulates into a different key; not, Where was God? but, Where was I? "But where was I when I was seeking you? You were there in front of me, but I had wandered away from myself. And if I could not find my own self, how much less could I find you?" (v.2). So much of the *Confessions* centers upon the image of homecoming. God waits for the soul to come back to its home with him; without that home in God, nothing can have any meaning. "What it is that I want to say to you, Lord God, is nothing but this, that I do not know where I came from into this world, into this—what should I say?—this deathly life, this living death; no, I do not know" (I: 6). Identity is ultimately in the hand of God: but this does not mean that it is a nontemporal thing. It is to be found, and in some sense *made*, by the infinitely painstaking attention to the contingent strangeness of remembered experience in conscious reference to God which makes up most of this extraordinary work. Augustine, says Peter Brown (op. cit., p. 164), "distils a new feeling" from the memory of uncomprehended emotion. The light of God can make a story, a continuous reality, out of the chaos of unhappiness, "homeless" wandering, hurt and sin. And so nothing can be left out of account—not even the very first inklings of experience, the origin of

consciousness itself. Augustine shows a wholly new concern with childhood experiences and a new understanding of their determinative importance. His field of study is, uncompromisingly, the whole mental history
of human beings. Rowan Williams, *The Wound of Knowledge*

SAINT BENEDICT OF NURSIA (C. 480–C. 547) Very little detail is
known of Benedict's life, yet here is the Father of Western monasticism,
whose Rule and teaching had such immense influence upon its development in Europe and beyond. He was born in Nursia, central Italy, and began to study in Rome. But he was so disillusioned by its worldly ways that
he soon withdrew and became a hermit in Subiaco, a remote mountain
district fifty kilometers east of Rome. There he was joined by others
whom he organized by offering them a rule. But this resulted in fierce dis-
agreements, culminating in an attempt upon Benedict's life; so he withdrew to Cassino.

And it was here that he completed his Rule, founding the monastery
of Monte Cassino and the order which bears his name. In his Rule he drew
upon the wisdom of both Cassian and Basil; with its emphasis on community life (stability), conversion, poverty, and obedience and its characteristic moderation in following the ascetic life in a balanced and humane
manner the Rule had enormous influence in the spread of monasticism in
the West.

JOAN CHITTISTER, O.S.B. Joan Chittister is a member and former
prioress of the Benedictine Sisters of Erie, Pennsylvania. Her work now
concentrates on modernizing the monastic tradition; she is executive director of Alliance for International Monasticism (AIM).

SAINT JOHN CLIMACUS (C. 579–C. 649) John Climacus (meaning
ladder) is the eponymous author of the most influential ascetical book in
the Eastern Church: *The Ladder of Divine Ascent;* it is read every Lent in Orthodox monasteries and has been studied and copied repeatedly across the
centuries. A monk from the age of sixteen, he spent his life of prayer and

meditation in Saint Catherine's monastery at the foot of Moses' Mount Sinai.

AELRED OF RIEVAULX (1109–1167) Aelred was abbot at Rievaulx, in the north of England, for the last twenty years of his life. By that time his reputation was at its height. Known as the "Bernard of the North," he was most famous for his *Treatise on Friendship*, the Christian counterpart to Cicero's *De Amicitia*. Aelred boldly describes how a monk might take a close spiritual friend as a means to perfection in the cloister. In the quoted passage, Dom Aelred Squire imagines the old abbot holding a recreation in his cell. His chronic arthritis was a result of his harsh penitential habit as a young monk of standing up to his neck in icy water to mortify his flesh.

SAINT BRUNO (1032–1101) Founder of the Carthusians, Bruno's early office in the Church was as Chancellor of Rheims cathedral, in his day, the most important see in the whole of France. Here, he distinguished himself not merely by his ability as a teacher and his own outstanding learning, but his administrative skills were equally demonstrated in building up Rheims to become the leading school in Europe. During Bruno's time a whole line of future abbots and bishops received their formation in Rheims at his hands. But a sudden and bitter dispute with the new bishop resulted in his exile. And from this unpromising misfortune, the Carthusians arose. Gathering a small group of like-minded men, Bruno conceived the idea of living as hermits in community.

Bruno first forged his plan for a hidden life in a conversation with three friends "in the little garden adjoining Adam's house." Their talk was clearly animated, for it led to all three vowing to give up the world for the cloister. Some years later, Bruno writes Raoul, who is still dean of the cathedral chapter at Rheims. His letter (this and one other are the only writings that survive) is part invitation, in part admonition, since he fears for his friend's integrity in not having fulfilled his solemn vow. This agenda aside, it gives a rare glimpse into the hidden world Bruno was exploring.

His *Credo* stems from a custom of his day which was to compose a personalized statement of lifelong faith, almost a spiritual last will and testament, so as to hand your soul back to God.

WILLIAM OF ST.-THIERRY (C. 1085—C. 1148) Educated by the Benedictines, he first joined the Order at their house in Rheims. In 1119, he was elected abbot of St.-Thierry and soon gained a reputation as a brilliant philosopher. Coming under the influence of Saint Bernard, who became a close friend, he entered the newly founded Cistercian monastery at Signy as a simple monk. He continued his studies and produced many solid written works as well as being the first authority to challenge the advanced thinking of Peter Abelard, whom Bernard later brought to heel. His *Golden Epistle* as it popularly became known is addressed to the Carthusians of Mont Dieu; it was presumably composed at their own request in response to their enthusiasm for his other writings.

SAINT BERNARD OF CLAIRVAUX (1090—1153) Bernard is one of the giants of the early Middle Ages. His influence in both the political and spiritual realm was enormous. He burst upon the Christian scene in 1113, when he dramatically presented himself as a novice at the gates of Cîteaux accompanied by thirty other young noblemen whose company included his brothers. The abbey, the first of the Cistercian reforms, was utterly impoverished at the time. Bernard's arrival reversed their fortunes; but within three years, he had been appointed abbot of a new foundation, Clairvaux. It was here that he was to consolidate the Cistercian reforms and spread them rapidly across the rest of Europe within his own lifetime.

Adviser to popes and kings, preacher of the Second Crusade, monastic reformer, abbot, writer, and spiritual guide, he was in every aspect of his character a complex man. He had a sweet, almost sentimental side; yet he could pursue his chosen quarry with utter doggedness, as when he ran Abelard to ground and persuaded him to end his life doing penance in a monastery. Yet he championed Hildegard of Bingen without hesitation, encouraging her by bringing her writings to the attention of the pope. His enduring influence comes from his writings, among them the *Memorare*, his prayer to Our Lady, and numerous hymns still in use today.

SAINT ANSELM (1033–1109) Anselm, like his exact contemporary Bruno, exemplifies the mobile nature of the Church in the early Middle Ages. Born in Lombardy, he left his dissolute life behind by crossing the Alps to study at the school of the monastery of Bec which had just been founded in Normandy. Lanfranc, also an Italian, the first prior, soon spotted his promising fellow countryman. Having persuaded Anselm to become a monk, he was eventually succeeded by him twice over, first as Prior of Bec and then as Archbishop of Canterbury. Anselm, a brilliant philosopher and pious monk, brought an integrity to his writings which shines in every word he wrote. Yet, as archbishop, he could also be resolute. His appointment was first of all opposed by the king, then agreed. But further disputes concerning church and state jurisdiction led to his exile until Rufus was killed in battle. Only then was Anselm able to resume his title. Yet it is as theologian and teacher that he is especially remembered. While in exile he wrote a brilliant examination of the Incarnation, *Cur Deus Homo* (Why Did God Become One of Us); this includes his famous "ontological" proof of the existence of God, ultimately more a passionate prayer than a success story.

MEISTER ECKHART (1260–1327) Born around the year 1260, Meister (John) Eckhart was a Dominican Master of Theology who early in his career was marked out for the front line when he was sent to teach at the Schools of Paris. From the start, Eckhart's teaching was fearless and incisive. One of his key ideas was the birth of the Word in every human soul, an idea that was set before his Cologne congregation in the sermon *Ave Gratia Plena*.

Although insisting all along on the free operation of God's grace and despite his clear statement that any idea of human perfectibility was a-Christian, he was summoned to the papal court of Avignon to face heresy charges. These were stoutly defended (his own Provincial accompanied him to the hearings); matters dragged on unresolved. But in 1329, two years after Meister Echhart's death, a papal bull solemnly condemned twenty-eight of his propositions. There is little doubt today of Eckhart's brilliance as a theologian of the mind and spirit or question of his orthodoxy. Because he wrote in both German as well as Latin his work gave great impetus to the development of the language; moreover the German idealists looked to him as a forerunner while scholars today trace his influence on both Protestantism and existentialism. But his chief legacy is his brilliant teaching on the life of the spirit, although the full extent of his contribution has yet to be assessed.

THE CLOUD OF UNKNOWING Alongside *The Revelation* of Julian of Norwich, this work is the most formative and influential mystical writing of the English mystics in the Middle Ages. We know little of Julian as a person, even less of the deliberately anonymous author of this authoritative treatise. One theory is that it was written by a Carthusian, which would explain its anonymity. Certainly, certain passages bear a striking similarity to the writing of Richard Metthley's brief journal, which suggests the Carthusians of Mount Grace were familiar with the work. Experts on early English dialect detect an East Midlands accent, which would point to the prior or novice master of the Leicester Charterhouse offering to instruct his young monks in the purpose and ways of contemplative prayer.

THE ANCRENE RIWLE As the numbers of women solitaries began to grow and and their vocations to flourish in the Middle Ages, need was felt for a rule to guide their way of life. Such women—Julian of Norwich is the best known—would live in a cell or anchorhold tucked in against the church wall. Here they would be looked after by a servant so that they might be free to pray and contemplate. The apparent danger of becoming a gossip rather than a prayerful anchoress is addressed in several places in the Rule.

JULIAN OF NORWICH (1342–1428?) Among the best-loved and wisest and humblest of the English mystics is the lady we call Julian of Norwich. A misnomer for a woman? Yet this is because we do not know her real name, merely the dedication of the tiny church tucked away down a side street of busy Norwich. It was here, after receiving sixteen "Showings" or her "revelation of love" that she attached herself as an anchorite and lived in seclusion for perhaps more than half a century. During all this time, she, like Mary before her, "pondered in her heart" their meaning.

She writes her story and toward the end concludes that "love was his meaning," the message of God's love toward mankind.

MARGERY KEMPE (1373–1440) Far from being an anchoress as it was thought at the beginning of the twentieth century, Margery Kempe, once delivered of her thirteen children and having come to an amicable, if delayed, accommodation with her husband, set out on a series of pilgrimages. This very first autobiography in the English language, *The Book of Margery Kempe,* tells the fascinating story of her travels: Not only did she visit York, the archbishop of Canterbury, and other worthy priests, but she also pilgrimaged to the Holy Land and to Santiago de Compostela. Now the object of keen interest, both by scholars and the wider feminist world, we will always be grateful to Margery Kempe for giving us the only historical account of Julian of Norwich whose anchorhold she had the wit to visit. If her many journeys were in truth an expression of her own inner restless search for God, her visit to Julian was probably the most important landfall in her lifelong trail.

RICHARD METTHLEY, CARTHUSIAN (FIFTEENTH CENTURY) Richard Metthley joined the Carthusians at Mount Grace in Yorkshire at the age of twenty-five. As an old monk he kept a brief personal diary running from the feast of Saint Bruno, October 6, 1487, until December 15 following. It presents a rare glimpse of the hidden Carthusian life. Metthley died shortly before the Reformation.

MARTIN LUTHER (1483–1546) Luther is one of the most misunderstood and misinterpreted Reformers, especially among Roman Catholics. These two short extracts show him zealous to safeguard the spiritual well-being of the Church yet all the while trapped in a political crossfire outside his control.

In January 1519, Luther wrote to Pope Leo X from Altenburg. It was here that an important meeting had taken place with the papal envoy. One of the topics discussed with the pope's special envoy, Charles von Miltitz, was how to secure on behalf of the curia Luther's support—and through him that of Elector Frederick—for a suitable successor to the late Emperor Maximilian I. But as a preliminary, Luther was asked to write a letter of apology to the pope himself.

Leo X (who was pope from 1513 to 1521) was, like his predecessor, a Medici, and far more a Renaissance prince than a pope. As a result, his main interest was the political, economic, and cultural expansion of the papal state—not forgetting his own family. More politician than priest, he had little idea of the implications of Luther's approach to him.

SAINT IGNATIUS LOYOLA (1491–1556) Former courtier and soldier, founder of the Society of Jesus, Ignatius was exactly the right man for his age, the soldier of Christ born onto the battlefield of the Counter Reformation. Yet it was not until the age of thirty, when he was gravely wounded at the siege of Pamplona, that Ignatius was stopped in his worldly tracks. Taking up a book of Lives of the Saints while recovering from a leg that had been shattered by a cannonball, he resolved to turn to Christ. A man of iron will, Ignatius began at once to forge his own spiritual formation. For ten months he lived the life of a hermit in a cave above Manresa in Catalonia. It was here that he shaped his Spiritual Exercises which were to have such an effect in changing and shaping countless individuals' lives from then on. A pilgrimage to Jerusalem was followed by his return to Spain in search of learning at Salamanca, something he regretted neglecting but now pursued with characteristic determination. Following this, his studies took him to Paris, where he began to attract a circle of companions, among them Francis Xavier, to whom he offered his Exercises. It was not until 1540 that the Society was formally instituted by Pope Paul III. Sixteen years later, his life's work accomplished, Ignatius died, leaving behind him a well-organized army who were known as the Jesuits.

SAINT THERESA OF AVILA (1515–1582) Innate common sense, rather than lofty wisdom, marks out this most remarkable and lovable woman. Her earthy, matter-of-fact approach to everyday affairs combines with a sure authority on spiritual matters: One senses at once from her writings that she knows precisely what she is talking about. Yet, somewhat belatedly, she was only made Doctor of the Church in 1970, the first woman to be so named.

Her writings are too numerous and varied to offer anything other than some few glimpses of all she has to tell us about our approach to God. It cannot be said too often that any truth that is valid for nuns or monks is equally applicable to every Christian who ever lived. Monks are not climbing Everest for nothing; like successful moon probes, they occasionally give rise to a technology that has everyday applications in the kitchen, such as non-stick saucepans.

Theresa, herself, far transcends so mundane a metaphor.

Like her nineteenth-century namesake, Saint Theresa also wrote her autobiography, which covers the first fifty years of her life. For the next sixteen she continued to receive great graces. The six "Relations," as they are known after the Latin *relatio* or report, belong to these latter years and rehearse her prayer life to more than one spiritual director.

JOHN OF THE CROSS (1542–1591) John of the Cross became a Carmelite at the age of twenty-one and was ordained four years later. Within the year, Theresa had spotted him, dissuaded him from joining the Carthusians, and enlisted him in her reform movement. His support for Theresa's work led to John being imprisoned by his own monks, a not uncommon form of corrective treatment for monks who were judged to be stepping out of line. It was while he was in prison—his cell without window measured barely his own length—that he began to compose his epic poem "The Dark Night of the Soul." It was to form the basis of his spiritual teaching and writings on the spiritual life.

GEORGE HERBERT (1593–1633) Poet and divine, George Herbert's talents as a classicist were soon recognized. Appointed public orator at Cambridge University at the age of twenty-seven, he surprised his friends by taking to divinity, whereas they had foreseen him in a courtly career. Once ordained, he accepted a quiet country parish near Salisbury where he spent the last few years of his short life. His most famous prose work, *A Priest to the Temple,* was well received in its day but is now quite eclipsed by his poetry. This broke fresh ground by leaving aside the florid imagery and conceits of the majority of his contemporaries and relying instead on homely, direct language instilled with simple piety. His accomplished and well-balanced use of both internal rhyme and deceptively sophisticated rhythms inspired many later poets such as Henry Vaughan and Samuel Coleridge. As a hidden country priest, his example was typical of numerous men who over the centuries unobtrusively taught and nurtured their congregations throughout their lifetime.

MARY WARD (1585–1645) Mary Ward was born in a small Yorkshire town in 1585, a terrible time to be born a Catholic; one year later, Margaret Clitheroe was crushed to death in York for refusing to plead to the charge of harboring priests. In 1600, at the age of fifteen Mary Ward knew she had a vocation. She spent these formative years at Babthorpe, a large recusant house in Yorkshire which followed a particularly fervent religious life with daily mass, vespers at four o'clock followed by matins. A period of exile on the Continent where she joined a convent of Poor Clares led eventually—not without enormous tribulation—to her founding her own Order, *the* Institute of the Blessed Virgin Mary, "the English Ladies." Their reputation for learning and their skills in education have led them to be compared to the Jesuits.

THOMAS TRAHERNE (1637–1674) Born the son of a shoemaker, Thomas matriculated as a Commoner at Brasenose College, Oxford, aged fifteen. Ordained eight years later, he became a country vicar. His spiritual verses—almost lost in the mud of history, before they were picked up by his brother—spring off the page today with a mystical originality that seems to echo Eden.

SAINT THÉRÈSE OF LISIEUX (1873–1897) In her twenty-four years of life, Thérèse proceeded from teenage brat to saint in a painfully joyous certainty that cost her all. Somehow she had glimpsed her God right away. Her middle-class, ordinary upbringing, albeit paved ahead into the Carmel by her elder sisters, did little to enable her progress. She should have ended up unknown: she succeeded in talking to the modern world in a language they at once recognized and appreciated as contemporary and uniquely novel.

THE BASILIAN NUNS OF MINSK After enduring seven years' persecution (1838–1845), the Abbess of the Basilian nuns of Minsk, Makrena Mieczyslawka, was asked by Rome to submit an account of their prolonged ordeal. This brief extract from a deposition to Propaganda in Rome, which took the Abbess one month to set down, spells out a particular incident which might be an icon of the sufferings and hardships that religious women have had to endure over the centuries.

CHARLES EUGÈNE DE FOUCAULD (1858–1916) Born in Strasbourg—son of Vicomte de Foucauld de Pont-Briand—on September 15, 1856. His mother died when he was eight and he was brought up in the home of his mother's mother. He went first to the lycée where, as he wrote later, he found at best a very neutral view of religion which fed his boyish independence. At the age of fifteen, he had passed on to the Jesuits with a military career at St. Cyr in mind; yet by now he was in open revolt. Pursuing at first a military career, as well as that of a dandy *de la belle époque*, he was stopped in his tracks by a chance encounter with a priest at the dinner table. In 1886 he first became a Trappist monk, then a hermit in the North African desert of Algeria. He endeared himself to the local Tuareg tribe, composing their first grammar and dictionary. He also transcribed their songs and folk tales. He was killed during the First World War by anti-French tribesmen. His mystic prayer life focused on the Eucharist and he wrote hundreds of meditations; it is said that he never made a single convert to Christ. Yet inspired by his example, the Little Sisters and Little Brothers of Jesus continue his work today.

BEDE GRIFFITHS, O.S.B. (1906–1993) Bede Griffiths was open to all routes by which all people seek God: his whole life was spent in a patient search for a way which had meaning for all. As a convert to Roman Catholicism, he soon found his way to the Cistercians at Prinknash. Later, as his world expanded, he found his way to India, again in search of the simplest possible way of life that would feed his spirituality. His ashram at Shantivanam, Southern India, was to become a center of spirituality which sought to bridge East and West. From there, he continued to pray and to write, influencing the world he had left behind. Toward the end of his life, he emerged from the ashram to undertake several grueling lecture tours that took him to Europe, Asia, and North America.

JOHN MAIN, O.S.B. (1926–1982) John Main was born in London into an Irish family. As with Bede Griffiths, he found that monastic life in the modern world failed to satisfy his hunger for God. Increasingly, his life became a continuing search for an effective method of prayer. Only in the last decade of his life did he succeed in developing the mantra which, he maintained, linked the Western monastic traditions of prayer with that of the East.

THOMAS MERTON (1915–1968) Born to American parents in Prades, France, Merton lost his mother when he was still a young boy of six; his father also died while he was still at school. He began his university education in England at Cambridge but a love affair ended in his girlfriend becoming pregnant. Legal proceedings followed and after only a year he moved to the United States. Here he taught English at Columbia University, taking his degree. Converting at the age of twenty-three, he worked at a Roman Catholic center in Harlem in New York City. In 1941 he entered the Trappist monastery of Our Lady of Gethsemani in Kentucky. He was ordained a priest in 1949, taking the name Father Louis. Merton was continually drawn to a greater solitude than the Cistercian routine could offer; and yet he sustained a busy writing schedule throughout his life. Achieving almost overnight fame with his autobiography, *The Seven Storey Mountain,* he sustained an active voice in such contemporary phenomena as the peace movement, the civil rights movement, and the spiritual revival of the Church associated with the Vatican Council. He died in a bizarre way, electrocuted by a fan in his hotel room while attending a Christian-Buddhist conference in Bangkok.

HENRI NOUWEN (1932–1996) Henri Nouwen, a Dutch Catholic priest, theologian, and spiritual writer, spent seven months with the Cistercian community of Genesee in upstate New York. Living the life of a monk rather than a mere guest, Nouwen was able to understand the inner experience of the monastic vocation for himself. His *Genesee Diary* covers the months June through December and tells how the abbot, Dom John Eudes, was able to guide him to sustain his life of solitude and prayer as a temporary "monk."

Henri Nouwen also spent long periods living and working in L'Arche Communities both in France and later in Canada. There he encountered the poverty and the riches of those handicapped by learning difficulties frequently physical in origin.

EVELYN UNDERHILL (1875–1941) Anglican mystic and writer of spirituality who pioneered the retreat movement. In addition to her continuous lecturing and retreat work, much of it undertaken in her own home, she wrote over seventy books. Recognition of her scholarly originality came with an honorary degree from Kings College, London, an unheard-of honor for a woman in her day.

By 1911, Evelyn Underhill had completed her major work, *Mysticism,* to critical acclaim; and it still remains the major work of reference in its field. Three years later, as the Great War engulfed Europe, she wrote *Practical Mysticism*, a work intended to offer the spiritual life to everyone. She continued her work right up to the Second World War. But as an ardent pacifist her spirit was crushed by the advent of a second European war in her lifetime and she died at the age of sixty-six during the London blitz.

A TOUCH OF GOD *(Benedictine Contributors) Maria Boulding* was born in Wimbledon, the daughter of a pioneer of radar. She entered Stanbrook Abbey in 1947 where she has been novice mistress and librarian. Editor and author of several books, since 1985, she has lived as a hermit, with the backing of her community.

Leonard Vickers was educated at Douai Abbey School and in 1953 entered the novitiate there. He was ordained priest, helped to run the farm, and served the Community as assistant bursar, junior master, parish priest, and novice master. For twelve years he was officiating chaplain to the WRNS ["Wrens": women sailors with the Royal Navy]. In 1983 he was appointed Prior Administrator of Saint Anselm's Abbey in Washington, D.C., and was elected abbot there in 1987.

Philip Jebb was born in Staffordshire but grew up in Sussex. He was educated at Downside School, from where he went straight into the monastery, though later he did a classics degree at Cambridge. For two years he was a curate in Somerset, and then successively a house master, deputy head master and head master of Downside. He has contributed many articles and written books which include *Widowed*, a book to help those who have lost a partner.

FRANCIS KLINE, O.C.S.O. Abbot of Mepkin, a Cistercian (Trappist) monastery near Charleston, South Carolina, whose house and land were donated to the Order in 1949 by Henry and Clare Boothe Luce. In his book, *Lovers of the Place,* Abbot Francis makes a passionate plea for the spirit of monasticism, its wisdom and power for good, to be spread back into the Church and the world at large. The "governing image" of his book is "the vision of the Church as communion in a vast building of great architecture." People are welcomed under this great roof and within its innermost depths find spiritual awakening and shared human experience that has been radically enlivened by Christ's Paschal Mystery. In this temple space, each individual is able to commune and communicate with growing awareness their inner spiritual journey of discovering the Father in Christ.

CARTHUSIAN REFLECTIONS *The Spirit of the Place* consists of a series of exhortations and sermons given by the Prior of Saint Hugh's Charterhouse, Parkminster, England, to his brethren. They form part of a growing corpus of spiritual writings emanating from the same source. Traditionally, the Carthusians never preach and rarely write books; but, in an attempt to share their rich teaching on the spiritual life, the present prior has boldly gone to print and even permitted his monks to record a CD of the Night Office of Matins.

BROTHER DAVID STEINDL-RAST, O.S.B. Born in Vienna, David Steindl-Rast studied art, anthropology, and psychology. In 1953, he joined the Benedictine monastery of Mount Saviour in Elmira, New York. Author of several books on the contemplative life, his key ideas as set out in *Gratefulness, the Heart of Prayer*, have been widely praised—Henri Nouwen declares that he has the ability to make old words fresh and new.

DAME FELICITAS CORRIGAN, O.S.B. Born of Liverpool Irish descent, Sister Felicitas is a member of the Stanbrook Abbey Benedictine community. During her long lifetime she has formed many literary friendships with notable writers of her day and written numerous books on spirituality.

FATHER PHILIP CARAMAN (1911–1998) Jesuit priest and writer who specialized in popularizing the lives of Jesuit saints and martyrs, especially those working on the English Mission in penal times.

PETER HEBBLETHWAITE (1930–1994) Former Jesuit priest and editor of *The Month*, Hebblethwaite became a specialist "Vatican watcher" and religious journalist. Among his several books were two major biographies dealing with the lives and times of Pope John XXIII and Paul VI.

BROTHER VICTOR-ANTOINE D'AVILA-LATOURRETTE A monk of Our Lady of the Resurrection, a monastery observing the Rule of Saint Benedict and drawing its inspiration from the ancient traditions of monasticism both East and West. The monastery is perched on a secluded hilltop outside Millbrook, in upstate New York.

THOMAS KEATING Abbot of the Cistercian community in Snowmass, Colorado, Father Keating is founder of the Centering Prayer Movement. As well as writing numerous books on prayer and spirituality, he has traveled extensively in order to lecture and teach about contemplative prayer.

IAIN MATTHEW Joined the Discalced Carmelites in Oxford in 1978. He has worked in parish and youth ministry and given retreats in Europe and Australia. He is presently prior of the Carmelite Community in Dublin.

RUTH BURROUGHS Sister Rachel is prioress of the Carmelite community at Quiddenham, Norwich. As Ruth Burroughs she has written numerous books on prayer and Carmelite spirituality.

EDITH STEIN (1891–1942) Edith Stein, Saint Edith as we must now learn to call her (she was canonized by John Paul II in 1998), was born the last of eleven children of a Jewish family in Breslau (now the Polish town of Wroclaw) on October 12, 1891. It was Yom Kippur, the holiest day of the Jewish calendar. Eighteen months later, her father died, leaving her mother to bring up the children and manage the family lumber business. Edith was bright and from the start sailed into learning. At nineteen, she entered university and as a postgraduate studied under Husserl, the father of phenomenology. Her doctorate was awarded *summa cum laude*, top marks, and she became Husserl's assistant.

A self-confessed atheist at the age of fifteen, Edith was suddenly surprised by Christianity on reading a life of Theresa of Avila. Aged thirty-one, she became a Catholic and later a Carmelite nun. She and her sister died in Auschwitz, Jewish-Christian victims of the Nazis.